Counselors' Perception of and Experiences with Empathy When Treating Male IPV Victims

Although the author and publisher have made every effort to ensure that the information in this book was correct at the time of first publication, the author and publisher do not assume and hereby disclaim any liability to any party for any loss, damage, or disruption caused by errors or omissions, whether such errors or omissions result from negligence, accident, or any other cause.

The resources contained within this book are provided for informational purposes only and should not be used to replace the specialized training and professional judgment of a healthcare or mental healthcare professional. Author and the publisher of this work cannot be held responsible for the use of the information provided. Always consult a licensed mental health professional before making any decision regarding treatment of yourself or others.

Copyright © 2025 by Moses Omane-Boateng

All rights reserved. No part of this book may be reproduced or transmitted in any form or by any means, electronic or mechanical, including photocopying, recording, or any information storage and retrieval system, without permission in writing from the author.

ISBN: 978-1-6653-1032-1 - Paperback
eISBN: 978-1-6653-1033-8 - eBook

These ISBNs are the property of BookLogix for the express purpose of sales and distribution of this title. The content of this book is the property of the copyright holder only. BookLogix does not hold any ownership of the content of this book and is not liable in any way for the materials contained within. The views and opinions expressed in this book are the property of the Author/Copyright holder, and do not necessarily reflect those of BookLogix.

Library of Congress Control Number: 2025918925

☉This paper meets the requirements of ANSI/NISO Z39.48-1992 (Permanence of Paper)

093025

Counselors' Perception of and Experiences with Empathy When Treating Male IPV Victims

An Evidence-Based Paradigm to Mitigate Intimate Partner Violence

Moses Omane-Boateng, PhD

ELAINE M. BARCLAY, PhD, Faculty Mentor, and Chair
MORGAN MCAFEE, PhD, Committee Member
PAMELA KLEM, EdD, Committee Member
LISA KREEGER, PhD, Dean School of Counseling and Human Services

I dedicate the task of this daunting academic journey to my family, whose relentless, sustainable prayers and support throughout this dissertation process inspired me to finish strong. To my beloved wife, Missionary Ruth Omane-Boateng (deceased November 28, 2021), your priceless, relentless, and steadfast prayers are appreciated. To my children, Gifty Omane, Rita Moss, Demertia Moss, William Moss (deceased), and Pastor Steve and Marchella Hopwood, I embraced the prayers and encouragements when I was frustrated with the barriers of academic episodes. My grandchildren, Samoria, Chris, Jarvis, Kwasi, Precious, and Zoe, I hope this academic work will catalyze your ambitions. I compliment my sisters, Joyce Omane and Dianne Larussa, as well as my brothers, Dr. Thomas Larussa's family, John Simon's family, and Jasper Simon. My parents (biological, deceased in Ghana), Moses and Juana Omane, taught me discipline, diligence, resilience, and hard work; I owe you gratitude, Mom and Dad. Grandpa Boateng (deceased in Ghana), you taught me patience, selflessness, decency, and discipline. My American adopted parents, (a) John and Anne Larussa (deceased), (b) Bud and Donna Young (deceased), and finally, Johnnie (deceased) and Emma Simons, your prayers, financial support, and encouragement sustained me. Family, this is your milestone; the dream is absolute now.

Above all, I dedicate this study to my Lord Jesus Christ, who defined my purpose and the imbued Spirit of discipline, patience, resilience, and perseverance in me. Lord, accept my gratitude for healing me from quadruple bypass surgery. I learned from Solomon; He said:

> One more thing I have observed here under the sun: speed does not win the race, nor strength the battle. Bread does not fit the wise, wealth to the gifted,

or success to the skillful; time and chance govern all.
(Ecclesiastes 9:11 (Crim, 1970))

Yes, this dissertation's academic journey is finished. This scripture was my inspirational armor.

*"The heart has its reasons,
of which reason knows nothing."*

—Blaise Pascal

Contents

Abstract	xv
Chapter 1: **Introduction**	1
Background of the Problem	3
Problem Statement	5
Study Rationale	6
Significance of the Study	7
Identified Gap	10
Research Question(s)	11
Overview of the Methodology	12
Chapter 2: **Literature Review**	21
Methods of Searching	23
Theoretical Framework for the Current Study	23
Review of the Literature	25
Synthesis of the Literature	47
Research Opportunities	50
Proposed Research	51
Chapter 3: **Methodology**	55
Research Design	56
Sampling	58
Target Population and Sample	59
Sample Size Rational	61
Procedures	61
Participant Selection	61
Data Collection	66
Instruments	67

Data Analysis	71
Ethical Considerations	72
Chapter 4: Results	**75**
The Study and the Researcher	76
Description of the Sample	78
Presentation of Data and Analyses	83
Summary of Results	102
Chapter 5: Findings and Conclusions	**103**
Summary of Findings	104
Findings in Context of the Theoretical Framework	106
Findings in Context of the Previous Literature	108
Discussion of Results	110
Limitations	113
Implications for Policy or Practice	116
Recommendations for Future Research	119
Conclusion	123
References	**125**
Appendix A: Publishing Agreement	**305**
Acknowledgments	**309**

List of Tables

Table 1   80
    IPV Professional Mental Health
    Counselors Demographic
    Characteristics

Table 2   85
Thematic Data Analysis
    Themes and Sub-Themes

"For by him were all things created, that are in heaven, and that are in earth, visible and invisible, whether they be thrones, or dominions, or principalities, or powers: He created all things, and for him."

—Colossians 1:16

Abstract

Researchers have noted that mental health providers reported male intimate partner violence (IPV) population mental disorders are from sexual, physical, emotional, anxiety, anger, and relational victimization experiences (Dim, 2021; Park et al., 2021; Peraica, 2021). The literature reviewed indicated that mental health counselors have limited insight into understanding experiences and feelings while working with male IPV victims. I addressed analytical, emotional, and mental illness recovery treatment services and programs to support male IPV clients, fostering empathic experiences and mental health professionals' beliefs. This study's primary question was, "What are the mental health counselors' experiences with and feelings about the role of empathy while working with male victims of IPV?" Thus, the research study used the purposive and snowball sampling approach to find an eligible sample of licensed mental health providers to explore the research question. A generic qualitative research approach about the meaning, understanding, and straightforward thematic data collection protocol and analysis sampling was right for this study. The study sample size included ten licensed mental health providers (cohort) in the South-Central United States. Concerning the inductive thematic analysis, six main themes emerged consisting of (a) experiences with empathy working with male IPV victims, (b) male masculinity ego issue "I am a man; I don't need help," (c) challenges working

Abstract

with male IPV victims, (d) perpetrators' victimization and abuse, (e) advice and training impact on mental health professionals, and (f) changes in mental health professionals' experiences and effects that affect the ability to empathize. The empathic simulation theory (EST) approach indicates mental health providers' support for male IPV victims' recovery treatment. Again, the findings showed how meaningfully masculinity compared to societal culture can change heterosexual male IPV survivors' cohort mental, emotional, psychological, and physical behaviors and well-being.

Introduction

Chapter 1

According to previous scholars Skoczek and Akram (2023) and Shortland and Palasinski (2019), intimate partner violence (IPV) and domestic abuse have been linked to several adverse outcomes in the past among male IPV victims. These adverse effects outcomes included (a) physical impairment (e.g., neurological symptoms, traumatic brain injury of cerebrovascular accident (CVA), (b) psychological effects (e.g., anxiety, timidity, distress, and emotions), (c) family dysfunction (e.g., high divorce rate), (d) academic cognitive impairment in children (e.g., unhealthy child academic functioning development), and (e) high human economic and public costs issues (e.g., impairment of economic conditions, mental health, and risk of food insecurity) (Cage et al., 2022; Davidson & Beck, 2017; Hamadani et al., 2020; Murali-Larson, 2023; Stubbs & Szoeke,

2022; Skoczek & Akram, 2023). Further, in collaboration with this study's findings, Hine, Bates, and Wallace (2020) asserted that:

> While previous scholars have begun to provide evidence on the experiences of male victims of IPV/DVA abuse, current understanding in this area is still limited and subject to narrow methods of inquiry. Moreover, we know little research information regarding the challenges of providing support for men in abusive relationships and how both men and service practitioners experience barriers to effective service engagement. (p. NP5594)

The topic for this study was mental health professionals' experiences with and feelings about the role of empathy while working with male intimate partner violence (IPV) victims. This study used the terms mental health provider and mental health professional interchangeably (Hamp et al., 2016). Mental health service providers need to have the compassion to support males who have experienced IPV abuse (Carlson et al., 2019, 2018; Crane & Easton, 2017; Harvey et al., 2018; McGinn et al., 2016; Romero-Martínez et al., 2019; Romero-Martínez et al., 2016; Watson, 2019). According to Singh (2016), a positive association exists between women's perpetration of partner violence (PV) against men and male victims' mental health issues. For this study, male IPV survivors' health issues included depression, anxiety, PTSD, and substance use problems such as alcohol and illicit drug use (Arroyo et al., 2017; Singh, 2016).

According to Romero-Martínez et al. (2019), cognitive and emotional empathy expresses moral reasoning and vitality, prosocial behavior, social and emotional adequacy, moods, and behavior regulation. For instance, McGinn et al. (2021) and McGinn et al. (2020) argued that IPV perpetrators' irrational cognitive malfunction, emotional instability, gendered social imperatives, and self-worth degradation issues are barriers that might deter motivational intervention programs. Hence, offsetting these functions may stimulate behavior domination and the embracing of specific types of violence, such as intimate partner violence (IPV) (Romero-Martínez et al., 2019).

Recent researchers posited that cognitive empathy is understanding how a person sees the world and consciously caring for another fellow (Godfrey et al., 2020; Romero-Martínez et al., 2019). Besides, emotional empathy is what someone else feels; thus, "experiencing sharing" is an effective stimulus that involves moral reasoning, positive social behavior, social and emotional adequacy, and mood behavior control (Paris, 2017; Romero-Martínez et al., 2019; Santos et al., 2019, Santos et al., 2017). This study focused on mental health service providers' past experiences and feelings of empathy while working with male IPV victims.

Earlier studies have noted that mental health providers have reported male IPV population mental disorders that stemmed from sexual, physical, and emotional distress, anxiety, anger, and relational victimization experiences (Emelianchik-Key et al., 2023). Male IPV victims are likelier to show their victimization experiences to an unofficial support group (Edwards & Dardis, 2020; Huntley et al., 2020, 2019). Debrowska and Boduszek (2017) found that mental health counselors' empathy in their treatment programs could help male IPV victims overcome their mental disorders and emotional distress issues. Nevertheless, there is a general shortage of research on male IPV victims' experiences. This information enhanced the understanding of developing rational emotional and mental illness recovery treatment services and programs to support male IPV clients (Burelomova et al., 2018; Debrowska & Boduszek, 2017, 2016).

Background of the Problem

Historically, intimate partner violence (IPV) has been a fundamental global, social, and public problem (Garland et al., 2019; Pichonet et al., 2022). Thus, it is pivotal for researchers to inquire into the nature of this IPV phenomenon to arouse community consciousness, moral reasoning, positive social behaviors, and emotional vitality (Burelomova et al., 2018; Romero-Martinez et al., 2019; Suleimenova & Ivanova, 2018). For this research, mental health–related issues, such as labeling, could be misused when working with IPV survivors. Nonetheless, studies showed that a collaboration of mental health providers can administer screening appropriately to help IPV survivors' cognitive-emotional distress (Simmons et al., 2017). Simmons et al. (2017) asserted that agencies could use screening concept mapping labeling to find mental health survivors' issues and barriers that prevent recovery treatment. The diagnoses include depression, posttraumatic stress disorder (PTSD), acute stress disorder, and anxiety-related conditions. Cognitive health assessment, diagnosis, and treatment can help these vulnerable populations significantly.

According to Capella (2023), "The theoretical orientation in qualitative studies tends to articulate the theoretical foundation of the method and framework used in the research rather than the theory relevant to the research topic" (p. 15). Thus, this study indicated a generic qualitative framework with an inductive constant thematic approach (Taylor et al., 2018; Xu, 2020). Augsburger et al. (2019) argued that empirical studies had concluded practitioners' concerns with IPV victims' violence and aggressive acts experienced from their perpetrators. Hence, it seems prudent that future researchers support the topic by addressing mental health professionals' experiences with and feelings about the role of empathy while working with male IPV victims. Furthermore, Contractor et al. (2018) and Bennett et al. (2020) asserted that clinicians and researchers are concerned with the low self-esteem, emotion, and anxiety outcomes of male IPV-abused victims. In Hardesty and Ogolsky's (2020) study, men's IPV victims reported significantly more victimization in the past year than women. However, they argued that no study reported a higher proportion of male victims than female victims.

Nonetheless, men reported more lifetime and past-year physical violence. In contrast, women generally reported more psychological IPV in the past six calendar months, and, throughout studies, women rationally reported higher rates of sexual victimization (Hardesty & Ogolsky, 2020). According to Hardesty and Ogolsky (2020), evidence in national survey data depicted that "one in three (35.6%) women in the United States reported experiencing IPV, including physical violence (32.9%), stalking (10.7%), rape (9.4%), in their lifetime" (p. 455). Compared with men, more than "one in four (28.5%) reported experiencing lifetime IPV physical violence (28.2%); (2.1%) experienced stalking, but few addressed rape experiences" (Hardesty and Ogolsky, 2020, p. 455). The foregone background suggested the need for complex collaborative research through disciplines in the next decade to broaden and enhance researchers' knowledge and inform prevention and intervention programs legislation to mitigate perpetrators' atrocious behaviors (Hardesty & Ogolsky, 2020).

Problem Statement

The primary problem/purpose of this generic qualitative study is to answer the research question related to mental health professionals' experiences with and beliefs of the role of empathy compared to male IPV survivor victims who are seeking recovery support. The literature on male IPV survivors showed a dearth of empirical research on mental health providers' empathy experiences of male IPV victims' experiences (Huntley et al., 2019; MacLeod, 2019; McCarrick et al., 2016, 2015). Another concern is a gap in the current research regarding the understanding of mental health counselors' experiences with and beliefs about the role of empathy while working with male IPV victims (Williams et al., 2020). Prior literature review depicted limited information about mental health providers' empathy role experiences of male victims suffering from cognitive distress and fear of how the perpetrator will blame them for the abuse (Huntley et al., 2019; Barkhuizen, 2015). Hence, this dissertation aims to fill the research literature gap on mental health service providers' empathic experiences of male IPV victims' mental health issues.

The risk of suicide, emanating from hopelessness, self-doubt/lack of confidence and worthlessness/lack of self-esteem, emotional dilemma, psychological distress, and anxiety is a grave public concern about the male IPV survivor's mental health well-being (Lim et al., 2015; MacLeod, 2019; Mossière et al., 2018). Understanding these issues is critical for mental health providers to implement suitable recovery programs for the male IPV victim population. Therapeutic providers can use empathy to develop preventive treatment programs, professional training, and research to support professionals working with male IPV victims (Di Napoli et al., 2019; Joe et al., 2020). Research findings of male victimization remain a subject of ambiguity that requires further research associated with the experiences of providers who work with the male IPV victim population (Clarke et al., 2017; Depraetere et al., 2020, 2018).

Study Rationale

Kulkarni and Kulkarni (2019) reported that support services could be used to foster the empathic relationship between counselors and marginalized male IPV victim clients. The authors suggested that mental health professionals' empathy for the marginalized male IPV victim population can appeal to the community for support (Kulkarni & Kulkarni, 2019). Studies indicated that while working with the male IPV victim population, the mental health service providers aimed to appeal to the community to operationalize primary healthcare equitable distributive resource support services (Bessaha et al., 2023; Nhedzi et al., 2022; Singh, 2016). Researchers have found that mental health providers received help from the cognitive knowledge and understanding of emotional healing support programs through spiritual and community advocacy support groups (Flasch et al., 2020, 2019; San-Martin et al., 2017). For McGinn et al. (2016), the fundamental rationale for the study highlighted the role of mental health professionals' empathy in treating male IPV survivors, improving their understanding of these clients, and perfecting their multidisciplinary social services.

Besides, Eckhardt et al. (2019) posited that mental health providers' empathy for the low- and middle-income class population associated with limited affordable healthcare systems for people experiencing poverty and marginalized IPV population cohort is vital for a new policy precept by public legislators. As Kulkarni and Kulkarni (2019) cited, Ogbe et al. (2020) articulated that "social support is vital for mitigating and moderating male IPV survivors' mental health concerns" (p. 1). However, some studies showed that social support services sustain the clients' empathic relational program recovery process (Shultz, 2020). Stylianou (2019, 2018) argued that mental health counselors offer programs describing support for men in advocating for male IPV victims. In contrast, government agencies provide legal programs such as family law and criminal justice systems guided by empowerment-based and survivor-centered approaches. Rossettini et al. (2018), describing psychotherapy and counseling intervention processes for victim-survivors of IPV, articulated a range of providers' empathic therapeutic procedures that have produced emotional functioning enhancements.

Significance of the Study

According to Capella Programs of Research (2020), Social and Community Services Specialization focuses on developing social services and community collaborations. Further, the study was significant for social and community service workers because it explored the insights and understanding of mental health service providers' feelings about and experiences implementing recovery programs and services for male IPV victims (Ferranti et al., 2018; Stylianou, 2019). The study's findings highlighted empathy's role in treating male IPV survivors. An improved understanding of these clients may improve the delivery of multidisciplinary social services.

Multidisciplinary social services insight would promote intervention programs and services more likely to meet these male IPV survivors' vulnerable population needs. Mental health professionals can use information from this study to better understand empathy's role in treating male IPV victims (McGinn et al., 2016). These experiences with compassion may provide mental health professionals with vital information for family advocacy, support groups, and treatment programs. Researchers asserted that male IPV victims are most likely to disclose their victimization experiences to informal individuals for support (e.g., friends and family) (Brooks et al., 2020; Edwards & Dardis, 2020). IPV disclosures presented positive empathic support and avoided victim-blame reactions (Edwards & Dardis, 2020).

On the other hand, the adverse reactions significant for IPV males' disclosures include ignoring and accusing the victim perpetrators (Ahrens et al., 2021; Sylaska & Edwards, 2014). Mental health service providers understanding the role of empathy in treating male IPV victims and social services support groups, such as a church, family, and friends, could improve the likelihood of these men's self-esteem improving (Ahrens et al., 2021; Dim, 2021; Sylaska & Edwards, 2014). Thus, the male IPV victims may feel confident enough to show their abuse and improve these treatment programs' efficacy (Ahrens et al., 2021; Dim, 2021). Mental health professionals administer empathy in inpatient care as a cognitive attribute for understanding the clients' experiences, concerns, and perceptions (San-Martin et al., 2017).

These service providers can articulate cognitive knowledge and understand intended emotional healing support programs through spiritual and community advocacy support groups (San-Martin et al., 2017). However, the public has less interest in male IPV survivors' well-being and has overlooked the need for mental health providers' emotional empathic support for victims' treatment (Huntley et al., 2019). Also, it is difficult to understand how mental health service providers measure the role of IPV perpetrators' behavior in providing empathic support for their male IPV victims (McGinn et al., 2016; Simmons et al., 2018).

According to Howell et al. (2016, 2014), clinicians have named risks and issues associated with the increased need for male IPV victims' mental health and well-being. Also, studies asserted that motivational empathy programs might significantly improve male IPV victims' treatment compliance (Romero-Martínez et al., 2019). However, researchers have little insight into mental health professionals' experiences with and beliefs about the role of empathy when working with IPV victims. For instance, while working with the male IPV victim population, the mental health service providers' roles may appeal to the community to operationalize primary healthcare fair support services (Kulkarni & Kulkarni, 2019). Furthermore, mental health providers' empathy for the low- and middle-income class population associated with limited affordable healthcare systems for the poor and marginalized IPV populations is crucial for public legislators' new policy precepts (Eckhardt et al., 2019).

Scholars' empirical studies indicated that social support services sustained clients' empathic relational recovery program process (Foye et al., 2022; Gunn & Miranda Samuels, 2020; Rollins, 2020; Stylianou, 2019, 2018). For example, "The family court system develops, implements, trains, supervises, and evaluates survivor-centered approaches to recovery programs" (Stylianou, 2019, p. 254). Stylianou (2019, 2018) further argued that mental health counselors offer programs describing support for men advocating for male IPV victims. Thus, for Gunn and Miranda Samuels (2020), support programs are essential for transforming IPV victims to treatment transitions to recovery from substance and alcohol addictions. In contrast, government agencies offer legal programs such as family law and criminal justice systems guided by empowerment-based and survivor-centered approaches (Bergman, 2020, 2019). Rossettini et al. (2018), describing psychotherapy and counseling intervention processes for victim-survivors of IPV, focused on various providers' empathic therapeutic procedures that have produced emotional-functioning enhancements.

Identified Gap

According to Sparrow et al. (2017), male IPV victims with mental illness are at increased risk of intimate partner violence victimization. Tarzia et al. (2020) posited that studies found that male IPV victims have experienced emotional, physical, and sexual abuse in their marital relationships. However, male IPV victims are reluctant to admit and show their marital relationship conflicts (Alsawalqa, 2023; Band-Winterstein, 2018; Nakalyowa-Luggya et al., 2022; Tarzia et al., 2020). Violent victimization is a unique stressor that may contribute to male IPV victims' physical and mental health (Schwab-Reese et al., 2017). Rizo and Rizo (2016) suggested that given the prevalence and harmful effects on male IPV victims, many researchers have focused on understanding the association between IPV and its adverse experiences for male survivors' well-being.

According to San-Martin et al. (2017), empathy in inpatient care is a cognitive attribute for understanding clients' experiences, concerns, and perceptions. Mental health service providers can articulate this cognitive knowledge and understanding in intended emotional healing support programs through spiritual and community advocacy support groups. However, the public has less interest in and has overlooked the need for mental health providers' emotional empathic support for male IPV victims (Huntley et al., 2019). Besides, it is difficult to understand how mental health service providers measure the role of IPV perpetrators' behavior in providing empathic support for their male IPV victims (McGinn et al., 2016; Simmons et al., 2021, 2018). Earlier articles indicated that clinicians had shown risks and issues associated with the increased need for male IPV victims' mental health and well-being (Howell et al., 2016, 2014). Furthermore, the findings of the literature reviewed suggested/indicated that mental health providers know that motivational empathy programs may significantly improve male IPV victims' treatment compliance (Romero-Martínez et al., 2019). Nonetheless, the gap is that the researcher may lack awareness of the roles of mental health professionals' experiences with and beliefs of empathy when working with IPV victims.

Research Question(s)

The research study's primary question was, "What are the mental health counselors' experiences with and beliefs about the role of empathy while working with male victims of intimate partner violence (IPV)?" The research study seemed to indicate the emotional experiences of how mental health counselors feel and understand working with IPV male victims/survivors' emotions, distress, and anxiety levels (Carlson et al., 2019, 2018; Eckstein & Eckstein, 2016). According to Taylor and Bates (2019), "The 1970s issues of intimate partner violence (IPV) have been explained through the patriarchal desire of men to dominate women; however, this gendered dynamic limited both counselors' understanding of IPV and its treatment" (p. 1312). To better serve male IPV survivors, practitioners must understand the role of aggressive behaviors associated with the development and incidence of IPV sexual abuse (Al-Modallal, 2016; Eckstein & Eckstein, 2016).

Falgares et al. (2018) have documented significant psychological (emotional), physical, sexual, and neglect as critical perspectives for mental health counselors fostering the development of strategic male IPV abuse programs. For example, in their integrated treatment options for male perpetrators of intimate partner violence, Crane Easton (2017) pointed out that motivational interviewing programs significantly improve intimate partner violence treatment compliance and diminish physical partner violence behaviors. This research study seems to indicate that intimate partner violence is physical, sexual, and psychological (emotional) harm to a sexually intimate partner that affects spouses in the United States (Doyle, 2020; Stöckl et al., 2021).

This research study provided insight into developing a holistic operationalized definition of an emotionally focused therapeutic model (Hardesty & Ogolsky, 2020). Finally, this research study adopted the IPV phenomena associated with the universal concept of violence defined by the World Health Organization:

> The deliberate use of natural force of power, susceptible or actual, in contradiction to any other person, or against a group or community that results in or has a high likelihood of injury, death, psychological harm, maldevelopment, or deprivation (WHO, 1996b, cited in Krug, Mercy, Dahlberg & WI, 2002, p. 1084)

Overview of the Methodology

Qualitative method was the best-suited approach for this study because it accounted for semi-structured open-ended interviews for focus groups, field observations, written materials, data collection, and inductive processes to develop research interpretation themes (Creswell, 2019; Kallio et al., 2016; Percy et al., 2015). Qualitative researchers make claims based on multiple meanings of individuals' experiences (Creswell & Poth, 2018; Coccia, 2020; Ebenau et al., 2020; Percy et al., 2015; Tavares et al., 2016). Thus, they used the qualitative method when the research question concerned respondents' experiences and feelings, while quantitative methods are suitable for testing a hypothesized relationship between variables (Creswell, 2019; Percy et al., 2015).

However, due to the non-quantitative paradigm of this study, a generic qualitative approach is significant in guiding this research because it is interested in the phenomena's actual and outer-world experiences (Percy et al., 2015). Generic qualitative inquiry is an exploratory approach appropriate for articulating an understanding of feelings, opinions, and event phenomena, such as mental health professionals' empathic roles with male IPV victims' recovery programs (Bryson et al., 2017; Percy et al., 2015). The generic thematic inductive process was administered with constant comparisons of the data analysis paradigm to foster meaning from the data sources (Creswell & Poth, 2018; Coccia, 2020; Percy et al., 2015).

Unlike generic qualitative studies, phenomenological research focuses on the individual's internal subjective psychological structures, the intent of opinions, and attitude experiences (Kennedy, 2016; Kallio et al., 2016; Percy et al., 2015). By contrast, Bellamy et al. (2016) and Nowell et al. (2017) reported that generic qualitative research deals with external and real-world experience, contrary to internal psychological and subjective beliefs. This generic qualitative research framework fills the gap in the literature by discovering, understanding, and developing knowledge suitable for professional counselors' empathy roles while working with IPV victims' experiences, thus conducive to this dissertation (Cheung, 2016; Falkenström et al., 2016; Kim et al., 2019).

Definition of Terms

This dissertation's practical operational terms fostering understanding and enlightenment include the following:

Empathy

Mental health professionals' empathic roles include expressing social-emotional responses and interpersonal feeling anataxis's (arrangements of parts again) reactivity to patients (Hall et al., 2021).

Intimate Partner Violence

IPV involves psychological aggression, bimodal classification of impulse instead of instrumental aggression, and the perceived need to control the partner instead of the ability to exercise self-control (Blake et al., 2018; Dim, 2021, 2020). According to Dim (2021), "Intimate partner violence (IPV) refers to acts of violence performed against intimate partners, spouses, and dating partners, either in current or former relationships" (p. 1029).

Mental Health Professionals/Providers

Mental health providers are state-licensed professionals who deliver psychological therapy, including diagnosis, treatment programs, and psychosocial interventions to patients (Apolinário-Hagen et al., 2017; Bartholomew et al., 2021).

Psychological (Emotional) Abuse

Male IPV victims' emotional abuse includes yelling, haranguing (i.e., lengthy, critical, and aggressive speech), criticizing, devaluing, demeaning, threatening, and coercing (Dim, 2020).

Research Design

The generic qualitative approach was essential for describing, interpreting, and analyzing the study's research question (Booth et al., 2018; Kennedy, 2016; Percy et al., 2015). The current research question was, "What is the counselor's experience with and belief in the role of empathy while working with male clients who experience IPV?" Percy et al. (2015) said that ethnography explores a defined culture's social groupings, customs, beliefs, behaviors, and practices. Moreover, unlike a generic qualitative study, phenomenological research focuses on the individual's internal subjective psychological structures, the intent of opinions, and attitude experiences (Kennedy, 2016; Percy et al., 2015). Moustakas (1994) and Giogi (2009) described this study approach as one that explores respondents' descriptive and interpretive lived experiences. On the other hand, the generic qualitative approach is suitable for this study because it is interested in actual and outer-world experiences (De Waard & Kalkman, 2022; Percy et al., 2015). A literature review of generic qualitative research about the meaning, understanding, and straightforward thematic procedure for sampling data collection and analysis was found proper for this study (Awenat et al., 2019; Bandara et al., 2015; Houghton et al., 2017; Gogo & Musonda, 2022; Percy et al., 2015).

Assumptions

According to Berland and Crucet (2016), the research question explained epistemological, ontological, and axiological assumptions. This scientific knowledge fostered understanding, explained, and developed meaningful information about mental health professionals' empathy with male IPV victims. The epistemological assumption was that these understandings supported the researchers' construction and evaluation of scientific knowledge (Berland & Crucet, 2016). Ontological assumptions describe the nature of reality, namely that multiple realities exist to effectively communicate the overall study design (McCrudden & Marchand, 2020).

Axiological assumptions promote an understanding of experiences with objectivity but inherently with misleading subjective values, intuition, and biases of social reconstruction dialogue and data interpretation (Greshilova et al., 2020). Greshilova et al. (2020) contended that axiological subjective values stem from (a) a person is subject to the cultural space of continuous education, (b) a person is a self-developing personality, and (c) a continuous education pursuit. The researcher used bracketing to set aside any biases and preconceptions to avoid negative implications during data collection and analysis in a qualitative study. Therefore, researchers must be aware of prejudices and preconceptions and how those might influence data collection and analysis. Sorsa et al. (2015) said that bracketing promotes scientific rigor, trustworthiness, and validity in any qualitative study.

General Methodological Assumptions

The researcher accounted for several methodological assumptions. A qualitative method design was the best-fitted approach for this study. The researcher used semi-structured open-ended interviews for focus groups, field observations, written materials, and inductive thematic analysis with constant comparison processes (Burelomova et al., 2018; Percy et al., 2015). The researcher assumed the inductive data analysis paradigm fosters meaning from the individual interviewed data sources to help explore repeated patterns (Creswell & Poth, 2018; Coccia, 2020; Percy et al., 2015; Patton, 2015). The researcher assumed this knowledge enriches the understanding of mental health counselors' feelings of and experiences with empathy while working with male IPV victims (Percy et al., 2015). Researchers assumed that a generic approach is significant for training novice clinicians to work with IPV persons with addictions and ease recovery treatment and substance abuse recovery treatment (Di Napoli et al., 2019; Mackowiak & Scoglio, 2018).

A purposeful sampling approach was used for the research because of the intentionally homogeneous selected clinicians' professional respondents. Semi-structured interview questions focused on the respondent's empathy experiences while working with male IPV victims. Percy et al. (2015) recommended data collection elements to ensure reliable thematic information. The researcher assumed the interview elements to include in-depth semi-structured and open-ended interview questions (Kallio et al., 2016; Percy et al., 2015; Patton, 2015; Santo-Tomás Muro et al., 2020). During the research, I assumed that thematic data analysis involves organizing data, then standing for the output in a way that defines them (Monteleone & Forrester-Jones, 2017; Phipps et al., 2018; Percy et al., 2015).

Theoretical Assumptions

Nonetheless, Burelomova et al. (2018) suggested that "theoretical frameworks for studying IPV appeared complex and multifaceted, with a dearth of empirical viability findings" (p. 128). Thus, a narrow theoretical stance might prevent a variety of exploratory insights for understanding the current topic: mental health providers' experience and feelings of the role of empathy while working with clients who experience IPV (Augsburger et al., 2019; Burelomova et al., 2018). According to Gabbay, Lafontaine, and Lafontaine (2017), the established significance of attachment theory promotes support for mental health clinicians to understand heterosexual IPV conflict outcomes. Besides, Ulloa & Hammett's (2016) empirical findings suggested that more petite empathic men were more likely to perpetrate IPV and be victimized.

Topic-Specific Assumptions

The rationale assumption of this study was to use generic qualitative methods to explore and understand counselors' empathic role experiences and beliefs when working with male

IPV victims (El Sayed et al., 2022). Percy et al. (2015) showed that when researchers want to understand a subject thoroughly from their participants' perspectives, a generic qualitative framework emphasizes individuals' reports of a real-life experience. Earlier authors argued that while investigating from a generic qualitative perspective, a researcher learns about mental health professionals' empathic thoughts, viewpoints, opinions, and attitudes about a topic or experience (Artioli et al., 2021; Barker et al., 2019; Percy et al., 2015; Kaligis et al., 2022). Braun et al. (2022) and Koning et al. (2022) assumed that the study problem is a lack of information about mental health providers' experiences with empathy when working with male IPV victims.

Limitations

Design Flaw Limitations

The limitation of the generic qualitative research approach used to explore the research question was the paucity of literature about administering it well. The validity of generic research design as a qualitative method seemed debatable (Bellamy et al., 2016). Preconception and pre-understanding are what was known and understood before interpretation. A core flaw aspect of the generic qualitative study is that the researcher is considered inextricable from assumptions and preconceptions about the phenomena under scrutiny. These assumptions and prejudices of constant data analysis were acknowledged and integrated into the research findings (Correa da Cunha, 2022; Lovegrove & Bannigan, 2021; Percy et al., 2015).

Delimitations (Intentional Areas Not Investigated)

Trustworthiness is essential in this generic qualitative study because it ensures that the research outcome is credible, transferable, and dependable for a correct result. Hence, Cloutier and Ravasi (2021) found that trustworthiness provides a study's transparency. The researcher's role as the critical study instrument might precipitate "biases and misconceptions" potential for the research limitation. Sesar and Šimić (2018) posited that their study findings highlighted the active, reactive, and adaptive needs for treatment services to screen and assess the wide range of psychological difficulties. These psychological issues include anger, anxiety, depression, suicide, personality disorders, alcoholism, gambling, and IPV perpetration to provide the best treatment approaches for survivors (Berry et al., 2020; Sesar and Šimić, 2018). Moreover, the researcher's roles depend on the situation and challenges posed by the inquiry's topic (Wilson et al., 2018), the results' primary users (Bjorkvold et al., 2018), the researcher's dominant style (Javed et al., 2020), the purpose of the investigations (Fedrigo et al., 2023), and the characteristics that the research incorporated into the inquiry (Hoogendijk et al., 2023).

Organization of the Remainder of the Study

Chapter 1 of this study presents the background of the study, the need for the study, the purpose, significance, research question, key terms definitions, research design, assumptions, and limitations. Chapter 1 shows the general methodological assumptions of the study. These assumptions include epistemological, ontological, and axiological to explain the research question. Male IPV survivors' hindrances hindered the respondents' empathic role experiences for providing support. These hindrances include (a) fear of disclosure, a challenge to masculinity, commitment to relationship, diminished confidence/despondency, and invisibility/belief of services; and (b) experiences of interventions and support: first contact, confidentiality, and proper, inappropriate professional approaches (Huntley et al., 2019).

Entilli and Cipolletta's (2017) research study showed gaps in service provision presented by a dearth of information perceived as prejudice toward abused IPV men. However, the literature reviewed indicated a lack of empirical studies on mental health providers' empathy experiences of male IPV victims' experiences (Huntley et al., 2019; MacLeod, 2019; McCarrick et al., 2016, 2015). Thus, the research problem was the lack of information about mental health providers' experiences with empathy when working with male IPV victims (Field et al., 2018; Woernle et al., 2019). Another concern was a gap in the current research about the understanding of mental health counselors' experiences with and feelings of the role of empathy while working with male IPV victims (Williams et al., 2020). Hence, to merit this gap, I proposed the mental health provider's empathic role in supporting male victims' treatment and prevention plans (Entilli & Cipolletta, 2017).

The rationale of Chapter 2 is to review the study's scholarly literature. The literature reviewed will indicate the preliminary information about the topic, terms of the research outcomes, and the theoretical orientation for the study. The chapter will indicate the synthesis of the research findings, the theoretical orientation's strengths, and its demerits, and show the earlier method and critique of the method.

Chapter 3 will show the protocol, methods, and procedures used in the study for future research. The chapter will indicate the study's purpose with a brief scholarly introduction, the research question, and design. The chapter will show the target population, the purposive sampling size, and the differences. It will also describe the methodology's procedures that explain the data collection procedure, analysis, and ethical considerations.

Chapter 4 will highlight the study results, the sample presentation, the methodization of the data collected, the data analysis, the description of the chapter, and the researcher's role, knowledge, and experiences of the topic.

Chapter 5 will show the study's conclusion, highlighting the significant limitations with delimitations to collaborate recommendations for future research studies regarding mental health providers' empathy experiences of male IPV victims' experiences.

Literature Review

Chapter 2

Scholars suggested that formal invaluable services, civic organizations, healthiness, or the iniquitous justice system are significant support resources for male IPV victims and mental health professionals' empathic programs (Robinson et al., 2021; Falcone & Meynen, 2019; Mackowiak & Scoglio, 2018). On average, IPV researchers and policymakers asserted that one in four women and one in ten men in the United States had experienced IPV issues. These IPV issues include physical violence, sexual violence, and stalking (Robinson et al., 2021; Harris, 2023). Forty-three million women and thirty-eight million men (about twice the population of New York) reported experiencing emotional IPV (Robinson et al., 2021; Harris, 2023). Recovery support is a significant community issue (Machado et al., 2017; Machado et al., 2020; Robinson et al., 2021). According to Machado et al. (2017) and Robinson et al. (2021), these help-seeking hurdles could constrain male IPV survivors to mitigate anxiety, depression, and emotional distress, including (a) limited social consciousness, (b) obstacles of fear of negative family response, (c) masculinity disclosure credibility, (d) dearth of recovery program resources, and (e) policymakers' failures to adhere to advocacy groups. Researchers addressed the need for mental health professionals to continue empathic education compared to available services (Kaspersen et al., 2022; Lentz et al., 2022).

Researchers found the significance of male IPV victims' physical and emotional issues and the continued development of resources to mitigate personal barriers that male survivors may face (Machado et al., 2017; Robinson et al., 2021). According to Carraro et al. (2023) and Vilamala et al. (2022), mental health professionals' treatment assessment of cognitive-behavioral treatment (CBT) has provided promising results in reducing aggression in IPV relationships. Thus, CBT shows measuring phenomena for male victims' mental health. Paterson et al. (2022, 2020) found that "intimate partner violence (IPV) is a global social issue distressing all populations irrespective of gender, race, and socioeconomic status" (Paterson et al., 2022, p. 2599). Thus, IPV is an essential target for mental health professionals' prevention and intervention recovery programs to mitigate victims' anxiety and emotional distress (Paterson et al., 2022, 2020; World Health Organization, 2013). Hence, this study merged to fill a knowledge gap in intimate partner violence in the aftermath of the violence on the victims (Adomako & Darkwa, 2021).

This chapter highlights the literature review compared to the topic. The chapter indicates the existing literature, search methods, and the study's theoretical orientation. In addition, the chapter shows generic and qualitative method design as the fitting framework for the analysis. Further, the synthesis of the findings is presented.

Methods of Searching

The literature reviewed for this study was done through electronic databases PsycINFO, Capella Library, Capella dissertations, Sage Journals, and the Google Scholar research engine. Furthermore, electronic resources were searched, including the World Health Organization website http://whol.int/topics/violence/en (Tarzia et al., 2020). The researcher garnered more than a hundred scholarly peer-reviewed articles via Capella and Google Scholar databases on the topic "mental health professionals' experiences with and perceptions of the role of empathy while working with male intimate partner violence (IPV) victims." The scholarly journals previewed included (a) *Journal of Interpersonal Violence*, (b) *Qualitative Social Work: Q.S.W.: Research and Practice*, (c) *European Journal of Social Psychology*, (d) *Mediterranean Journal of Clinical Psychology*, (e) *Journal of the Society for Social Work and Research*, (f) *Journal of Motivation and Emotion*, (g) *Journal of Psychology in Russia: State of the Art*, (h) *Journal of Social Philosophy & Policy*, (i) *Journal of Psychiatry Research*, (j) *Journal of Attachment and Loss*, (k) *Journal of Aggressive Behavior*, and (l) *Journal of Psychology of Men & Masculinity*. In addition, the study method and overview of basic design concepts were workable resources for the existing systematic reviewed criteria.

Theoretical Framework for the Current Study

Empathetic simulation theory guided this study design to address the topic of mental health professionals' experiences with and perceptions of the role of empathy while working with male IPV victims (Bates et al., 2020; Bui & Pasalich, 2021; Hardesty & Ogolsky, 2020; Lopez, 2010; McCarrick et al., 2016; Ulloa & Hammett, 2016; Velotti, 2020; Zosky, 2016). Heng (2020) said that research theory provides the understanding of a phenomenon, such as the mental health of male IPV victims, and describes, designs, interprets, analyzes, and pluralizes the study design. Furthermore, theory and practice indicated comprehensively a critical association between male IPV victims and their problems in healthcare and socio-legal contexts (Cascardi et al., 2020). Hence, theoretical perspectives underpinned inquiries into the nature and etiology of the IPV phenomenon of fundamental importance in fostering mental health providers' understanding of preventing, reducing, or cutting male IPV mental health disorders (Burelomova et al., 2018).

Social and Community Services (Human Services) researchers recommend theoretical and conceptual frameworks for dissertation programs (Cunningham-Williams et al., 2019; Klag & Langley, 2013; Locke & Boyle, 2016; Wansink & van Ittersum, 2016). Abramo et al. (2017) articulated that the empathic simulation paradigm tries to collaborate the mind-body unity through the neuronal brain structures from a neuroscientific perspective. The neuroscientific process explored the interconnecting links between the mind, implicit memory, and mirror neurons. Abramo et al. (2017) further posited that mind-body integration inquiry fosters theoretical understanding and practice of the psychotherapeutic process. Thus, the insight into the psychotherapeutic process enhanced mental health professionals' recovery program development for male IPV victims.

Schadler's (2016) study indicated that about fifty years ago, Talcott Parsons and Robert Bales (1956) described the nuclear family system as a male and a female adult. At least one child is the social norm. Nonetheless, the nuclear family model restructures North American and European society's structural level to the trinity of marriage, sex, and childbirth. However, this covenant relationship appears disconnected (Schadler, 2016). Again, according to Bowen (1978), social learning and family system theories served as a mechanism for investigating the potential role of offspring maternal forgiveness in the intergenerational transmission (IGT) of violence (Rivera & Fincham, 2015). However, theory and practice articles previewed posited that the IPV concerns included healthcare and socio-legal contexts (Burelomova et al., 2018). Significantly, theoretical perspectives underlying inquiries into the nature and etiology of the IPV phenomenon were of fundamental relevance in fostering researchers' and mental health professionals' understanding of preventing, reducing, or cutting the problem (Burelomova et al., 2018; Peled & Krigel, 2016; Spencer et al., 2021; Thorvaldsdottir, 2022, 2021).

Review of the Literature

Earlier research findings indicated that intimate partner violence (IPV) seemed to be a major global problem, camouflaging/masking as a challenge to public health and clinical practice (Burelomova et al., 2018; Tarzia et al., 2020; Walker et al. 2020; World Health Organization, 2013). Walker et al. (2020) found that intimate partner violence is a global problem of social, health, and cultural disparities. Due to the cultural, economic, social, and political uncertainties, intimate partner violence has become a severe global public health issue (Adjei, 2017; Cofie, 2020; Magezi & Manzanga, 2020; Morris et al., 2022, 2020; Walker et al., 2020). Also, Huntley et al. (2019) found that counselors' empathy in their treatment programs could help male IPV victims overcome their mental disorders and emotional distress issues. Researchers Dim (2021) and Huntley et al. (2019) have explored mental health issues to support counselors in developing recovery programs. For example, according to Santos et al. (2017), an eight-week group cognitive-behavioral intervention program with psychological self-assessment for male victims of IPV revealed a positive impact on the participants. This program (GCBIP) evaluation indicated a decrease in revictimization and in beliefs toward legitimizing IPV. A decrease in levels of depression and a significant improvement in general clinical symptoms were also evident (Santos et al., 2017). For Santos et al. (2017), self-esteem and social support were enhanced through group intervention. The effect of the GCBIP program may indicate a decrease in male IPV victims' emotional distress, depression, and anxiety and improve their self-esteem (Dabrowska & Boduszek, 2017, 2016). Shah et al. (2018) have proven a relationship between trauma exposure and psychotic experiences. However, there was a universal lack/dearth of research literature to mitigate adult trauma exposure, including IPV risk factors for psychotic experiences such as schizophrenia (Galletly et al., 2016; Machisa et al., 2018; Shah et al., 2018; Volpe et al., 2018).

IPV Historical Context

Most current signs/signals related to IPV come from Western countries like the United States (Walker et al., 2020). However, unlike in the United States, there is limited evidence of IPV in developing countries like Saudi Arabia (Alhalal et al., 2021, 2019). Currently, scholars informed that the concerns of IPV are in Saudi Arabia with a paucity of data outcomes (Alhalal et al., 2021, 2019). Male IPV victims reported experiencing physical, sexual, verbal, threatening, and coercive abusive behaviors in their relationships (Burelomova et al., 2018; Dim, 2020; Huntley et al., 2019; Walker et al., 2020). According to Dim (2020) and Abudulai et al. (2022), there is a paucity of studies on the experiences of anger, control, jealousy, and emotional coercion among mental health providers' role of empathy feelings and opinions on male victims of intimate partner violence. Researchers have little empirical generic methodologies framework research designs on male IPV victims (Burelomova et al., 2018; Huntley et al., 2019; Walker et al., 2020).

According to Walker et al. (2020), in 2010, in the United States, 24.3% of females and 13.8% of males accounted for lifetime IPV physical violence experience that included fists and objects, beating, and slamming. The scholars premised that during the prior year, out of 48% of females, 14%, and 48.8% of males, 18% reported experiencing IPV psychological dilemmas (Walker et al., 2020). Furthermore, 30% of females and 10% of males reported experiencing the IPV aftermath: fear, injuries, and posttraumatic stress disorder symptoms (Bryngeirsdottir & Halldorsdottir, 2022; Gilmore & Flanagan, 2020, 2019; Kelly & Garland, 2016). In Canada, 6% of people in a relationship from 2007 to 2012 reported being victims of physical or sexual violence, while 17% affirmed having been victims of psychological or economic violence (Walker et al., 2020).

Male IPV victims' issues have influenced victims' and perpetrators' social and legal interventions (Cofie, 2020; Corbin & Strauss, 2008; Magezi & Manzana, 2020; Strauss & Corbin, 1990). According to this viewpoint, IPV is a behavior that addresses patriarchal values that contribute to men's control and domination of their spouses (Asiimwe, 2021). Mental health providers noted that female IPV perpetrators cause serious harm to male victims (Jewkes et al., 2021; Labarre et al., 2019). Hence, male IPV victims' poor emotional and mental health is a social problem that deserves much public attention and resources (Dim, 2021; Labarre et al., 2019). Hence, this generic qualitative method indicated the research process to fill the mental health providers' knowledge, understanding, and social and public consciousness gap.

Machado et al. (2017) found intimate partner violence a worldwide phenomenon. Nonetheless, limited qualitative research explored male IPV survivors victimized by female partner perpetrators. According to Taylor and Bates (2019), history has shown that the 1970s IPV problems stemmed from patriarchal men-dominated women—however, this gendered dynamism limited counselors' understanding of IPV and its treatment. To better serve male IPV survivors, practitioners must understand the role of aggressive behaviors associated with the development and incidence of IPV sexual abuse (Al-Modallal, 2016). Thus, the research problem was a lack of information about mental health providers' experiences with empathy when working with male IPV victims (Johnson et al., 2020; Ravi et al., 2022). The following information will further provide an understanding of this study's topic.

Male Victims of Intimate Partner Violence

Park et al. (2021) found that, like in the United States, males in other cultures, such as Korean men, experience spousal IPV victimization. Dim (2021) in Canada also upheld that despite the existing arguments that IPV significantly affects female victims, he suggested that men, too, are victims of IPV, universally in heterosexual relationships. For Dim (2021), intimate partner violence refers to acts of violence enacted against intimate partners, spouses, and dating partners in current or former relationships. Park et al. (2021) found empirical research that intimate partner violence involves physical, psychological, and sexual violence in a personal connection. For the victims, it often leads to devastating outcomes such as physical injuries and posttraumatic stress disorder (PTSD). Research on IPV has been conducted for several decades. Scholars argued about male-to-female perpetration, but men's victimization has been neglected. According to Park et al. (2021), men's IPV victimization experiences in Korean society are impeded by a lack of understanding and information on how men are victimized.

Nevertheless, Dim (2021) contended that there had been few studies on the experiences of physical and psychological abuse among men and the aftermath effects. Psychological IPV uniquely differs from physical, especially its indifferent impacts on male IPV victims (Dim & Elabor-Idemudia, 2018; Doherty & Berglund, 2008). Spencer et al. (2024) and Cowlishaw et al. (2022) reported that emotional distress in IPV harms men's mental and physical health. However, there has been a paucity of generic qualitative studies on how emotional distress IPV affects male victims. Nevertheless, Dim and Elabor-Idemudia (2018) found that the masculine ego in one society can shape male victims' thoughts, emotions, reactions, and behaviors. Thus, the masculine ego assumes that male IPV victims in the United States are not indifferent to Korean male IPV victims seeking help (Dim & Elabor-Idemudia, 2018; Park et al., 2021). Furthermore, Machado (2021) of Portugal reported that intimate partner violence is a well-known social, criminal, and health problem. However, intimate partner violence against male victims has a dearth of academic, social, and scientific attention (Machado, 2021).

According to Tarzia et al. (2020), in 2010, in the US, intimate partner violence was common in patients attending healthcare services and is associated with various health problems. Most IPV perpetrators are men, while a significant minority are victims

(Tarzia et al., 2020). Nonetheless, healthcare professionals have little evidence or guidance on responding to male patients who experience violence in their intimate relationships (Dim & Elabor-Idemudia, 2018). Overall, mental healthcare providers' treatment services have limited and weak intervention services and resources to mitigate male IPV perpetrators' aggressions and behaviors (Heim et al., 2018; Heim et al., 2019). Thus, this study showed the gap in mental health providers' empathic treatment needs protocol for male IPV victims.

Bates's (2020, 2019) study found that men's IPV experiences affect their physical, mental, and emotional health relationships. The impact of attitudes toward male victims of IPV is significant because the survivors felt society disbelieved men who described these experiences, often perceiving them as "weak" yet perpetrators (Bates, 2020, 2019). Society stigmatized men's IPV disclosures as a weakness, preventing them from seeking help (Sivagurunathan et al., 2019). Thus, this cultural masculinity identity discouraged and hindered men's experiences seeking and exiting the relationship/marriage (Gage & Lease, 2021, 2018). Dim (2021, 2020) reported that male IPV victims experienced physical and psychological IPV, as well as the consequences of such abuse, resulting in physical, controlling, and threatening behaviors and verbal abuse. The aftermath of the male victims' abuse resulted in physical and psychological setbacks such as emotional distress, poor mental health, and PTSD (Dim, 2021; Gage & Lease, 2021, 2018).

Masculinity and Male IPV Victims

The concept of masculinity has been employed to understand the nature and the epidemic of the gendered experiences of men's IPV victimization in society (Dim, 2021; Cofie, 2020). Hegemonic masculinity tends to involve a high degree of cruel competition, an inability to express emotions other than anger, refusal to admit weakness or reliance, devaluation of women and all-female characteristics in men, and homophobia (Brooks et al., 2020; Dim, 2021). However, researchers argued that hegemonic masculinity is socially constructed and orients men's belief of feeling vulnerable toward denying or suppressing their feelings (Dim, 2021). The construction of masculinity might also mold men not to have the skills to deal with emotional pains (Dim, 2021, 2020; Peretz et al., 2020). This traditional masculinity paradigm precludes mental health professionals' empathic recovery treatment change insight (Jordan & Bedi, 2021).

Dim (2021, 2020) found that despite uncertainties with the experiences, male IPV victims acknowledged their masculinity instead of meeting the sexual expectations of their peers and society. Brooks et al. (2020) reported that male victims of IPV tend to resist showing their victimhood status but reframe their status as a "victim" to keep their unity. Thus, abused men tend to delude their abuse narrative to dissociate their identities as men from that of an abused person (Corbally, 2015). Eckstein (2010) also used the concept of masculinity for mental health providers to explain that men adhere to their victimization through societal and self-blame. Thus, this male identity creates misconceptions about how mental health professionals administer empathic recovery treatment programs.

On the contrary, Aragbuwa (2021) and Dim (2021, 2020) attested those male victims upheld their power and control while still under victimization bondage. Researchers contended that the abused men resisted the perpetrators yet shrewdly defended their spouses' aggressive behaviors and falsely claimed acceptance for their spouses' actions. Other scholars have employed the concept of masculinity to understand how men make sense of IPV (Dim, 2021, 2020; Di Napoli et al., 2019; Gage & Lease, 2021, 2018; Morgan & Wells, 2016). Thus, these studies indicated that masculinity distorts the experiences, realities, and beliefs of IPV male victims (Dim, 2021, 2020; Brooks et al., 2020; Holiday et al., 2019, 2018). Hence, the present study seeks to explore the mental health providers' empathic roles and feelings in collaboration with the masculinity concept to make sense of male IPV victims' recovery program experiences (Dim, 2021, 2020; Di Napoli et al., 2019; Gage & Lease,

2021, 2018; Morgan & Wells, 2016). This behavior seems to challenge mental health providers' empathic role dispensation.

Multicultural Challenges of Male IPV Survivors

Scholars attested that African American males are more likely to report experiencing IPV than any other racial group (Al'Uqdah et al., 2016; Bent-Goodley, 2004). Researchers found that prevalent male IPV populations in the American Indian community and a spectrum of adverse health outcomes are associated with IPV among the general population (Kafka et al., 2021; McKinley et al., 2020; Shultz et al., 2021). They have also partnered with many providers to aid in the school setting and link students to outside resources. Spiritual dogma as sanctification and forgiveness is paramount to deter male IPV victims' minds, souls, and hearts from the spiritual transformation (Carroll & Prickett, 1998; Crim, 1970; Romans 12:1–5). Hence, Houston-Kolnik et al. (2019) found that religious leaders provide and respond to male IPV victims' emotional-help seekers.

Furthermore, religious leaders acknowledged training and support for mental health empathic provider programs (Dim, 2021, 2020); however, they reported a paucity of IPV resources and community organization interaction (Houston-Kolnik et al., 2019). Nonetheless, "We know that intimate partner violence (IPV)" against women is a breach of human rights and one form of discrimination (Benebo et al., 2018; Gracia et al., 2019; Lundberg-Love & Marmion, 2006). What about women's perpetration against men? Hence, mental health professionals, social workers, and public policymakers are implored to design effective strategies for meeting the demands and needs of the male IPV victim population (Noel et al., 2022; Martin et al., 2018; Manjunatha, 2023). Intimate partner violence is a severe epidemic among Asian immigrant communities (Kim & Hogge, 2015; Lacey et al., 2016; Lee & Hadeed, 2009). However, we know little about the scope, nature, context, and cultural and social factors of IPV among this Asian population (Lin et al., 2018; Tripathi & Azhar, 2022). Male IPV victims are susceptible to stigmatization, and fear vulnerability and safeguarding efforts (Thorvaldsdottir et al., 2021). This fear of male IPV victims' masculinity is an affront discouraging zeal for mental health providers' empathic services to sustain male IPV victims' resilience passion (Alsawalqa, 2023; Childress et al., 2024; Doyle & McWilliams, 2020; Lysova et al., 2022; Rubini et al., 2023).

 Ndlovu et al. (2022), Yonga et al. (2022), and Santos et al. (2019) said that intimate partner violence is a noteworthy public health challenge for emotional and mental distress. Healthcare providers (e.g., physicians, counselors, and social workers) have the empathic privilege to transform male IPV survivors via screening and referral. For instance, Bird (2016), Brown et al. (2021), and Nasrallah et al. (2023) studies found that a traumatic brain injury (TBI) is an injury caused by frequent hitting of the IPV victim to the brain. This behavior caused head, neck, and face injuries (Brown et al., 2021; Esterov et al., 2024; Nasrallah et al., 2023). Male IPV survivors are vulnerable to TBI. Thus, empathetic mental health practitioners could adopt this screening instrument to explore and analyze their clients' feelings and experiences to enhance a reliable and practical data collection protocol (Brown et al., 2019; Esterov et al., 2024; Nasrallah et al., 2023). In the past, public domestic violence (DV) programs were standard in communities across the country, intending to support survivors but with futile outcomes (Goodman et al., 2015; Goodman & Walker, 2016; Tarzia et al., 2016). The lack of resources to mitigate IPV issues challenges community advocates and policy authorities for new legislation (Hoare et al., 2022, 2021; Heron et al., 2022; Murshid & Bowen, 2018) and education to combat IPV's social, political, and economic marginalization limitations (Kimuna et al., 2018; Sutton et al., 2021). This study fills the gap with the depicted community collaborators (e.g., policymakers, researchers, and mental health providers) for mental health professionals' empathic services for male IPV victims and spouses (Chatterji et al., 2020; Di Napoli et al., 2019; Mackowiak & Scoglio, 2018).

Mental Health Providers' Empathic Roles for Male IPV Victims

Transformation Challenges. Hardesty et al. (2020) found that resolving IPV family issues requires individual, social, legal, and ecological collaborative efforts to mitigate this social dilemma. However, mental health professionals have a dearth of resources, information, knowledge, and understanding to deal with male IPV victims (Labarre et al., 2019; Roy et al., 2020). This study's literature review suggested that mental health professionals' experiences with and perceptions of the role of empathy while working with male IPV victims are suitable to fill this gap (Romero-Martínez et al., 2019; Romero-Martínez et al., 2016; Watson, 2019). This study found that mental health professionals' empathic roles seem fit for males who have experienced IPV abuse (Crane & Easton, 2017; Harvey et al., 2018; McGinn et al., 2016; Romero-Martínez et al., 2019; Romero-Martínez et al., 2016; Stern & Carlson, 2019; Watson, 2019).

For Stern and Niyibizi (2018), IPV gender transformation requires communities' and society's fair attention, beliefs, and attitudes for impactful outcomes. For Stern and Niyibizi (2018), a pragmatic development to resolve the IPV issue in Rwanda is the Indashyikirwa program. This program aims to mitigate IPV concerns and foster healthy, hospitable relationships (Stern & Niyibizi, 2018; Tarshis & Baird, 2019; Tarshis et al., 2022). This five-month program is designed for heterosexual couples to explore economic, emotional, physical, and sexual IPV limitations to build a more amicable relationship (Stern & Niyibizi, 2018). The title of this IPV transformation program is Engaging Men through Accountable Practice (EMAP) (Stern & Niyibizi, 2018). This study indicated this resource gap for mental health providers fostering male IPV empathy roles (Dekel et al., 2019; Dekel & Abrahams, 2023; Tan et al., 2023).

Male IPV Empowerment Tenets

Researchers held that the association between the mental health providers' empathy advocate and male IPV survivors fosters significant IPV traumatic abuse healing protocol (Cislaghi & Heise, 2018; Chatterji et al., 2020; Dichter et al., 2019; Dichter et al., 2022). However, there is a paucity of research on advocate-survivor alliance for male IPV victims for a cordial spousal relationship (Goodman et al., 2016; Hardesty & Ogolsky, 2020). Community-based interaction and education promotion are vital for social cohesiveness. Scholars reported that community-based relationships carry out and empower changing social norms (Dichter et al., 2022; Dim & Lysova, 2022). However, due to limited literature, obscure community dialogs take part in interconnections to effect change (Dichter et al., 2022; Dim & Lysova, 2022; Valandra et al., 2019). Participants in community-based IPV interventions are empowered to collaborate knowledge, experiences, and understandings systematically with others in their networks, eventually helping change social norms (Mittal et al., 2023; Valandra et al., 2019). Future community-based interventions and social norms would help mental health practitioners by coordinating strategies to mobilize mental health for program information networks to empower peers (Dichter et al., 2022; Valandra et al., 2019). For instance, researchers believe that African American male solutions-focused IPV empirical study could offer ideas of Black men propagating programs, policies, and male IPV intervention efforts in African American communities (Bent-Goodley, 2004; Dichter et al., 2022; Valandra et al., 2019). Mental health providers collaborating with African American men with untapped resources could respond to and prevent IPV in African American families in rural southern communities of the US. (Dichter et al., 2022; Valandra et al., 2019). According to Valandra et al. (2019), little research examined IPV/DV from the spectra of African American views, feelings, experiences, and socio-demographic backgrounds within rural African American communities. Hence, the vitality of this study topic, mental health professionals' experiences with and beliefs in the role of empathy while working with male IPV victims, indicates the need for future research (Dichter et al., 2022; Valandra et al., 2019).

Male IPV Survivors' Adverse Experiences

This study's primary focus explored the mental health professionals' beliefs of and experiences of the role of empathy while working with males who experience IPV psychological distress, depression, and anxiety (Kimber et al., 2015; Ridings et al., 2017). This research problem was significant for IPV sexual abuse, social support, and spiritual prevention programs (Jung et al., 2019). According to Brooks et al. (2020), researchers have focused on women's experiences of intimate partner violence. However, researchers have lacked researching qualitative studies on men who experience IPV (Dim, 2021). Brooks et al. (2020) reported that male IPV victims' mental health concerns include fear, anxiety, victimization, and distress that harm their cognitive health. Mental health service providers understanding these empathic mental health experiences may develop and promote intervention strategies to foster a more positive impact on male IPV victims' experiences with sexual maltreatment and domestic violence levels of distress, depression, anxiety, and emotions (Kimber et al., 2015; Ridings et al., 2017). Ridings et al. (2017) contended that social support and family resources are pivotal empathic protective factors in buffering against IPV-risk families' homes. The authors also suggested that the counselor's empathic role may include domestic parenting programs to target core risk and protective factors for male IPV abuse (Ridings et al., 2017). Applying these prior approaches could guide counselors in empathic home-based delivery services and support programs for males' IPV counseling decision-making process (Ridings et al., 2017).

Empathy Experiences Associated with Male IPV Survivors

San-Martín et al. (2017) reported that empathy is associated with male IPV clients' cognitive attributes for understanding their experiences, concerns, and perceptions. Collaborating on these attributes can improve mental health counselors' understanding of support services and programs such as spirituality for IPV victims' treatment. San-Martin et al. (2017) posited that counselors' empathy associated with patient care is a significant cognitive attribute that involves a capacity to dialogue this understanding and intent to help male IPV victims appreciate their emotional treatment experiences that enhance their self-worth. Counselors may better serve male IPV victims with empathy if they first seek to understand the perpetrator's problem and its solution and correlate that to the perpetrators' aggressive behavior (Al-Modallal, 2016; Eckstein & Eckstein, 2016; Labarre, 2019; Roy et al., 2020). According to McGinn et al. (2016), mental health counselors could successfully empathize with IPV victims by understanding male IPV victims' mental issues by learning how and why perpetrators change their aggressive behavior. McGinn et al. (2016) posited that counselors might adopt new perspectives, such as conflict interruption techniques, new communication skills, and belief systems, to understand perpetrators' behavioral changes. Falgares et al. (2018) also have presented significant psychological (emotional), physical, sexual, and negligence maltreatment as critical perspectives for the counselor's empathic role experiences. Clinicians' empathic understanding of psychological and sexual beliefs inspired them to plan strategic abusive treatment programs for male IPV survivors.

Treatment and Male IPV Victims' Compliance Protocol

Mental health professional treatment protocol compliance for male IPV survivors may diminish/reduce the client's next physical and sexual partner violence behaviors. Crane et al. (2017) contended that alcohol was an adverse risk factor for male IPV victims' high nonadherence to treatment program protocol. The noncompliance treatment behaviors were associated with unfavorable recidivism. Recidivism means repeated offenders of issues. Crane et al. (2017) and Satyanarayana and Krishnamachari (2022) noted that the male IPV victims' alcohol use hinders counselors' empathy counseling programs to promote male IPV treatment well-being. Counselors' empathy experiences with male IPV victims' alcohol control would be the catalyst to address their spouses' maltreatment of physical, sexual, and psychological (mental health) issues. The IPV victim's adherence to treatment program protocol compliance inspires counselors' empathic insight to understand their clients' experiences and develop a more holistic emotional therapy counseling plan (Crane et al., 2017; Satyanarayana & Krishnamachari, 2022).

Low-Income IPV Male Victims Sustainable Programs Implications

According to Weobong et al. (2017), several empirical studies have reported that Healthy Activity Programs (HAP) promoted male IPV victim mental health awareness. Thus, HAP could transform and sustain male IPV victims from posttraumatic stress disorder (PTSD). Volp et al. (2017) also noted that narrative exposure therapy (NET) helped male IPV victims' therapeutic recovery processing to overcome PTSD and depression. Narrative exposure therapy was an innovative intervention model that significantly improved patients' mental health (Volp et al., 2017). Hence, this study indicated that it was essential for mental health service providers to express their empathy by providing social-seeking, friendship, and environmental support. These support services for IPV men's victims inspired them to express genuine thoughts, feelings, fears, and views about IPV and abuse (Huntley et al., 2019). Nikolova et al. (2023) suggested that mental health counselors should express concerns for the poor and low-income male IPV victims' financial empowerment programs such as TANF to improve their financial well-being. Mental health providers should recommend the Temporary Government Assistance for Needy Families Program (TANF) to improve their clients' housing and food insecurity needs. Corbally (2015) reported that IPV has a global economic and severe social, physical, and psychological individual well-being cost for male IPV victims. Nonetheless, mental health counselors have little knowledge and literature to explore female-started male IPV victims' concerns (Corbally, 2015).

Also, there was limited literature on how male IPV victims accounted for their physical, emotional, social, economic, spiritual, and mental cost experiences (Corbally, 2015).

Mental Health Professionals' Coping Strategies for Male IPV Victims

IPV Individual Rational Cognitive Behavior Trends. Di Napoli et al. (2019) found that domestic violence generally stemmed among intimate partners through emotional, psychological, economic, physical, and sexual concerns. Forms of violence include verbal (e.g., stalking) and physical abuse, control, threats, and coercion (Brooks et al., 2021; Logan & Landhuis, 2022; Tarzia & Hegarty, 2023). Scholars asserted that conflict violence among couples precipitates intimate partner violence (Kilgallen et al., 2022; Sutton & Dawson, 2021). However, perpetrators' cognitive psychological (emotional) behavior explains that aggressive IPV individual personality disorder significantly precipitates IPV perpetration (Yakeley, 2022; Maldonado & Murphy, 2021; Nesset et al., 2019). Therefore, mental health professionals' empathy roles can influence an ecological approach focusing on spousal behavior to reflect social power and control (Dim, 2020; Cheung & Huang, 2022; Kulkarni & Kulkarni, 2019). Thus, ecological scholars assert a collaborative model for exploring violent behavior risk factors for male IPV victimization (Di Napoli, 2019). Ecological construct deals with humans' cognitive, social, and physical interactive behaviors and environments (Di Napoli, 2019; Huard Pelletier et al., 2020). The ecological approach collaborates on collective/community, organizational, relational, and individual levels to find feminist cognitive-behavior and psychodynamic approaches, following a group protocol to respective ranks (Di Napoli, 2019; Lopez, 2020; Wood et al., 2020). Thus, scholars found that legal, social advocacy groups' consciousness, church, and family support for male IPV victims' transformation empowered the recovery paradigm (Dako-Gyeke et al., 2019; Di Napoli, 2019; Murray et al., 2016; Wood et al., 2020).

Men's aggressive and rigorous behaviors tend to discredit them in conflict management and anger control (Di Napoli, 2019; Gilchrist et al., 2015; Sileo et al., 2022). A Di Napoli (2019) study found that men develop a distorted understanding of relationships and hostile attitudes. These attitudes heightened executive attitudes, experiences, and relational interactions. According to the cognitive-behavioral approach, re-education increases IPV victims' awareness of their behavior and emphasizes substitutes for violent behaviors (Cotti et al., 2020; Di Napoli, 2019; Murphy et al., 2020). These changes might compel men to be conscious of their emotions and value their shortcomings for mutual hospitality with their spouses (Di Napoli, 2019; Lester et al., 2017; Wong & Bouchard, 2021). The forgone literature review analysis can equip mental health professionals with empathy and understanding in fostering male IPV recovery treatment programs (Coyle et al., 2019; Eiroa-Orosa & García-Mieres, 2019; Jackson-Blott et al., 2019).

Community Resilience Recovery Coping Strategies. For Poleshuck et al. (2018), intimate partner violence is a public health setback that includes social, physical, and mental health concerns with a dearth of policymakers' support. Besides, mental healthcare professionals have inadequate resources and information to inform victims of complex, compelling needs (Bonagura & Widom, 2023; Poleshuck et al., 2018). Depression and chronic pain are prevalent for male IPV survivors and can impede participatory program collaboration and self-worth outcomes in traditional community healthcare treatments (Bonagura & Widom, 2023; Poleshuck et al., 2018). According to Poleshuck et al. (2018), intimate partner violence resolution consciousness is reciprocal to community continuing medical education pursuits. Mental health providers' empathic services should promote gender-oriented services to inspire (resilience) and improve mental health among male IPV survivors (Kennedy et al., 2022; McIntyre et al., 2011).

Public advocacy awareness of the role of gender and its impact on mental health treatment should be a fundamental part of mental health professionals' education and practices to support male IPV depressive patients (Kennedy et al., 2022; McIntyre et al., 2011). However, higher suicide rates among men than among women show a need for gender-specific services for men with depression (Guerrero, 2016; Kennedy et al., 2022; McIntyre et al., 2011). Mental health professionals must focus their feelings and empathic attitudes toward men's depressive symptoms (Cole & Davidson, 2019). In addition, pursuing treatment resources, needs, and barriers also eases male IPV victims' recovery (Cole & Davidson, 2019; Kennedy et al., 2022; McIntyre et al., 2011).

Male IPV Spiritual Coping Strategy. Male IPV victims' spirituality coping strategy experiences may include engaging in defined ritual, doctrine, and specific practices to meditate and invoke a divine presence for firsthand experiences (Bowland et al., 2012; Ravi et al., 2022). Scholars believe spirituality is self-experience promoting unique understanding, emotional healing, growth, and meaning (Bowland et al., 2012; Good & Willoughby, 2008; Istratii & Ali, 2023; Ravi et al., 2022). Researchers found that male IPV survivors' spiritual coping promoted mental therapy, moderated stress and depression, enhanced vitality, and increased social interaction for fulfillment (Bowland et al., 2012; Good & Willoughby, 2008; Istratii & Ali, 2023; Ravi et al., 2022). Male IPV victims with emotional traumatic experiences are imbued with hope, joy, and tranquility in religious engagements (Bowland et al., 2012; Istratii & Ali, 2023; Ravi et al., 2022). Male IPV victims use spiritual engagements for meditation (mind, soul, and spirit) and seek pastoral support and hope (Bryant-Davis & Wong, 2013; Ravi et al., 2022).

Impact of Mental Health Providers' Spiritual Training. The collaboration of spirituality in mental health training allows counselors to develop empathic vitality to understand the positive and negative transforming impact of male IPV recovery treatment programs (Banfield, 2019; Hullenaar et al., 2023; O'Connor et al., 2021; Richards et al., 2023). Galan-Cisneros et al. (2023) and Richards et al. (2023) found a significant association between mental health professionals' spiritual recovery programs and improvements in client treatment outcomes. Thus, the literature reviewed indicated the productive spiritual effects of fostering support, comfort, and coping skills to diminish clients' stress levels (Banfield, 2019; Galan-Cisneros et al., 2023; O'Connor et al., 2021; Richards et al., 2023). Scholars found that mental health providers are ethically bound to collaborate with IPV victims' spiritual treatment programs. Spirituality program treatment can transform and perfect clients' self-worth, beliefs, and emotional vitality (Rivas et al., 2015). Spirituality hedges IPV effects and reduces future mental and emotional risks (Rivas et al., 2015). However, IPV victims with constant perpetrator abuse seem to believe God is endorsing the ongoing threat of abuse or violence and often find it exceedingly challenging to adhere to beliefs (Szcześniak et al., 2020; Van Hook, 2016). Nonetheless, developing a need for comfort and protection, heightened by the isolation experience, victims of IPV reach out for God's sustenance (Szcześniak et al., 2020; Van Hook, 2016).

IPV Mental Health Professionals' Training Impact on Male IPV Victims. Burns et al. (2022) found intimate partner violence to be a world public health issue that has precipitated a severe mental health epidemic. IPV is a perpetual co-occurrence with mental and emotional disorders (Burns et al., 2022). IPV concerns are significant for mental health professionals' assessment of IPV in the mental health realm to improve treatment protocol and publication. However, a lack of training in showing and responding to IPV victimization is a barrier to assessing IPV victims in treatment settings (Burns et al., 2022). This study presents a better understanding of this IPV-related training gap by evaluating international mental health professionals' experiences compared to training and factors contributing to training implementation (Burns et al., 2022; Wojcik et al., 2022).

Public advocacy to institutionalize the legislative enactment has been an affront to improve and promote IPV mental health professionals' training practices to cater to male IPV mental health (Burns et al., 2022; Forsdike et al., 2019; Tarzia et al., 2020;

Trevillion et al., 2016; Wojcik et al., 2021). For Burns et al. (2022), barriers impeding IPV professionals' training programs are attributed to a lack of leadership to address the mental health IPV education crisis. In addition, other hindrances include inadequate IPV resources and expert response to IPV perpetration (Forsdike et al., 2019; Hultmann et al., 2013; Trevillion et al., 2016).

Finally, mental health IPV providers' regional training experiences have a dearth of mandatory regional enforcement of professional training programs and what to include in training curricula (Kamimura et al., 2015). In addition, surveys in the U.S. and U.K. presented 41% to 46% of trained mental health professionals (Burns et al., 2022). Tol et al. (2019) found few studies on mental health victimization and perpetration in low- and middle-income countries (LMIC). Thus, well-informed mental health providers engaging with formal IPV services can buffer the impacts of violence and reduce future risks in community settings (Voth Schrag et al., 2021).

Furthermore, Stiawa et al. (2020) found that limited mental health professionals' knowledge might account for uncertain findings of depression among men. This peculiar depression symptom ascribed to men refers to psychosocial depression that hinders male IPV help-seeking behavior (Di Napoli et al., 2020; Duchaine et al., 2019; Stiawa et al., 2020). According to Jackson et al. (2015), psychosocial factors consist of risk variables of IPV victims, including the demographic population with lower socioeconomic status, lower education levels, and unemployment. Stiawa et al. (2020) argued that IPV mental health professionals with vested knowledge must analyze psychosocial depression symptoms for treatment programs. However, higher suicide rates among men than women showed a need for gender-specific services/programs for male IPV victims with depressed mental health (Stiawa et al., 2020). Wilson et al. (2021) found that in the U.S., about 20% of IPV victims have contemplated suicidal beliefs (suicidal thoughts or behaviors). Stiawa et al. (2020) suggested that mental health professionals' attitudes and knowledge are significant assets in administering depressive treatment. Mental health professionals must analyze barriers such as masculinity and help-seeking constraints undermining treatment. Thus, the male IPV victims' emotional program requires a qualified professional perspective for male patients' treatment (Di Napoli et al., 2020; Duchaine et al., 2019; Stiawa et al., 2020).

Professionals can use the psychosocial paradigm to articulate the causes of depression and provide sociological explanations for fostering masculine culture among male IPV victims. Professionals are concerned that psychoeducation is an affront to depressive diagnosis (Stiawa et al., 2020). The mental health professionals' (MHPs') advocacy for consciousness of the role of gender and its repercussions on mental health treatment should be a central theme of MHPs' education and daily implementation of mental health treatment practices (Stiawa et al., 2020; Di Napoli et al., 2020).

Mental Health Professionals' Empathy Challenges with Male IPV Victims

For the aim of this study, the primary question platform was, "What are the mental health counselors' experiences with and feelings about the role of empathy while working with male victims of intimate partner violence?" (Harvey et al., 2018; Huntley et al., 2019; Di Napoli et al., 2019; Inman & Rao, 2018; McGinn et al., 2016; Romero-Martínez et al., 2019). Researchers are concerned with limited empirical studies on mental health providers' empathy experiences of male IPV victims' experiences (Huntley et al., 2019; MacLeod, 2019). Another concern was a gap in the current research about the understanding of mental health counselors' experiences with and feelings of the role of empathy while working with male IPV victims (Williams et al., 2020). There was a dearth of literature about mental health providers' empathy role experiences of male victims suffering from self-doubt, anxiety, emotion, cognition, and distress (Barkhuizen, 2015; Huntley et al., 2019). The male IPV victims fear how the perpetrator blamed them for the abuse (Barkhuizen, 2015; Huntley et al., 2019). Hence, this study is significant because it fills the research gap about mental health service providers' experiences of male IPV victims' mental health disorders. The Kaiser Family Foundation (2021) reported increased demands for mental health providers (America's Health Rankings analysis of U.S. HHS, 2022). In 2021, only 26.9% of mental health providers accounted for male IPV survivors' mental health well-being (America's Health Rankings analysis of U.S. HHS, 2022). The National Council of Behavioral Health (NCBH) also reported that 77% of counties in the United States face a severe shortage of mental health providers (HHS, 2022). The estimated demand for mental health professionals increased during the COVID-19 pandemic period. According to NCHW analysis, by 2025, mental health professionals would have a 45,000 to 250,000 shortage (America's Health Rankings analysis of U.S. HHS, 2022).

According to Machado et al. (2017), intimate partner violence is a common phenomenon worldwide and a significant cause of male IPV mental health concerns. Although 80% of the world's population lives in low- and middle-income countries (LMICs), health system responses to IPV are poorly understood (MacLeod, 2019). However, researchers also seemed to possess little literature on qualitative studies exploring and interpreting male IPV survivors' victimization issues (Machado et al., 2017). A generic qualitative of this study aimed to understand mental health service providers' empathy experiences of male IPV victims' mental health issues and develop recovery support plans.

Overview of the foregone literature seemed convincing and rational to uphold the current study topic: Mental health professionals' experiences with and beliefs of the role of empathy while working with male IPV victims dissertation research. Overall, the literature reviewed for this research encompassed a comprehensive and rigorous protocol to present all relevant recommended published research and scholarly sources (peer-reviewed articles) in the literature review (Bardus et al., 2020; Hughes et al., 2016).

Review of Methodological Literature

According to Creswell (2003), the researcher makes knowledge claims based on multiple meanings of individuals' experiences.

The inquirer also could construct social and historical data into analytical patterns (Coccia, 2020). Researchers use qualitative methods because the research question concerns respondents' experiences and feelings, while quantitative methods are suitable for testing a hypothesized relationship between variables (Creswell, 2019; Percy et al., 2015). Percy et al. (2015) further noted that the researcher collects open-ended interview data to develop themes for the research interpretation. Qualitative research focuses on discovering, understanding, and developing knowledge suitable for professional counselors' empathy while working with IPV victims' experiences (Cheung, 2016; Falkenström et al., 2016; Kim et al., 2019). A qualitative method is the best approach for this study. The qualitative method uses inductive processes with semi-structured open-ended interviews, field observations, and written materials to interact with focus groups of respondents (Percy et al., 2015). The generic thematic inductive with constant comparisons data analysis paradigm fosters meaning from the data sources (Creswell & Poth, 2018; Coccia, 2020; Percy et al., 2015). Generic qualitative inquiry is an exploratory approach appropriate for articulating an experience of a particular event, opinions, and events or phenomena, hence suitable for this research respondent's pursuit (Bryson et al., 2017; Percy et al., 2015). The generic qualitative approach was suitable for this study because it is interested in actual and outer-world experiences (Percy et al., 2015).

Generic Qualitative Framework. The researcher examined and described the empathic roles of the mental health providers (respondents) relative to their attitudes, opinions, beliefs, feelings, and experiences (Percy et al., 2015; Viverito et al., 2018). Generic qualitative research focuses on external and real-world experiences and perceptions, contrary to internal psychological and subjective feelings (Bellamy et al., 2016; Nowell et al., 2017). For Holtrop et al. (2018), a generic qualitative research approach explored counselors' experiences working with male IPV victims. This knowledge enriched the understanding of mental health counselors' beliefs of and empathetic experiences while working with male IPV victims (Percy et al., 2015). Researchers suggested it is significant to train novice clinicians to work with IPV persons with addictions and substances for recovery treatment (Gerass, 2018; Mackowiak & Scoglio, 2018). Hence, this research explored clinicians' experiences with empathy for male IPV victims' experiences while helping recovery treatment services (Di Napoli et al., 2019; Weiss et al., 2016).

For Percy et al. (2015), the rationale purpose of this study is to use generic qualitative methods to explore and understand counselors' empathic role experiences with and feelings while working with male IPV survivors. These experiences and beliefs of male IPV victims consist of victimization and recovery support treatment protocol (Di Napoli et al., 2019; Schachner et al., 2021). A scholar's premise is generic qualitative research to thoroughly explore and understand a subject from their participants' environmental perspectives. This framework is consistent with the researchers' assertion because this study emphasized individuals' reports and beliefs of a real-life experience (Emezue & Udmuangpia, 2022; Percy et al., 2015). While exploring from a generic qualitative perspective, a researcher learns about people's thoughts, beliefs, opinions, and attitudes about a topic or experience (Emezue & Udmuangpia, 2022; Percy et al., 2015).

On the contrary, the research problem was a lack of information about mental health providers' experiences with empathy when working with male IPV victims. Hence, this study is essential in filling the research gap about mental health service providers' role in empathy experiences of male IPV victims' mental health problems (Dim, 2021, 2020; Voth et al., 2021). This study's findings show a first creative understanding of mental health providers' empathy experiences working with the emotional problems of male IPV victims (Di Napoli et al., 2019; Heron et al., 2021; Wilson et al., 2021). Empathy creativity fosters more mental health professionals' training opportunities to cater to the acute licensed providers' shortages (Heard et al., 2020, 2017).

Overall, this study's analytical task was to answer the research question related to mental health professionals' experiences with and feelings about the role of empathy while working with male IPV victims (Carlson et al., 2019, 2018; Crane & Easton, 2017; Harvey et al., 2018; Kimber et al., 2015; McGinn et al., 2016; Watson, 2019). The study's research question was: What are the mental health counselor's experiences with and perceptions of the role of empathy while working with male victims of intimate partner violence?" However, the literature reviewed indicated a dearth/paucity of empirical studies on mental health providers' empathy experiences about male IPV victims' experiences (Huntley et al., 2019; MacLeod, 2019; McCarrick et al., 2016). Hence, this research is significant because it shows the gap in mental health service providers' role in the empathy experiences of male IPV victims' mental health problems (Hamdani et al., 2020; Pope et al., 2019).

Synthesis of the Literature

The research literature reviewed to explore the topic for this proposed study provided a background to understand the experiences of mental health professionals working with male victims of intimate partner violence. Some of the literature reviewed lacked plans/programs to measure the mental health of counselors working with male victims of intimate partner violence (MacGregor et al., 2016). The literature review suggested that African Americans are more likely to report experiencing IPV than other racial groups (Al'Uqdah et al., 2016). However, academics and counselors have not investigated why they might be part of the high IPV rates in the African American community (Al'Uqdah et al., 2016). Despite controversy over the indications of couple therapy for IPV, current counselors and clinicians lack focus on (a) significant IPV couples' therapeutic strategic programs on avoiding aggressive domineering and power abuse and (b) sustainable economic/financial health plans (Päivinen & Holma, 2017; Silva-Martinez et al., 2016; Silva-Martinez, 2016).

Literature Review

The research study did not indicate a new theory but enhanced mental health providers' support to set up positive relationships with their male IPV victims' recovery treatment process. Empathy enabled mental health providers to establish rapport with their clients to make them feel heard through words and service support needs. The study indicated and showed the empathic simulation theory (EST) execution/implementation for the study (Annion et al., 2023; Atzil-Slonim et al., 2019; Bechtoldt et al., 2019; Molas, 2022). According to Capella Programs of Research (2020), the Social and Community Services Specialization indicates developing social services and community collaborations with stakeholders. This research study is helpful for social and community service workers because it explored and reported the insights and thoughts of mental health service providers' beliefs about and experiences with implementing recovery programs and services for male IPV victims. Thus, the findings from the study highlighted the role of empathy in treating male IPV survivors. An improved understanding of these clients can lead to improved delivery of multidisciplinary social services.

The EST framework gives mental health counselors the ability to understand what the male IPV victims are thinking or feeling (Annion et al., 2023; Atzil-Slonim et al., 2019; Bechtoldt et al., 2019; Bollmer et al., 2020; Molas, 2022). Also, researchers found that empirical studies articulated that empathic theory fosters organizational leadership motivation (Mayfield et al., 2015; Roy, 2020; Yue et al., 2021). For example, according to Shortland and Palasinski (2019), the UK community seems to uphold that for a mental health counselor to understand what a male IPV victim feels, a client's emotional experiences should be felt. Shortland and Palasinski's (2019) study found that contrary to what the media typically portrays, males are also often the victims of DV/IPV abuse. In the United Kingdom, for example, more than 40% of males in heterosexual relationships are victims of DV/IPV abuse (Behounek, & Hughes, 2022; Zafar et al., 2022). This study was guided by EST because, as Xiao et al. (2016) pointed out, the framework provided a helpful association between a counselor's role and clients' experiences. It required sharing an emotional state and taking collective responsibility for opinions and beliefs. In searching for a cognitive capacity to know another's internal states, including thoughts and feelings, counselors developed programs to normalize male IPV victims' emotional pain by allowing compassion and supporting behavior (Xiao et al., 2016).

The study indicated the EST impact on mental health professionals' treatment and program services dispensation (Annion et al., 2023; Atzil-Slonim et al., 2019; Bechtoldt et al., 2019; Bollmer et al., 2020; Molas, 2022). Radzvilavicius et al. (2019) claimed that keeping the vitality of empathy was essential to keeping the community's collective consciousness. Moudatsou et al. (2020) reported that empathy was significant to the social care professions and professionals. Moudatsou et al. (2020) also suggested that mental health providers might be supported with continuous and personal development education programs and supervision sessions to develop empathetic role skills to care for their male IPV victims' intervention recovery programs. Nonetheless, mental health counselors' empathic experiences and understanding of male IPV victims' emotional, sexual, and physical experiences could develop community psychosocial rehabilitation clinics for IPV-related treatments. For instance, psychotherapists are more effective than the average population in regulating negative emotions. Duquette (2017) suggested that mental health counselors receptive to patients' distress and down-regulating negative emotions (e.g., anxiety and depression) are essential for psychotherapists to provide practical help and sustain their well-being.

The mental health counselor's community psychosocial rehabilitation clinics could create a therapeutic context to diagnose comprehensive program assessment to foster male IPV victims' recovery treatment planning (Mackowiak & Scoglio, 2018). This information implication requires mental health counselors with empathy while working with male IPV victims to develop intervention programs to bridge family bonds (Di Napoli et al., 2019; Gibson et al., 2015). This focus could change how mental health providers are trained to treat this marginalized population (Kendall et al., 2020). Focusing on using empathy effectively and avoiding judgment improves the treatment of the male IPV population. These implications are relevant to researchers, policymakers (e.g., legislators), counselors, social workers, counselor learners, and human services professionals who affect this study population with programs and treatment services support (Hash et al., 2017).

Research Opportunities

The Kaiser Family Foundation (2021) analysis reported that approximately 119 million Americans live in mental health shortage areas, and only 26.9% accounted for the need in 2025 (America's Health Rankings Analysis of U.S. HHS, 2022). According to research by the National Council of Behavioral Health (NCBH), there is a significant shortage of mental health practitioners in 77% of U.S. counties (America's Health Rankings analysis of U.S. HHS, 2022). Based on an analysis of U.S. HHS (2022) by America's Health Rankings, there was an expected increase in demand for mental health practitioners during COVID-19. According to the National Center for Health Workforce Analysis, there will be between 45,000 and 250,000 fewer mental health professionals in the United States by 2025 (America's Health Rankings Analysis of U.S. HHS, 2022).

A report from the U.S. Health and Human Services conducted in 2021, premised that by 2030, multiple mental health–related objectives would include the following:

- Pursuing the proportion of adults with depression who get treatment
- Showing the segment of adults with endemic/chronic mental illness (e.g., distress) who get treatment

- Increasing the proportion of essential healthcare visits to screen adolescents and adults with depression issues (America's Health Rankings analysis of US, 2022; U.S. HHS et al., 2021)

The study's findings showed an understanding of mental health providers' empathy experiences working with male IPV victims' emotional problems (Korsbek et al., 2021; Mott & Martin, 2019). Empathy and creativity fostered more mental health professionals' training opportunities to cater to the acute licensed providers' shortages (Heard et al., 2020, 2017). Issues facing male IPV victims included the risk of suicide, self-blame, and anxiety, which were of grave public concern (Lim et al., 2015; MacLeod, 2019; Mossière et al., 2018). Hence, understanding these issues is critical for mental health providers to implement suitable recovery programs for the male IPV victim population. Therapeutic providers can use empathy to develop preventive treatment programs, professional training, and research to support professionals working with male IPV victims (Cimino et al., 2019; Renzetti et al., 2017; Sugiyama & Hunter, 2020).

Proposed Research

Critique of the Previous Research Methods

Research outcomes about male victimization remained ambiguous and needed further research on the experiences of providers who work with the male IPV victim population. According to Machado et al. (2017), intimate partner violence is a common phenomenon worldwide and a significant cause of male IPV mental health concerns. Although 80% of the world's population lives in low- and middle-income countries (LMICs), health system responses to IPV are poorly understood (MacLeod, 2019). However, researchers also have a dearth of qualitative studies exploring and interpreting to mitigate male IPV survivors' victimization issues (Machado et al., 2017; Sprague et al., 2017).

Literature Review

Researchers have posited inadequate literature about mental health providers' empathic role experiences of male IPV victims suffering from self-doubt, anxiety, emotion, cognitive distress, and fear of how the perpetrator will blame them for the abuse (Bernardi & Steyn, 2019; Huntley et al., 2019). This study used generic qualitative methods to explore and understand counselors' empathic role experiences with and beliefs about male IPV victims' experiences of victimization and recovery support. Besides, this generic qualitative study's constant thematic analysis indicated mental health service providers' empathic experiences of male IPV victims' mental health issues, looking to develop recovery support plans.

Thus, this belief reinforces the individualistic bias in which domestic abuse advocates focus on reporting abuse against women within a framework that does not account for men (MacLeod, 2019; Mossière et al., 2018). Mental health professionals' understanding of experiences with empathy and its role in treating male IPV survivors is significant in creating suitable recovery programs for the male IPV population (MacLeod, 2019; Mossière et al., 2018).

According to Depraetere et al. (2020, 2018), research findings on male victimization remain a subject of ambiguity that requires further research on the experiences of counselors who work with the male IPV victim population. Thus, the research problem was a gap in information about mental health providers' experiences with empathy when working with male IPV victims (Hamel et al., 2020; Woerner et al., 2019). Hence, this study's little literature challenged researchers' future investigatory pursuits about the premised question: What are the mental health counselors' experiences with and feelings of the role of empathy while working with male victims of intimate partner violence? (Harvey et al., 2018; Inman & Rao, 2018; McGinn et al., 2016; Romero-Martínez et al., 2019).

Summary

Clinicians and IPV scholars are concerned with the low self-esteem, emotion, trauma, toxic relationships, and mental health disorders through PTSD, sexual abuse, anger, and anxiety experiences outcomes of IPV-abused victims (Angelidis et al., 2019; Campoverde et al., 2022; Oshri et al., 2017). This study added theoretical knowledge about how counselors might use empathy to treat a poorly understood population. Meyer and Frost (2019) noted that:

> The theory was crucial for practice because it helped make sense of the complex array of factors, including individual, interpersonal, and social factors involved in IPV. It also informs practitioners what to look for in assessing risk and guides them in acting. (p. 33)

Issues facing male IPV victims include the risk of suicide, self-blame, and anxiety, which are a grave public concern (Lim et al., 2015; MacLeod, 2019; Mossière et al., 2018). Hence, understanding these issues was significant for mental health providers to implement suitable recovery programs for the male IPV victim population. Therapeutic providers could use empathy to develop preventive treatment programs, professional training, and research to support professionals working with male IPV victims (Blackmore et al., 2017; Di Napoli et al., 2019; Renzetti et al., 2017; Rhodes & Iwashyna, 2009). Research findings on male victimization remained vague/uncertain and require further research on the experiences of providers who work with the male IPV victim population (Barrett et al., 2020).

Thus, a narrow theoretical stance might prevent a variety of exploratory insights for understanding the current topic: mental health providers' experience and feelings of the role of empathy while working with clients who experience IPV (Augsburger et al., 2019; Burelomova et al., 2018). Finally, this study indicated a need for future scientific research work on the current topic:

mental health providers' experiences with and belief in the role of empathy while working with clients who experience IPV victims' emotions, anger, distress, and anxiety to fill this dearth information gap (Hamp et al., 2016; Vandewalle et al., 2016). In the next chapter (Chapter 3), the study's generic method dynamics, including research design, sampling, population size, procedures, and ethical considerations, will be presented/discussed in further detail. This chapter sums up a shift and conversion of Chapter 2 into Chapter 3.

Methodology

Chapter 3

The study's research problem statement indicated how mental health providers' experiences with and feelings of empathy while working with male intimate partner violence victims for transformation to sustain their self-worth and self-esteem to boost victims' egos (Hellemans et al., 2015; Voth et al., 2021; Wilson et al., 2021). The most significant outcomes of males' IPV mental illness were the associations between IPV experiences with depression, post-traumatic stress disorder (PTSD), and anxiety (Ahmadabadi et al., 2020; Moreira et al., 2022). However, scholars found a dearth of qualitative method studies exploring and interpreting male IPV survivors' victimization issues (Machado et al., 2017; Spraque et al., 2017). A generic qualitative study aims to explore understanding mental health service providers' empathy experiences of male IPV victims' mental health issues and develop recovery support plans (Tarzia, 2021). Thus, this feeling reinforces the individualistic bias in which domestic abuse advocates tend to focus on reporting abuse against women within a framework that does not account for men (MacLeod, 2019; Mossière et al., 2018). Hence, understanding mental health professionals' experience with empathy and its role in treating male IPV survivors is critical to creating suitable recovery programs for the male IPV population to fill this gap.

This chapter shows the method and procedures (protocols) used in the study for future scholars' collaborative replicative research work. Besides, this chapter provides the purpose of the study, the research question, the research design, the target population, and the sampling of the respondents' inclusive participation. Also, the chapter describes the steps used for data collection and analysis. In addition, the chapter indicates an ethical no-harm paradigm to protect the participants' confidentiality, rights, and human value endowment with the Belmont Ethical Compliance (Belmont Report, 1979). Finally, the chapter summary collaborates, synthesizes, and aligns the central conceptual tenets for the study's meaning and understanding for future researchers' replication.

Research Question

The research study's primary question is, "What are the mental health counselors' experiences with and feelings about the role of empathy while working with male victims of intimate partner violence (IPV)?"

Research Design

The generic qualitative approach is essential for describing, interpreting, and analyzing the study's research question (Booth et al., 2018; Kennedy, 2016; Percy et al., 2015). Percy et al. (2015) said that ethnography explores a defined culture's social groupings, customs, beliefs, behaviors, and practices. Moreover, unlike generic qualitative study, phenomenological research focuses on the individual's internal subjective psychological structures, the intent of opinions, and attitude experiences (Kennedy, 2016; Percy et al., 2015). Moustakas (1994) and Giogi (2009) described this study approach as one that explores respondents' descriptive and interpretive lived experiences. A rigorous literature review of generic qualitative research about the meaning, understanding, and straightforward thematic procedure for sampling data collection and analysis was found right for this study (Awenat et al., 2019; Bandara et al., 2015; Houghton et al., 2017; Gogo & Musonda, 2022; Percy et al., 2015). Thus, the researcher used the counselors' empathic role in subjective opinions, attitudes, and beliefs about the experiences and feelings of their male IPV clients (Emezue & Udmuangpia, 2022; Percy et al., 2015; Saletti-Cuesta et al., 2018).

Furthermore, generic qualitative research was suitable for the study because the researcher examined and described respondents' attitudes, opinions, beliefs, feelings, and experiences (Percy et al., 2015; Rejeh et al., 2017; van Leeuwen et al., 2019). Generic qualitative research focuses on external and real-world experiences and perceptions, contrary to internal psychological and subjective feelings (Percy et al., 2015). According to Holtrop et al. (2018), a generic qualitative research approach explores counselors' experiences working with male IPV victims. This knowledge will enhance the understanding of mental health counselors' beliefs of and empathetic experiences while working with male IPV victims (Percy et al., 2015).

The researcher used a purposeful sampling approach because of the intentionally homogeneous professional respondents of the selected clinicians (Ohlsson Nevo et al., 2020, 2019; Williams et al., 2019). Semi-structured interview questions focused on the respondent's empathy experiences while working with male IPV victims to answer the study question, "What are the mental health counselors' experiences with and beliefs of the role of empathy while working with male victims of intimate partner violence (IPV)?" (Kallio et al., 2016; Percy et al., 2015; Patton, 2015; Santo-Tomás Muro et al., 2020). Levis et al. (2018) attested that semi-structured interviews are less structured, informal, and conducive for the researcher to obtain similar information from each participant. Percy et al. (2015) recommended data collection elements that ensure reliable thematic process information. These elements include in-depth, semi-structured, and open-ended interview questions (Kallio et al., 2016; Percy et al., 2015; Patton, 2015; Santo-Tomás Muro et al., 2020). Scholars found that inductive analysis is suitable for analyzing group and individual interview data to ease and explore repeated patterns (Percy et al., 2015; Patton, 2015). Data analysis involves organizing data into common themes, categorizing, describing, classifying, and interpreting the process. The researcher stands, visualizes, and implements the data in a way that represents this analysis protocol (Monteleone & Forrester Jones, 2017; Phipps et al., 2018; Percy et al., 2015).

The researcher used bracketing to set aside biases and preconceptions to avoid negative implications during data collection and analysis in a qualitative study (Tufford & Newman, 2012). Bracketing is used in qualitative research to mitigate the adverse impact of preconceptions that may deter the research process (Tufford & Newman, 2012; Soule & Freeman, 2019; Zhu et al., 2018). Sorsa et al. (2015) posited that bracketing promotes scientific rigor and validity in any qualitative study. Hence, Sorsa et al. (2015) asserted that trustworthiness enhanced the study findings for future research replication because bracketing would mitigate critical approach, empathy, distancing, and the awareness of personal values influencing the respondents and researcher interaction (Sorsa et al., 2015). Trustworthiness is crucial in this generic qualitative study because it ensures that the research outcome is credible, transferable, and dependable for a correct and authentic result. Hence, Cloutier and Ravasi (2021) posited that trustworthiness ensures the study's transparency.

Sampling

Sampling is selecting individual participants within a population to explore the study topic to understand the entire population (Atif et al., 2021; Cooper & Schindler, 2008; Fearon et al., 2020; Jacobs & Niekerk, 2017). Purposive and snowball sampling were used to explore the research question (Nally et al., 2019; Perryman & Appleton, 2016; Xiang et al., 2020, 2019). The fundamental rationale for using the purposive sampling technique is to investigate the participants' experiences and feelings for a specific purpose (e.g., male IPV victims' mental health) to meet specific holistic criteria program for treatment (Mwendera et al., 2016; Xiang et al., 2020, 2019). Snowball sampling is the word-of-mouth convenience sampling process (Huntley et al., 2019; Perryman & Appleton, 2016). Recruiting using purposive and snowball sampling techniques helped to find an eligible sample population (Geddes et al., 2018; Nally et al., 2019; Perryman & Appleton, 2016; Xiang et al., 2020, 2019). This study used 10 participants to enhance the understanding of mental health counselors' experiences with empathy while working with males who have experienced IPV abuse (Moser & Korstjens, 2018, 2017; Percy et al., 2015).

Target Population and Sample

The study's target population was mental health providers in the South-Central USA. The researcher also gave credence to ethnic population diversity in the South-Central USA region. The respondents included whites, African Americans, Hispanics, Asian Americans, and others based on availability. The researcher provided this extensive statistical data from the national 2015 APA—Survey of Psychology Health Service Providers report (Hamp et al., 2016) because mental health practitioners lacked cumulative demographic statistical data in the area and the local sectors. Psychologists with master's and doctoral degrees who were licensed in the United States were eligible to take part in the study. Staff from APA's Information Technology Services standardized, combined, and de-duplicated the State licensing board lists that the researcher had gathered from all 50 states and the District of Columbia (Hamp, 2016). A summary of the licensed mental health data findings revealed the following: (a) professional license categories, (b) demographic and educational information, and (c) gender-specific services offered (Hamp, 2016). In terms of gender identity, 2,730 respondents (59.2%) versus 1,871 respondents (40%) were female (Hamp, 2016). Less than 0.1% of transgender respondents, according to the survey, were professionals (Hamp, 2016). According to survey results, the mean age was 55.7 years, while the median age was 58 years (Hamp, 2016). Around 5.4% of the respondents were younger than 35, while over half were 55 or older (Hamp, 2016). About race/ethnicity, white respondents included 4,029 (87.8%) of the sample, while less than 1% did not (Hamp, 2016). 12.2% of Asian Americans, 2.5% of Black/African Americans, 2.6% of Hispanic Americans, and 4.4% of Asian Americans were members of racial minorities (Hamp, 2016). The degrees that were questioned were PhD, EdD, and PsyD. Nonetheless, a few participants owned licenses at the master's degree level (Hamp, 2016). There were 2,112 (58.5%) female respondents with doctorates among those surveyed. In comparison, 1,501 (41.5%) of the PhD responders were men. With 3,139 (87.7%) doctoral degrees, white men and women made up the majority (Hamp et al., 2016).

I explored and targeted the mental health licensed professional population with one year of experience working with male IPV survivors. The specific mental health specialties included Licensed Social Workers (LCSW), Licensed Professional Counselors (LPC), and licensed marriage and family therapists. Participants' other academic eligibility criteria formed bachelor's or master's and PhD degrees. Further, the inclusion criteria included mental health licensed providers/practitioners and professional counselors in the South-Central USA. Respondents were 18 years old and had at least one year of experience working with male IPV survivors. I excluded unlicensed professional clinicians/providers and those who are personally and professionally affiliated (Hamp et al., 2016; Williams et al., 2019).

Sample Size Rationale

The sample size was 10 licensed mental health providers (Creswell et al., 2014). Also, de Jong et al. (2016) and Percy et al. (2015) suggested a range of 10 to 15 subjects for this exploratory study, and data were collected using semi-structured face-to-face and online interviews. Considering a rational perspective, the researcher investigated the understanding and knowledge of mental health providers' experiences with and feelings of the role of empathy when working with heterosexual men who experienced IPV abuse (Chiba et al., 2018; Feddersen et al., 2022; Langenderfer-Magruder et al., 2019, 2018; McCauley et al., 2019; Powers & Lajoie, 2021). By contrast, other qualitative research methods, such as grounded theory, require more than 15 to 20 (n=15–20) participants from various sites to support theory development (Corbin & Strauss, 2015; Strauss & Corbin, 1990). Data collection continued until saturation was reached (Abi Khalilet al., 2022; Helou et al., 2021; Percy et al., 2015; Ward et al., 2017). Saturation is reached in qualitative research when no other information is obtained from the interviewees (Alsufyani et al., 2023).

Procedures

Participant Selection

Means of Recruiting/Selecting. Participants were recruited through flyers placed in mental health organizations, emails, and word of mouth (e.g., snowball sampling) (Creswell, 2013; Patton, 2015; Percy et al., 2015). Snowballing was the most effective selection strategy (Creswell, 2019; Patton, 2015; Percy et al., 2015). Before any recruitment, the researcher presented site permission letters and flyers face-to-face and via email to all the selected sites for endorsement (Bellamy et al., 2016; Patton, 2015). The authorized representative signed the site's official notes to authenticate recruitment (Bellamy et al., 2016; Patton, 2015).

Recruitment Sites. Capella University Institutional Review Board (IRB) approved an identified South-Central USA region counseling center for the snowballing protocol consultation. The researcher consulted the counseling center to discuss an approved IRB's recruiting materials to present the snowballing process. The approved IRB's materials consisted of a note designed for the center, a recruitment flyer, a screening process, researcher-designed interview questions, and an informed consent form. This interactive, collaborative meeting was held in the counseling clinic director's office on July 8, 2022. The meeting was focused on fostering and administering the snowballing through the clinic's professional allies and organizational members. The enthusiastic dialogue outcome was pivotal for the respondent's sample size (n=10) recommended for the study. Meetings were carried out via phone calls and personal interactions. The researcher appreciated the clinicians' collaborative spirit and resilience in the study's protocol success.

Steps of Recruitment. The researcher presented flyers at the approved location, screening and recruiting materials via telephone and emails to the potential respondents, and expected responses by email or phone. Any missed calls were returned to the potential participants to conduct a screening protocol to decide eligibility and negotiate for the volunteer's face-to-face interaction, as well as emails to introduce the informed consent form and the research study synopsis. Also, the researcher emailed the informed consent form at least 24 hours before the interview. The researcher pursued a follow-up call to the potential respondents to discuss the informed consent form and articulate the concerns that they might have. The researcher sought respondents' permission to audio-record the interview. Finally, the participants provided information about the study to share with other potential respondents after the interviews (Sherratt et al., 2022; Husebø et al., 2021).

Screening Process and Questions. A telephone screening interview was conducted to decide if the prospective respondents met the study's inclusion criteria. If the respondents met the inclusion criteria, the researcher asked if they would like to participate in a scheduled interview. Participants must have at least one year of working experience with male IPV victims to be eligible for the study. However, any potential participant who did not meet the study's inclusive protocol/criteria would be excluded to avoid coercion or undue harm and thanked for their time (Al-Baghdadi et al., 2019; Fletcher et al., 2021). After the screening, the researcher emailed the informed consent to each potential volunteer. The researcher asked the interested volunteers to print, sign, scan, and email the informed consent form. The researcher scheduled the interview after receiving the informed consent form. The researcher discussed the screening questions on the phone for the respondents' inclusion and exclusion criteria to take part in the research.

Data Coded Compliance. After the screening, the researcher emailed each potential/screened volunteer the informed consent. The researcher asked that the interested volunteers print, sign, scan, and email the informed consent form. After accepting the informed consent form, the researcher scheduled the interview and enforced semi-structured interview data collection, which lasted approximately 60 minutes. The researcher assigned alphanumeric codes such as R-1 and R-2 to each participant to ensure confidentiality (Alonso et al., 2020; Wolf et al., 2020).

Hence, I followed and adhered to the data collected and coded process ethics confidentiality of the study participants (Rudolph et al., 2020, 2018). The participants articulated their experiences without coercion because they are experts in their profession (Jöbges et al., 2022; Wolf et al., 2020). The researcher's interview recording began with Sony's digital phone/equipment. The participants ended the data collection process without coercion (Jöbges et al., 2022; Wolf et al., 2020). Respondents answered questions satisfactorily to conclude the recording. I thanked the participants for their time and offered them a $25 coffee gift card. As the interview was completed, upon request, I sent a copy of the study to the respondents. As the COVID-19 virus concerns persisted, I utilized online interaction, face-to-face semi-structured, and open-ended interviews for the data collection.

Informed Consent. Capella University requires researchers to use an informed consent form for all human subjects and legal guardians before research activity. The informed consent form protocol follows

Belmont 45 CFR 46.111, 45 CFR 46.116, and 45 CFR and the applicable subpart requirements (Anderson, 2014; Doig et al., 2019). Finally, this study collaborated and enforced the researcher's compliance with the Informed Consent Form (IFC). Participants received informed consent at least 24 hours before the interview and needed to ask questions. No discussions were conducted before receiving informed consent from the participants. The researcher conducted open-ended semi-structured interviews for the data collection that lasted approximately 60 minutes. Each participant was assigned alphanumeric code numbers (e.g., P1 and P2) to follow confidentiality. Data collected and coded followed the confidentiality of study participants. The participants can end the data collection process without coercion (Jöbges et al., 2022; Wolf et al., 2020).

Possible Risks to Participants. Overall, the potential risk to the participants includes the loss of privacy and breach of confidentiality, which is the risk of professional status if the researcher does not support secured data collection and security procedures (Choi, 2020; Kienzler & Sapkota, 2020, 2019; Treloar et al., 2016). Possible participant risks include physical harm, unforeseen side effects, emotional distress or embarrassment, monetary costs, physical discomfort, and loss of time (Berenguera et al., 2020; Clark & Sousa, 2018). Also, psychological or emotional risks may include fear, stress, confusion, and guilt (Rodríguez-Almagro et al., 2019; McCormack et al., 2017).

Besides, this research is a minimal-risk study with discomfort that should not exceed daily life experience. Thus, the bracketing technique is used to mitigate biases and private opinions. Nonetheless, participants can stop participation at any time without coercion. However, according to Hasking et al. (2019), shared areas of ethical challenges in this generic qualitative research that guided the study included (a) respondents' vulnerability, (b) records storage confidentiality, (c) data security, and (d) enforced identity confidentiality. Ethical concerns pose risks to the subjects and the researcher (Hasking et al., 2019).

Capella University's IRB focuses on (a) protecting the privacy and confidentiality of participants, (b) respecting the autonomy and dignity of participants, and (c) minimizing risks to the participant (Capella Institutional Review Board, n.d.; Wessels & Visagie, 2017; Young et al., 2022). In addition, (d) ensuring participants have adequate information to make informed decisions, (e) weighing the benefits and risks of research, and finally, (f) adhering to the federal regulation governing research under 45 CFR 46 (Belmont Report of 1979; Young et al., 2022).

Belmont Ethical Compliance. According to Hasking et al. (2019), the researcher must report on their research's ethical protocol and be capable of conducting it. According to Hasking et al. (2019), the following ethical issues were covered: (a) disclosure and confidentiality, (b) the possibility of an iatrogenic effect, (c) duty of care, and (d) researcher safety. The fundamental tenets of the ethical frameworks in this study are based on the Belmont Report of 1979. Thus, the basic premises of the Belmont Report (1979) about human subjects' care for the current study consist of (a) respect for persons, (b) beneficence, and (c) justice. Based on the Belmont Report (1979), the researcher followed these three principles to protect individuals' rights to take part in this research study. The precepts of respect for persons relate to two moral obligations: acknowledging the respondent's liberty to choose or refrain from participation in the research without coercion or any adverse effect on their care or education (Abadie et al., 2021; Hasking et al., 2019). Regarding beneficence, the researcher should respect the participant's voluntary decisions and ensure their well-being. However, the researcher saw and enforced the risk of the do-no-harm protocol to ensure respect, beneficence, and justice to protect participants' identity and confidentiality (Hasking et al., 2019).

Written Materials. The researcher presented materials and paperwork related to the study to keep and sustain the participants' confidentiality (Abadie et al., 2021; Patton, 2015). Also, the researcher ensured that all written materials were understood through ongoing review by the mentor and the committee members (Gibbs et al., 2018). All materials were scripted at the eighth-grade reading level.

Data Collection

Semi-structured interviews were used for the data collection, which lasted approximately 60 minutes. Code numbers were given to each respondent to ensure confidentiality (Audette et al., 2020, 2019; Mathur et al., 2019; Schmidlin et al., 2015). The participants could articulate their experiences without coercion because they are experts in their experiences and knowledge (Abadie et al., 2021; Jöbges et al., 2022; Lawn et al., 2016; Livingston et al., 2016; Renedo et al., 2018). The interviews were recorded, and an audio soundtrack began once the informed consent process was completed (Abadie et al., 2021). Once the interview is completed, the researcher thanks the participants for their time and issues a $25 gift card and, upon request, serves them with a copy of the study once it is completed (Moser & Korstjens, 2018, 2017; Bellamy et al., 2016).

Data Collection Location. It is vital to decide where the data was collected (Creswell, 2014; Patton, 2015). Data collection occurred in an assigned public library conference and respondents' offices for confidentiality (Creswell, 2014; Patton, 2015; Schmidlin et al., 2015). However, as the COVID-19 restrictions persisted, the online platform interactions eased the semi-structured interviews. It was necessary to ensure confidentiality and privacy at these interview locations (Schmidlin et al., 2015).

Informed Consent Form Process. Capella University requires researchers to use an informed consent form for all human subjects and legal guardians before research (Abadie et al., 2012; Alexa-Stratulat et al., 2018; Hattingh et al., 2016, 2015). The informed consent form protocol followed Belmont 45 CFR 46.111, 45 CFR 46.116, and 45 CFR, plus the applicable subpart requirements (Barton et al., 2018; Ethicist, 2018). The Belmont Report (1979) required human subjects' care (mental health providers) for the current study as stated above.

Researcher-Designed Open-Ended Questions. Semi-structured open-ended questions are proper for this study because they allow in-depth information from the respondents about their experiences and feelings (Hayes et al., 2016; Percy et al., 2015; Roberts, 2020). The respondents had the opportunity to articulate in-depth responses vital to the topic (Roberts, 2020). Finally, during the interviewing, the interviewer (researcher) and respondents collaborated to understand mental health providers' experiences with and beliefs about the role of empathy while working with male IPV victims (Brinkman & Kvale, 2015; Roberts, 2020).

Instruments

The Role of the Researcher as a Primary Instrument. The researcher was the primary instrument in the study to coordinate the research protocol. Thompson (2018) found that data analysis in qualitative research presents preparing and organizing the data to transcribe data into transcripts for assessment, then reducing the data into themes through coding and reducing the codes, and finally standing for the data figures, tables, and discussions.

Qualitative Inquiry. Shadish et al. (2016) suggested that the researcher's role is significant for qualitative inquiry. The researcher can be active, reactive, or adaptive (Barton et al., 2018; Shesar et al., 2018). Thus, Shesar et al. (2018) posited that their study findings highlighted the active, reactive, and adaptive need for treatment services to screen and assess a range of psychological difficulties. These psychological issues include anger, anxiety, depression, suicide, personality disorders, alcoholism, gambling, and IPV perpetration to provide the best treatment approaches for survivors.

Moreover, according to Shesar et al. (2018), the situation and problems presented by the inquiry's topic, the key users of the results, the dominant style, the inquiry's aim, and the qualities included in the inquiry all influence the researcher's duties. Regardless of the researcher's method, they must learn to bracket their biases and understand the study, preconceived notions, and prior learning throughout the research process to address researcher bias (Chwang, 2014; Soule & Freeman, 2019). Thus, the researcher was primarily responsible for being conscious and mindful of biased issues (Tufford & Newman, 2012). Hence, the study's thematic inductive analysis with a constant comparison generic approach enhanced the designed method protocol to perfect competency skills and fieldwork rigor (Percy et al., 2015; Soule & Freeman, 2019; Zhu et al., 2018).

Bracketing. Bracketing is used in qualitative research to mitigate the probable adverse impact of preconceptions and biases that may deter the research process (Tufford & Newman, 2012). Moreover, proactive measures to reduce bias and bracketing ensured that participants' narratives and empathy care were uncensored, and the study's integrity was upheld (Chwang, 2014; Soule & Freeman, 2019; Tufford & Newman, 2012). This dichotomy fosters self-control to enhance understanding and minimize biases. Sorsa et al. (2015) reported that the bracketing protocol intentionally minimizes biases in interpreting the earlier phenomenology (p. 8). Hence, bracketing sets aside preconceptions and pre-understandings that further prevent the influence of the researcher's bias in this study. However, bracketing might be exceedingly difficult to apply by a researcher who has experienced the phenomenon under investigation. Thus, the interview questions were re-investigated in voice-aloud speech forum practice (mock interview) to avoid biases (Tufford & Newman, 2012). By bracketing one's experiences, the researcher did not influence the participant's understanding of the phenomenon (Johnston et al., 2017). Therefore, the task of bracketing was achieved by keeping a reflective journal to document any thoughts, feelings, and preconceptions throughout the research study relating to the topic of mental health counselors' experiences with and beliefs of the role of empathy while working with male IPV victims (Gill et al., 2021; Pool, 2018; Romero-Martínez et al., 2016).

Professional and Personal Experience. According to Cockburn et al. (2016) and Nyström et al. (2015), the researcher's roles in the generic qualitative study included knowledge broker, reflective scientist, self-reflexive scientist, and process facilitator. These barriers, such as masculinity taboos, precluded candid disclosure of the counselor's empathic recovery program for male IPV victims' insight interpretation (Malatras et al., 2019; Venäläinen, 2020). Finally, revisit the collaborative literature for feedback loop premises and attest conclusions for validation (Compaoré et al., 2021). The researcher's personal research experience began at the University of North Texas in a medical sociology program. That qualitative study explored the coping experiences of male breast cancer patients. The prior study applied generic qualitative study elements. The respondents consisted of male professionals who were male breast cancer patients. The open-ended semi-structured interview articulated the respondents' experiences with breast cancer. An example question was, "Please tell me about your breast cancer recovery experiences" (Percy et al., 2015). According to a Robinson et al. (2017) empirical study, participants found many barriers, such as male IPV victims' disclosures of identity associated with masculinity identity experiences. These barriers include fear of seeming less masculine and hindered candid disclosure of the counselor's empathic recovery program designed for male IPV victims (Venäläinen, 2020).

Preconceptions and Pre-Understandings Biases. Preconception and pre-understanding of what was known and understood before interpretation. A core aspect of the generic qualitative study is that the researcher was attached and inextricable from assumptions and preconceptions about the phenomena under inquiry. These assumptions and prejudices about constant data analysis must be acknowledged and integrated into the research findings (Percy et al., 2015; Schäfer et al., 2022). This prior knowledge guided the inquiry, fostering meanings that blend participants' and researchers' knowledge. However, bracketing can be invoked to avoid study biases. To do so, researchers should separate themselves from the study by showing personal and professional experiences relating to the topic to undo any bias associated with the study phenomenon (Creswell, 2014).

Guiding Interview Questions. The researcher's semi-structured, open-ended questions are proper for this study because they allow in-depth information from the respondents about their experiences and feelings (Hayes et al., 2016; Percy et al., 2015; Roberts, 2020). The respondents could articulate in-depth responses that were vital to the topic (Montgomery et al., 2019). Rubin and Rubin (2012) reported that interviews provide researchers with critical, comprehensive data to understand and explore participants' experiences and transform them into meaning. Overall, during the interview, the interviewer and respondents collaborated to understand mental health providers' experiences with and beliefs about the role of empathy while working with male IPV victims (Brinkman & Kvale, 2015; Roberts, 2020). The interviews lasted approximately 60 minutes. See below the open-ended questions used during the interviews:

1. Tell me about your experiences with empathy while working with male IPV victims.
2. Please illustrate/explain any challenges you have faced in using empathy in your work with male IPV victims.
3. How do you think empathy, or lack thereof, affects your work with male IPV victims?
4. Describe the training that helped prepare you to work with male IPV victims.
5. What advice would you give to another mental health professional about the use of empathy with male IPV victims?
6. What do you think training programs need to prepare mental health professionals to work with male IPV victims?
7. Describe any changes you have experienced in your ability to be empathic while working with your male IPV clients.
8. Please describe the factors affecting your ability to empathize with your male clients who have experienced IPV.

Data Analysis

As Percy et al. (2015) cited, Braun and Clark (2006) reported that generic data analysis focuses on exploring a data set for repeated patterns of meanings. The inductive relative with thematic analysis was used to analyze data collected through semi-structured, open-ended interviews. Hence, for Percy et al. (2015), the step-by-step thematic analysis in collaboration with constant inductive study began with the data analyzed as they were collected.

Step-by-Step Analysis. According to Percy et al. (2015), research transcription starts the theme analysis by comparing everything directly from the field notes, interviews, records, documents, and journals. The researchers explored (a) the patterns' meanings and sought the emergence to develop and cluster for meaningful themes to elucidate the patterns, (b) pertinent information that would be significant in creating coding themes related to the theory, (c) highlighted data for information associated with the research question, (d) previewed the critical data, applied the research question for the related data, and observed deviations from the original transcript information, (e) previewed the highlighted data to ensure the relationship with the research question, (f) previewed the critical data, applied the research question for the related data, and observed deviations from the original transcript information, (g) excluded all unrelated, unhighlighted data contrary to the study question but stored the excluded files for future reference and assessment, (h) coded and named the data to track individual data terms, (i) clustered the related data to develop interconnecting patterns to describe them in phrases, (j) sought specific patterns and correlated them to typical trends, (k) created themes matrix format to develop associated supportive patterns, (l) articulated a detailed abstract analysis to describe the scope and substance of each theme, (m) utilized this process for each respondent's data outcome, (n) collaborated the patterns and themes consistent across the participants' data for meaning and understanding, and finally, (o) synthesized the themes for holistic composite data analysis (Percy et al., 2015).

Backup copies (master copies) were kept in a computer-locked cabinet for seven years to follow the personal data confidentiality protocol (Dagi, 2017; Jahns et al., 2019; Lévesque et al., 2015). After seven years, all the data will be sanitized and destroyed, but the excluded files will be preserved for future reference (Jahns et al., 2019).

Ethical Considerations

This study's findings relatively indicated Gone et al.'s (2020) methodological improvement, conceptual clarity dynamics, and ethical awareness of fundamental research characteristics. The study's participants were professional clinicians with satisfactory academic standing who understood minimal ethical risk. In this study, respondents and counseling professionals reduced the risk associated with the research because the researcher used the bracketing technique conception to set aside biases and opinions (Roberts, 2020). Eight common areas of ethical dilemmas and considerations for this generic qualitative research framework encompassed (a) respondents' vulnerability, (b) records, data, and identity confidentiality, (c) safeguard no-harm philosophical perspective, (f) benefits and risks, (g) informed consent form, (h) unethical breaches, (i) safeguarding participants from physical, psychological, and legal harm, and (j) voluntary participation. Thus, in this study, the sample population (n=10), the researcher, and the design were adhered to and aligned with the Federal Regulation governing research under 45 CFR 46 (Belmont Report of 1979).

Summary

The generic qualitative method was the most appropriate to describe, interpret, and analyze the study's research question. The inductive data analysis paradigm fosters meaning from the data sources (Creswell & Poth, 2018; Coccia, 2020; Percy et al., 2015). Thus, this study indicated necessary knowledge about how counselors might use empathy to treat a population that is not widely understood. The methods and procedures (protocols) used in the study were covered in this chapter in preparation for future researchers' collaborative, replicable research projects. The chapter showed an overview of the study's aims, research questions, design, target population, and sampling procedures to ensure the respondents' inclusive participation. The chapter also showed the procedures used for gathering and analyzing data. Furthermore, the chapter presented a no-harm ethical paradigm that safeguards the participants' rights, privacy, and human values by using the Belmont Ethical Compliance (Belmont Report, 1979). The chapter summary indicated information for future researchers' replication and collaboration, and synthesized and harmonized the key conceptual premises for the study's significance and understanding. To develop general qualitative data-collecting saturation patterns (Malik et al., 2022; Guest et al., 2020), the study findings that resulted from the data collection and analysis are discussed in Chapter 4.

Results

Chapter 4

The primary purpose of this chapter is to utilize the data and findings of this study to answer the research question, "What are the mental health counselors' experiences with and beliefs of the role of empathy while working with male victims of intimate partner violence?" The data collected and analyzed from mental health professionals in Chapter 3 indicates experiences and beliefs about their role of empathy while working with male IPV victims. This chapter addresses the description and vitality of the purposive and snowballing paradigm of the 10 sampled volunteered professional respondents for the study data collection. In addition, the qualitative method was the best approach for this study because it utilized semi-structured, open-ended interviews for the focused professional respondents, written materials, and an inductive process model to nurture meaning from the data-collection sources.

Chapter 4 shows the generic qualitative framework as the most relevant approach to describe, interpret, and analyze the above-stated study's research question. Above all, the conclusive section of Chapter 4 indicates the catalyst for future research in Chapter 5 implications. I conclude this chapter with mental health professionals' experiences and beliefs of the outcome effect of their role of empathy while working with male IPV victims (Dim, 2021; Dziewa & Glowacz, 2022; Machado et al., 2024; Machado et al., 2016; Sivagurunathan et al. 2022). These male IPV survivors experienced mental health professionals' physical, emotional, sexual, psychological, and spiritual well-being treatment programs associated with the aftermath of abuses such as controlling, verbal, and aggressive stalking behaviors (Dim, 2021; Dziewa & Glowacz, 2022; Machado et al., 2024; Machado et al., 2016; Rana et al., 2022; Walker, 2020; Wörmann et al., 2021; Sivagurunathan et al. 2022).

The Study and the Researcher

I am passionate about studying mental health professionals' experiences with and beliefs of the role of empathy while working with male IPV victimization due to the relatively little information about this phenomenon. The literature reviewed revealed a dearth of qualitative research for exploring male IPV victims in the heterosexual cohort (Carlson et al., 2019, 2018; Crane & Easton, 2017; Harvey et al., 2018; Kim & Hogge, 2015; McGinn et al., 2016; Watson, 2019). Thus, my greatest interest in the study was due to the exposure to the gap in the literature review and little understanding of the size of male IPV victimization in the heterosexual community that hinders recovery treatments (Hine et al., 2022).

According to the literature reviewed, mental health providers' experiences and feelings have reported male IPV population mental disorders that stemmed from sexual, physical, and emotional distress, anxiety, anger, and relational victimization experiences

(Sparrow et al., 2017; Tarzia et al., 2020; Walker et al., 2020). As Edwards and Dardis (2020) cited, Huntley et al. (2019) reported that male IPV victims are likelier to show their victimization experiences to an unofficial support group. The unofficial support groups include friends, families, and the church. As I interviewed the study respondents, it became apparent that Hine et al. (2022), Huntley et al. (2019), and Watson's (2019) assertion that (a) fear, shame, and denial of disclosure, (b) challenge to masculinity, (c) commitment to relationship, (d) poverty, (e) manipulation and isolation, (f) serious injuries, (g) humiliation, and (h) coercive control are significant factors that can hinder male IPV victims' recovery treatment. I explored these issues to support counselors in developing programs that could mitigate male IPV victims' emotional distress, depression, anxiety, and low self-esteem and improve their quality of life (Angelidis et al., 2019; Oshri et al., 2017). Shah et al. (2018) said that earlier studies have examined the connection between exposure to trauma and psychotic episodes. However, research on adult trauma exposure, including IPV as a risk factor for psychotic symptoms, was generally lacking. My literature review revealed that mental health providers have a dearth of experiences with and beliefs in the role of empathy for male IPV victims (Asad & Chreim, 2016; Choudhury et al., 2022).

From a spectrum of beliefs and experiences to shape the study's trustworthiness, my role as a researcher underpinned the study's significant primary instrument resource (Cloutier & Ravasi, 2021; Perryman & Appleton, 2016; Schmälzle et al., 2019; Silvestri et al., 2022). Trustworthiness is a crucial tool in this generic qualitative study because it ensures that the research outcome is credible, transferable, and dependable for a correct result. Hence, Cloutier and Ravasi (2021) asserted that trustworthiness provides a study's transparency.

I developed professional and subjective experiences and skills through Capella University's post-graduate advanced courses in ethics, method, research design, and qualitative generic analytical skills. I screened respondents and conducted data-collection interviews, transcription, Internet search, and article searches. I conducted a video medium interactive search, mentor and faculty references, critique, and thematic analysis (Cockburn et al.,2016; Giardino & Hickey, 2020; Novak et al., 2022; Nyström et al., 2015; Percy et al., 2015; Sesar et al., 2018). The paradigm of other academic resources enhanced my generic qualitative inquiry design skills to explore other researchers' literature (Foster & McCloughen, 2020; Percy et al., 2015).

Addressing biases was essential for this generic qualitative inquiry because I was the primary collector of the data. Thus, I was cautiously responsible, conscious, and mindful of bias issues and used bracketing to avoid biases (Tufford & Newman, 2012). To do so, I bracketed myself out of the study by showing personal and professional experiences relating to the topic to undo any bias associated with the phenomenon (Creswell, 2013). Therefore, the task of bracketing was to support a reflective journal to document any thoughts, feelings, and preconceptions throughout the research study relating to the topic of mental health counselors' experiences with and beliefs of the role of empathy while working with male IPV victims (Gill et al., 2021; Pool, 2018; Romero-Martínez et al., 2016).

Description of the Sample

The study respondents were volunteered licensed mental health providers in the South-Central USA region. The sample size was 10 licensed mental health providers (Creswell et al., 2014). I used purposive and snowball sampling to explore the research question (Nally et al., 2019; Perryman & Appleton, 2016; Xiang et al., 2020, 2019). Snowball sampling is the word-of-mouth convenience sampling process for the data-collection protocol (Huntley et al., 2019; Perryman & Appleton, 2016). Recruiting using purposive and snowball sampling techniques helped me to find an eligible sample population (Geddes et al., 2018; Nally et al., 2019; Perryman & Appleton, 2016; Xiang et al., 2020, 2019). I used the 10 participants for the semi-structured data-collection protocol to enhance the understanding of mental health counselors' experiences with empathy while working with males who have experienced IPV abuse (Moser & Korstjens, 2018, 2017; Percy et al., 2015).

Table 1 presents the data depicting/indicating the respondent's demographic profile. I explored and targeted the mental health licensed professional population with one to thirty years of working experience with male IPV survivors. The following are the providers' specific mental health specialties acronym credentials and meanings: CART (Certified Anger Resolution Therapist), LCSW (Licensed Clinical Social Worker), LPC (Licensed Professional Counselor), LMSW (Licensed Master Social Worker), LCDC (Licensed Chemical Dependency Counselor), QMHP (Qualified Mental Health Professional), NCC (National Certified Counselor), and RYT 200 (Registered Yoga Teacher 200). Participants' other academic credentials were bachelor's and master's degrees. Further, the inclusion criteria included mental health licensed practitioners and professional counselor residents in the South-Central USA. Respondents were over 18 years old and had at least one year of experience working with male IPV survivors. The pseudonyms and the acronyms used for the respondents were R-1 through R-10. Specifically, the participants' experiences ranged between two and thirty years, and they were referred to in the study as professional participants. I excluded unlicensed skilled mental health clinicians and those who are personally and professionally affiliated (Hamp et al., 2016; Williams et al., 2019).

Results

Table 1
IPV Professional Mental Health Counselors

Respondents' (Pseudonyms)	Ethnicity	Gender	Education	License	Years of IPV Experience
R-1	African American	Male	Master of Social Work	CART & LCDC	30
R-2	Non-Hispanic	Female	Master of Social Work	LPC, NCC &-RYT-200	Less than 2
R-3	Caucasian	Female	Master of Social Work	LMSW	20
R-4	Caucasian	Female	Master of Professional Counseling	LPC	27
R-5	Caucasian	Female	Master of Professional Counseling	LPC	2
R-6	Caucasian	Male	Master of Professional Counseling	LPC	8
R-7	Caucasian	Female	Master of Counseling Social Work	LCSW	20
R-8	Hispanic	Female	Master of Social Work	LCSW	10

R-9	African American	Male	Master of Social Work	LCDC & QMHP	20+
R-10	African American	Male	Master of Professional Counseling	LPC	12

- Note. R=Respondents=n=10, Pseudonyms: R-1, R-2 & R-3 ... R-10

Research Methodology Applied to the Data Analysis

The qualitative method was the most advanced method for this study because it indicated semi-structured, open-ended interviews for focus groups, field observations, written materials, and inductive processes to ease and explore repeated thematic patterns (Creswell, 2003; Percy et al., 2015). I conducted inductive research using the Percy (2015) stepwise protocol approach. The inductive data analysis model showed meaning from the data sources (Creswell, 2003; Creswell & Poth, 2018; Coccia, 2020; Mørk et al., 2023; Tavares et al., 2016; Westas et al., 2022). According to Holtrop et al. (2018), qualitative methods such as generic frameworks promote understanding why and how the research results describe different data themes and patterns. Data analysis involves organizing data into common themes, categorizing, describing, classifying, interpreting, presenting, and visualizing the data in a way that defines them (Monteleone & Forrester-Jones, 2017; Phipps et al., 2018; Percy et al., 2015).

The data analysis was consistent with Chapter 3's systematic protocol collaboration, and the transcribed audio-recorded interviews were verbatim through the https://otter.ai transcribing software link. As Percy et al. (2015) cited, Braun and Clark (2006) reported that generic data analysis showed a data set for repeated patterns of meanings. Concerning the Percy et al. (2015) step-by-step thematic protocol approach, I transcribed and started the data analysis with constant comparison "through direct quotes from the respondents' interviews, field notes, records, documents, and journals" (p. 83). Further, I explored the following step-by-step protocol:

> (a) Patterns' meanings to develop themes, (b) searched pertinent information to create coding themes, (c) highlighted data for information associated with the research question, (d) previewed the critical data to observe deviations from the original transcript information, (e) excluded all unrelated, unhighlighted data contrary to the study question but stored them for future reference and assessment, (f) coded and named the data to track individual data terms, (g) clustered the related data to develop interconnecting patterns and phrases, (h) sought specific trend patterns, (i) created themes matrix format for patterns, (j) articulated a detailed abstract analysis for themes scope and substance, (k) accounted for each respondent's data reported/provided, (l) collaborated the patterns and themes for meaning and understanding, and finally, (m) synthesized the themes for holistic composite data analysis. (Percy et al., 2015, p. 83)

In their studies, Huntley et al. (2020) and Taylor et al. (2022) argued that respondents must not feel that they have been coerced and have the right to relent (withdraw) from the interview without fear of retaliation toward their well-being or education during the interview process. Backup copies (master copies) were kept in a computer-locked cabinet for seven years to follow Capella University's data confidentiality protocol (Dagi, 2017; Jahns et al., 2019; Lévesque et al., 2015). After seven years, all the data will be destroyed by sanitizing but stored in the excluded files for future reference and assessment (Jahns et al., 2019).

Presentation of Data and Analyses

The fundamental purpose of the data-collection protocol was to present the data collected from the diverse 10 volunteered mental health professionals (Respondents: R) interviewed and the results of the analysis to answer the research question (Madden et al., 2020; Olani et al., 2022). The study's primary question that guided this research was, "What are the mental health counselors' experiences with and beliefs of empathy while working with male victims of intimate partner violence (Atance-Pereira et al., 2020; Langenderfer-Magruder et al., 2019, 2018)?"

Hence, based on the outcomes of the question's open-ended semi-structured interview data, I developed, synthesized, and organized six emerging themes presented in Table 2 developed on the next few pages. I used three overarching themes to catalyze and support the direct quotes associated with the data transcripts addressed in the research study. However, the mental health providers' experiences with and feelings of empathy while working with male IPV victims were linked with clinicians' understanding of the male IPV survivors' mental health experiences (Burns et al., 2022; Pointet Perizzolo et al., 2022; Voth Schrag et al., 2021). The male IPV victim experiences include emotional distress, suicide, PTSD, and anxiety (Løkkegaard et al., 2019; Lysova et al., 2022).

According to Machado et al. (2017), intimate partner violence is a shared phenomenon worldwide and a significant cause of male IPV mental health concerns. As Eckstein (2016) cited, Easterbrooks et al. (2018) reported that victims of intimate partner violence often met adverse societal reactions to their abuser. Earlier authors Goodman and Walker (2016), Eckstein (2016), Easterbrooks et al. (2018), and Turner & West (2015, 2014) suggested differences in how diverse victims experienced and communicatively managed IPV attachment to mitigate perpetrators' aggressions. Interpreted through an applied lens for IPV practitioners and victims, findings also showed nuance/intricacy to existing theories of IPV, interpersonal communication, and social stigma (Aguillard et al., 2022; Berlinda Majola et al., 2023; Emezue et al. 2021). Mental health professionals described intervention strategies to combat, for instance, African American male victims' experiences with sexual maltreatment and mental health levels of substance addiction, distress, anxiety, and emotions (Kimber et al., 2015). This research study indicated mental health providers' empathic understanding of recovery treatment plans (Martin et al., 2020; Senneseth et al., 2022; White et al., 2019). Mental health providers lack the potential knowledge to address how the fundamental dynamics, such as regaining and recreating one's identity, are involved in the recovery plan processes (Flasch et al., 2017; Mookerjee et al., 2015). Augsburger et al. (2019) argued that "empirical studies had concluded practitioners' concerns with IPV victims' violence and aggressive acts experiences from their perpetrators" (p. 1776).

Clinicians and researchers are concerned with the low self-esteem, emotional, and anxiety outcomes of IPV-abused victims (Maiuro, 2015; Oshri et al., 2017). The research study indicated additional knowledge about how counselors might use empathy to treat a population that was not widely understood, such as male IPV victims' experiences with illicit drug use and mental disorders, emotional distress, depression, suicide, PTSD, and anxiety (Chen et al., 2021; Liu et al., 2020; Løkkegaar et al., 2019; Lysova et al., 2022; McCabe & Day, 2022; Miller, 2016).

I used coding to label, interpret, and organize the study of qualitative data collected to show different themes and their relationships (Cooper, 2016; Salanda, 2016). I analyzed the same datum in this study to create compositions, concepts, categories, and subcategories (Cooper, 2016; Percy et al., 2015; Saldana, 2016). I used symbolical codes (e.g., a word or short phrase) to assign the themes a summative, salient, and essence-capturing meaning (Cooper, 2016; Saldana, 2016; Saldaña, 2015). To Salanda (2012), "Coding is not a precise science; it is primarily an interpretive act" (pp. 3–4). Finally, compared to the Percy et al. (2015) step-by-step clustering and axial approach, I listened to the interviews, reviewed the transcripts again, and applied inductive thematic analysis by sorting out the respondents' repeated data patterns and tenets.

Following Otter.ai software audio transcriptions and exploring the transcripts again, I developed a new 52 sub-themes clustered into six themes presented in Table 2 stipulated below. I described thematic analysis to postulate the protocol for data exploration analysis to set up generic qualitative data-collection saturation patterns (Malik et al., 2022; Guest et al., 2020).

Table 2
Data Analysis: Themes and Sub-Themes

Themes	Sub-Themes Collaborated to Form Themes
Theme 1: Experiences With Empathy Working With Male IPV Victims	**Sub-Themes:** Disclosure constraints Female perpetrator's behaviors Domestic violence escalation Cultural dynamics Spirituality Social stigma and cultural taboos
Theme 2: Male Masculinity Ego Issue "I am a Man, I Don't Need Help."	**Sub-Themes:** Societal biases and cultural norms Cultural taboos Preserve self-esteem and shame Self-blame Social and cultural stigma
Theme 3: Challenges Working with Male IPV Victims	**Sub-Themes:** Trauma perspective Mental health professionals' burdens and heart issues Perpetrators' aggressive/violence Types of anger Shelter for females and lack of coping Resources for male IPV survivors

Results

Theme 4: Perpetrators' Victimization and Abuse

Sub-Themes:
Suicidal and homicidal feelings Justified
Embarrassment and disrespect
Burdens of PTSD and mental health
Molesting and physical behaviors of
Throwing objects
Verbal and sexual abuse
Stalking
Unhealthy toxic
relationship disruption

Theme 5: Advice and Training Impact on Mental Health Professionals

Sub-Themes:
Counselors' experiences with male IPV clients
Understanding and knowing male IPV victims
Read, Study, and conduct research to educate yourself
Mental Health Professionals acknowledge domestic violence victimization
Develop programs and questions for Treatment
Bracket yourself and avoid biases
Ensure clients' accountability
Question cultural and societal taboos advocacy for Government legislation and resources for Male IPV victimization

	Sub-Themes:
	Exercise compassion in treatment With Understanding the training that equips Mental health providers to know what a man is and that IPV victims and social biases DV/IPV is always against women but the reality is that it is against against men Avoid social stigma, cultural taboos and biases
Theme 6: Changes in Mental Health Professionals Experiences and Effects That Affect the Ability to Empathize	Proposals for a new government Legislation and resources for male IPV victims View domestic violence Seriously, to understand male IPV victims' situation The size of love for couples Change of perspective and understanding that domestic violence goes against men Trauma sometimes makes men susceptible DV/IPV Trauma and promote self-esteem Spirituality and Belief Ideal For coping with physical issues

Presentation of Data and Results of the Analyses

The primary research question that guided and synthesized the perspective and feelings of this study's participants was, "What are the mental health counselors' experiences with and perceptions of the role of empathy while working with male victims of intimate partner violence?" Hence, in the articulation and collaboration of the research data-collection semi-structured interview protocol, six themes indicated in Table 2 above emerged. These six themes in

Table 2 indicate mental health providers' beliefs and experiences relevant to explaining and enhancing the understanding of the research study question and purpose (Bouchard & Wong, 2021; Rogers et al., 2021).

Overall, the 10 mental health professional respondents (R) that took part in the study expressed empathy experiences and beliefs concerns based on the male IPV survivors' masculinity ego (Gateri et al., 2021; Sattar et al., 2022). San-Martín et al. (2017) described empathy in patient care as a cognitive attribute encompassing understanding the patient's experiences, concerns, and perspectives. However, the 10 respondents and other researchers affirmed empathy compared to masculinity stigma constraints of men's ego for not seeking legal redress. Instead, they used indirect criteria methods such as reporting to friends and family members and self-blame (Lelaurain et al., 2018; Mwayuli et al., 2019). The participants expressed empathy for clients' treatment from the perspective of (a) lack of disclosures, (b) female perpetrator's behaviors, (c) domestic violence escalation, (d) cultural dynamics, (e) spirituality, (f) social shame, (g) self-blame, and finally, (h) social and cultural stigma.

Theme 1: Experiences with Empathy Working with IPV Victims. Respondents 1, 2, 3, 4, 7, 9, and 10 shared the same perspectives that aligned with this theme. For example, R-10 stressed his concerns as:

> We take women's aggressive behaviors, such as stalking, as a form of abuse. These alone need much empathy. Men are motivated by ego; hence, most of the time, they will not share their victimization with other men, so we have a societal construct of what we think men should be. When that happens, we must show empathy. These behaviors alone needed extra empathy without judging the victims.

Unlike the rest of the respondents listed above, R-1 reported on Theme 1 in the context of first-time DV/IPV offenders. R-1 said:

> I feel empathy cognitively because I have experienced the phenomena from so many angles; "being empathetic means you put yourself in that person's shoes; cognitively, you can physically feel their pain."

In addition to R-1 and R-10's reports on Theme 1, R-2 articulated that her empathic experiences and perceptions developed through the lens of societal biases toward male IPV victims. R-2 reported that she had developed a strong empathy for that population because she thinks it is societally biased as often as it exists. She tends to connect well with male clients who have experienced either specifically physical violence, emotional distress, or mental illness.

For R-3, empathy is "how she feels to be in someone's shoes." According to her, the factors that influence her ability to dispense empathy include masculine characteristics such as:

> (a) shame, self-blame, trauma, timidity, isolation, drinking, embarrassment, and self-loathing, (b) victimization issues, nondisclosures, (c) policy passivity and defenseless of perpetrators' behaviors, and finally, (d) egg-shelling anxiety, which means being cautious about provoking conflict—suggesting that he had to be more cautious like you cannot, you have to watch what you say and do. For her, it is a shame when you blame yourself.

Theme 2: Male Masculinity Ego Issue, "I Am a Man; I Do Not Need Help." Respondents 1, 2, 3, 4, 7, 9, and 10 shared the same perspectives that aligned with this theme. For example, R-10 described empathy and masculinity ego through victimization by stating:

> Most men will not disclose. Male victimization is just a social stigma on how a woman has abused and

beaten the male victim. However, sociocultural stigmatized it to undermine masculinity. Thus, the victim is a man and does not need help for his wife's perpetration. They are not going to disclose their victim's behaviors.

For masculinity in men's behaviors, R-2 further stated that research and experience showed masculinity in men's behavior. She reported that in terms of mitigating programs for male intimate partner violence, a cultural dynamic of socioeconomic power and control prevents males from showing their victimization experiences. For example, R-2 said, he has often seen people on probation, especially county and federal probation systems, with poor economic status.

For example, R-2 stated:

> I have seen men who are the victims themselves come through counseling.
> The female threatens to call the police and has them arrested for intimate partner violence.

Concerning spirituality and the impact of expressing empathy while working with a male IPV masculinity ego, R-7 reported a meditation scenario that prepared and guided her to deal with her clients. Compared with R-1 and R-10 spiritual dynamics protocol for male IPV victims' treatment programs, R-7 said:

> Yes, and truthfully, I sought my faith in God for understanding constantly in this office. When faced with a treatment challenge, I sat back in my chair and silently prayed. God, please give me the right words. I closed my mouth and opened my ears, and somehow, some way to seek help. I sought the Lord to touch my heart. For example, physical issues such as stalking, traumatic brain injury, and multiple sexual assaults

were the basis of my empathy, and I tried to build trust in them through meditation.

R-9 further elaborated on neutral and nonjudgmental male victims' disclosure dynamics expressions to explain Theme 2. He reported:

> I can share that empathy of understanding what abuse is like because throughout my work with women whom men have abused, sometimes it is an odd situation that some women open up and share those experiences a little bit better because they do not have that judgment. Or the feeling of judgment to say that this guy did this to me versus another female introducing me to this, you know, so I guess it kind of ties into that challenges of what you face with the male spouse's interjections that cause (our treatment program composition/protocol to concentrate more on the company of male IPV victims') disclosure barrier for sure.

Theme 3: Challenges Working with Male IPV Victims. All 10 respondents (Rs) shared the same perspectives that aligned with this theme, ranging from physical to emotional victimization and abuse (Dim, 2021; Emezue et al., 2022; Sesar et al., 2018). From the R-1 perspective, victimization is skewed more toward males (aggressive behaviors). R-1 articulated that the offenders' pretrial diversion intervention program statistics success percentage rate was about ninety percent (90%). For example, R-1 reported that:

> These types of female perpetrators' anger management associated with male IPV victims impeded mental health professionals' intervention treatment programs. The victimization treatment success ratio was 60 to 40 females to males.

Results

Unlike R-1's anger management protocol that hindered his treatment of male IPV survivors, R-2, R-3, and R-4 reported that (a) mental health burdens, (b) perpetrators' aggressive and violent reactions, (c) unhealthy toxic relationships, and (d) burdens of PTSD tested their empathy while counseling male IPV clients. The Moreira et al. (2022) study found PTSD associated with complex posttraumatic stress disorder (CPTSD). The World Health Organization (2018) reported that CPTSD experiences show the aftermath of a person (e.g., male IPV victim) who has met a series of extreme perpetual stalking behaviors. For example, R-2 expressed:

> I have seen male IPV victims experiencing homelessness living in their cars. Because, you know, the social, cultural, and justice system empowered the wives to decide whether the man is allowed to be a resident in the home. Where is the victim going to live? And then the woman decided when he could come back.

Theme 4: Perpetrators' Victimization and Abuse. Throughout the interviews, the 10 participants shared the same perspectives such as perpetrators' aggressive and violent reactions, and unhealthy toxic relationships that aligned with this theme. A study indicated that IPV increases the risk of (a) depression, (b) anxiety, (c) injuries, (d) chronic pains, and (e) gastrointestinal disorders for male IPV victims. The study findings related to Theme 4 aligned with the results of previous research (Dim, 2021; Lysova et al., 2022; Zinzow et al., 2022). Men do not seek support for victimization disclosures to effect a change (Dim, 2021; Lysova et al., 2022; Zinzow et al., 2022). They are passive, ashamed, timid, and accept guilt. In R-2's view, male IPV victims' failure to hold their spouses' accountable precipitates unhealthy, toxic relationships. Furthermore, R-10 expressed that:

> It is interesting to say that because of the self-blame, men allowed victimization to happen because

their hands were not clean and allowed this to happen.

Besides, R-3 reported a strong case for embarrassment, disrespect, and stalking as a catalyst for describing perpetrators' victimization and abuse that posed challenges related to her while working with male IPV victims. She said victimized men are reluctant, feel embarrassed, and avoid masculine characters to show their perpetrators. Society and the legal system are biased toward them. Male IPV victims are vulnerable. I am empathic toward them. For R-3, empathy is natural and always there. She often thinks men prefer and are comfortable with female counselors' treatment because they see women as more trustworthy and safer for showing their victimization hurts. However, R-3 said:

> It's not a struggle or a challenge because empathy is a natural experience in handling real-life issues. If a man confides in me that he is a victim of a spouse, then empathy is there. It's not a struggle or a challenge for me. Victimized men have a victimized mentality. Victimized men are reluctant, feel embarrassed, and detest masculine traits to show their perpetrators. Society and the legal system are biased toward them. I recommend that other mental health providers avoid being judgmental but have compassion for therapeutic resolution.

Compared with R-3, R-1, R-2, and R-4 shared a common perspective consistent with explaining Theme 4. For example, R-1, R-2, and R-4 asserted that female manipulative characteristics and behaviors, such as nagging and belittling, may cause the aftermath of male IPV survivors' mental health disorders. In collaboration with R-3 and R-4 reports, R-5 buttressed perpetrators' aggressive behaviors and aggression associated with anger to affirm the unhealthy, toxic relationship that confronted mental health providers' treatment protocol while working with male IPV victims. I would say an unhealthy relationship pattern is suffering regardless of the gender of the person in the relationship. It is imperative for mental health professionals to develop anger management programs to mitigate the practice of perpetrators' estrange behaviors and not so much focusing on addressing gender social differences. R-5 augmented her report with this scenario:

> I guess to understand male victims and how that changes their identity. I'd say like an ordinary couple would be defensive, placing the blame on somebody else when you were the one who brought it. I would say, obviously, physical and emotional violence. Those things are also crucial in sexual violence, which we rarely discuss.

Compared with R-1, R-2, R-3, R-4, R-5, and R-7's perceptions on Theme 4, R-6 asserted a contrasting argument with the following scenario:

> I would like to tell people (refute) that it is seemingly imbalanced to blame women as aggressive perpetrators of victimization and abuse to men. Men have every emotion that women do; we're just taught not to express them as openly, but we have them all. And I think, in many ways, we're probably more sensitive in some areas than our female counterparts.

Contrasting with R-6, R-7 expressed that she was emotionally empathic for the male IPV victim's plight from their spouses' hostile reactions. Respondent 7 presented a dialogue with the following concerning confrontational victimization behaviors:

> When discussing intimate partner violence, will it include military sexual assault? Yes! I have much

training in military and male sexual assault. I am telling you that I have a male client in the heterosexual community whom three females assaulted. So, I know that the tiny part is a whole other study. Well, I've got a male client who was drinking and was sexually assaulted in the military by three females. This guy is struggling in his marriage to his current wife, who has been married for twenty years, and has never told her. Yes, on average, it seems one in four is sexually assaulted in the military, and the public doesn't want to talk about their sexual assault or physical assault.

Further, R-10 articulated that in dealing with disclosure issue concerns, the government should be interested in detaining female perpetrators instead of males. He said that education tells the community that research has revealed aspects of human life experience for government contribution to resolving male IPV and domestic violence dilemmas. R-10 revealed that:

Domestic violence shelters or support programs at the local or national level should equip mental health providers with resources to support male IPV treatment programs. However, we do not find programs dealing directly with male victimization. Ninety-eight percent (98%) of victimization disclosure issues are right for women, but less attention and service for male victims.

Theme 5: Advice and Training Impact on Mental Health Professionals. Respondents 1, 2, 3, 4, 5, and 6 shared the same perspectives that aligned with this theme. For example, the R-3 report aligned with cultural taboos and masculinity that impact her ability to dispense treatment for male IPV clients (Dim, 2021; Emezue and Udmuangpia, 2022; Huntley et al., 2019). R-3 believes research and study programs must continue discussing training programs to promote and affect professional experiences. For government consensus support for changes in mental health professionals and training that may affect their ability to empathize with clients coping treatment program protocol. Furthermore, R-10 suggested that training resources could guide and prepare mental health providers to understand and mitigate the victimization dynamic presented, such as unhealthy, toxic relationships, embarrassment, and relationship disrespect. On the contrary, he said, resources are unavailable for male IPV-victimized survivors' well-being. Thus, R-3 stated:

> For me, time experiences ultimately figure out the mental health providers' ability to offer male IPV clients treatment. However, treatments related to the current justice system bias, cultural disparities, beliefs, and societal taboo changes (substance abuse, drinking habits, sexual indulgences, spiritual failures) for spousal role changes affect mental health professionals' training program outcomes. Clients' different issues correlate with intervention programs for healing and restoration programs for male IPV victims' treatment.

R-3 reported that, unlike men, women unite and support each other for changes for a cause in the communities. For policymakers, no significant legislation exists for intervention in this family conflict tension on male and female DV/IPV content.

For R-1 and R-2, spiritualizing and believing are ideal advice for male IPV victims to cope with treatment for physical, mental, and emotional health well-being. In addition, from the lens of spiritualizing and believing, R-1 reported that:

> Some emotional issues are going on with the male IPV survivors. Everybody needs help. The victim needed help, and the perpetrator too. I try to be sensitive to the function of my therapeutic role and the service I am assigned to give. My connectivity to my Creator is the most significant factor in helping me to understand humanity.

R-4 reported an interesting academic endeavor that aligned with Theme 5 concerning reading and studying research to educate mental health providers. She stated that her master's program in counseling increases her empathy training for clients. Moreover, I learned a whole lot about domestic violence relative to a dual program that indicated victims of domestic violence and sexual assault. R-2 stated that mental health professional training that empathizes with male IPV victims must focus on hyperarousal or hyperarousal depression and anger, because these dynamics precipitate male IPV concerns. R-2 said many male IPV victims struggle with trauma and possibly hypervigilance concerns. The respondent said the characteristics of hyperarousal include defensiveness, impulsiveness, and hypervigilance. However, it depends on whether persons respond to hyperarousal or emotional levels and how they tend to flow. Siegal's et al. (1999) window-of-tolerance model supports feelings and reactions to adapt to a situation.

R-5 reaffirmed that her personal experience was one of the most significant factors that influenced her to see things differently and empathize with her clients. R-5 declared that being trained and taught as a workplace counselor helped her. Further, she said:

> My time working with victims and perpetrators of domestic violence influenced my empathy for male IPV victims. I didn't—I didn't even know that I have experienced perpetrators' behaviors until I sat there to listen to what abuses and, you know, hearing what emotional abuse and verbal abuse were, that I was able to find that had been part of my experience.

Understanding and knowing male IPV clients through a conducive counseling environment concur/acquiesce with Theme 5. A healthy counseling environment with safety, trust/transparency, and confidentiality strengthens professional, ethical authentication.

Results

Thus, R-6 asserted that an amiable, empathic, skilled clinician should consider the following positive environment:

> More experienced, I feel like you fall back on your basic counseling and skills training. It's some basic things you would do or need to provide for the environment. I mean, safety is critical. If people don't feel safe, they won't tell you anything. So, if you prepare the environment, then it will happen.

R-7 reported critical concerns about the government's dearth of information, few resources, and limited legislative policy programs to mitigate male IPV survivors' victimization and mental health. R-7 presented the following scenario to bolster her empathic position against the government's little support for VA male IPV veteran victims. R-7 emphasized that only the veteran administration and only one percent of the population are veterans. Overall, R-7 said that recommending that the government hasten the legislative process, be more aggressive, and encourage men to show female perpetrators' aggressive behaviors is significant for government consensus support for changes in mental health professionals and training that affects their ability to empathize. R-5 commented:

> I see where the government sometimes perpetuates male IPV victimization. Males are stuck in situations where mental health problems continue. It seems the problem is PTSD. Posttraumatic stress disorder and depression are interesting. I feel like many more men victimized may go more on the depression route. The women are more anxious about aggressive behavior; I think part of that is just the suppression of their feelings.

R-7 described researching to educate the following advanced changes in mental health professionals' experiences and training that affects her ability to empathize while treating male IPV survivors' mental health well-being. Trauma motivational interviewing training experiences advanced her empathetic treatment of male IPV survivors who struggled with trauma. R-8 reported that gender role (masculinity) experiences challenged her ability to empathize. According to R-8, professional mental health clinicians' understanding and experiencing male IPV training associated with societal biases fostered prominent effects on their ability to empathize while dispensing male IPV survivors' mental health treatment programs (Huntley et al., 2019). R-8 explained her standing through the lens of the following account by stressing:

> My recommendation for the training is that it should not just be a checklist of questions or a review of the frequency of what you see. Instead, it should focus on the individual and their unique presentation, while also considering the societal classes and ethnic diversity that may be influencing their behavior.

From these perspectives, R-9 had the following empathic viewpoints about mental health:

> The training that helped me was working with the male IPV crisis. Okay, for example, seeing clients who were suicidal based on that feeling while working with them, and I think these experiences get them to show about help and be able to aid those dealing with some of the problems of being victims of mental and physical abuse. Training programs must be prepared to be open for mental health providers.

The following were R-10's comments that aligned with this theme. He articulated:

> My buildup of experiences, through working with male IPV victims, studying, and researching, these resources helped me handle the study and research materials to understand IPV/DV effects on male IPV victims' abuse dilemma/predicament.

Moreover, R-10 said:

> Love is one key factor affecting his ability and practice to empathize. Our job is to love people, which "I call spiritual." Spiritual stuff manifests as we deal with the physical issues of stalking and work to discover what people believe about this clinic's practice. Our mission is to love our neighbors as ourselves, as shown in Matthew 22:39 (Crim, 1970). We love people for spiritual and physical wellness. The mission of this clinic is to empathize with people.

Theme 6: Changes in Mental Health Professionals' Experiences and Effects That Affect the Ability to Empathize. All the respondents (R-1–R-10) and scholars, including Coyle et al. (2019), Burns et al. (2022), Levit, (2020), and Negus & Grobler (2021), shared relatively the same perspectives that aligned with this theme. All the respondents (from R-1 through R-10) and scholars such as Coyle et al. (2019), Burns et al. (2022), and Levit (2020) pointed out that Changes in Mental Health Professionals' Experience and Training impacts mental health initiatives that provoke/arouse ability to empathize, fit, and deepen their holistic understanding. R-5 reported that personal experiences were the most significant crucial factors that influenced her to see things differently and empathize with her clients. R-5 said that being trained and taught as a workplace counselor helped her. For example, R-2 stated that one-to-one client interactions, treatments, and intentional program developments boosted her empathetic service experiences with male IPV victims. Also, she attested that her clients' interactive treatment experiences provided progressive training, learning, and knowledge tools for her clinical dispensation. Thus, R-2 stated:

> Counselors' experiences with male IPV clients' victimization and understanding of the training equip them to understand domestic violence and social biases.

R-5 buttressed empathic understanding and knowing male IPV oppression through her mother's perpetration (victimization experienced) of her father. In her testimony, R-5 reported the following domestic abuse scenario:

> I grew up in a household where my mom was, I don't know if I have described her as an abuser or anything like that, but she was a strong hand in the household. I often saw where she would put my dad down, targeting his self-esteem or manhood at times. So, I think this is probably one of the factors.

R-6 reported that an amiable, empathic, skilled clinician should consider a positive environment. Overall, R-6 shared that this statement affected his empathy while treating male IPV victims.

> My understanding of humanity is that people can be violent just as they can. I do see where society, for many years, has placed specific pressures on men and women for different character traits. So, I can see the impact of those characteristics a lot in male IPV survivors' responsiveness to coping treatment program.

Unlike R-1, R-2, and R-7, R-5 attested concerning spirituality and beliefs that presenting her work's beliefs with perpetrators helped her empathize with male victims, and because she was privileged enough to serve over time, it took a long time to break down some of the barriers with the perpetrators. She addressed that you would find that the male victims experienced domestic violence themselves during childhood. So, that helped her to understand that we either act out or internalize the traumas we meet. R-5 shared:

> Many men who become victims have internalized much of the pain they experienced in life rather than externalizing it.

Summary of Results

The primary purpose of this chapter is to use the data and findings of this study to answer the research question compared to mental health professionals' experiences with and beliefs of the role of empathy while working with male IPV victims. The study question presented was, "What are the mental health counselor's experiences with and beliefs of the role of empathy while working with male victims of intimate partner violence?" The chapter's findings indicate understanding mental health providers' empathic experiences and feelings of working with male IPV victims' emotional problems through six themes. Chapter 4 shows the tenets of the study's theoretical framework and earlier researchers' work.

Overall, the generic qualitative study framework paradigm was utilized to guide this research study to show and support the foundation for holistic analysis, synthesis, and alignment of the research work in Chapter 5. In addition, this conclusive chapter will show the study's interpretation, implications, limitations, and future scientific research relative to male IPV victimization.

Findings and Conclusion

This conclusive chapter of the research study indicates a generic qualitative method to support, summarize the results, and discuss the research organization, and the central sections. A description is provided in Chapter 5 that outlines this research study's results about mental health professionals' empathic role experiences, perceptions, and beliefs while working with male IPV victims who have experienced female victimization (Aiyenigba et al., 2019; Bandara et al., 2015; Bouwman et al., 2018; Dumesnil et al., 2018; Pelkowitz et al., 2023). Chapter 5 shows how 10 volunteered mental health professional respondents' input reported on their experiences, a summary of the results, the organization, and the central sections (Fagerlund et al., 2022; Griffiths et al., 2019; Huntley et al., 2019; Loo et al., 2021; Steffensen et al., 2023).

An outline was presented in Chapter 4 that provided the data-collection process with a logical understanding of the findings. Chapter 5 is replete with a thorough discussion of the findings. The results were interpreted through the lens of the research question and supported by earlier literature reviewed. The research question was, "What are the mental health counselors' experiences with and beliefs of the role of empathy while working with male victims of intimate partner violence?"

There is a description and contrast of the study's limitations and delimitations for the design flaws and other problems. Lastly, the conclusion of the chapter highlights the following headings and subheadings: (a) Summary of the Findings, (b) Comparison of the Findings with the Theoretical Framework and Previous Literature, (c) Discussion of Results, (d) Limitations, (e) Implications for Policy or Practice, (f) Recommendations for Future Research, and finally, (g) the Conclusion.

Summary of Findings

The findings of the research indicated six themes consisting of (a) experiences with empathy working with male IPV, (b) male masculinity ego issue, "I am a man; I do not need help," (c) challenges working with male IPV victims, (d) perpetrators' victimization and abuse, (e) advice and training impact on mental health professionals, and finally (f) changes in mental health professionals' experiences and effects that affect the ability to empathize. These six themes are relatively associated with sociocultural taboos and biases, stigmatized female perpetration abuses (e.g., sexual, stalking, power and controlling, physical, emotional, psychological), and male masculinity victimization (Alsawalqa & Alrawashdeh, 2022; Brooks et al., 2020; Huntley et al., 2019).

Purposive and snowball sampling was utilized to explore the research question. The fundamental rationale for using the purposive sampling technique was to explore participants for a specific purpose to meet particular criteria (Mwendera et al., 2016). Recruiting using purposive and snowball sampling techniques helped to name an eligible sample population (Ozodiegwu et al., 2023). Semi-structured interview questions with 10 volunteered contributors indicated mental health professionals' empathy experiences were screened based on the inclusive and exclusive criteria (Morriss, 2015) and shown in Chapter 4. I used Percy et al. (2015), which recommended data-collection elements to ensure reliable inductive thematic data analysis information. The data collected indicated, defined, and described the participants' realities (Appel et al., 2022; Ramalho et al., 2023; Rovira & Slater, 2022). The privacy and confidentiality of the respondents were preserved relative to the fundamental tenets of the ethical frameworks based on the Belmont Report (1979).

The purpose and rationale for this qualitative generic research study was to align and synergize the research question associated with the study topic of mental health professionals' experiences with and perceptions of the role of empathy while working with male IPV victims' experiences about victimization and seeking recovery support (Huntley et al., 2019; MacLeod, 2019; Schäfer & Löwer, 2021; Weibl & Hess, 2020). Hence, mental health professionals tended to find the need to understand the role of empathy in treating male IPV victims for recovery and intervention treatment programs (Romero-Martínez et al., 2016; Magaletta et al., 2020; Xiao et al., 2016; Zosky et al., 2016). However, one significant concern of this current research was a gap in the holistic knowledge of mental health counselors' experiences with the beliefs about the role of empathy while working with male IPV victims (Williams et al., 2020).

All 10 respondents and earlier authors, Brooks et al. (2021, 2020), Machado et al. (2016), Sathyanarayana Rao et al. (2022), and Hine et al. (2022), reported that male IPV victims' mental health concerns including fear, anxiety, victimization, and distress harm their cognitive health. Ridings et al. (2017) argued that social support and family resources were pivotal empathic protective factors in buffering against IPV-risk families' homes. Mental health service providers understanding these male IPV victims' empathic experiences may develop and promote intervention strategies to mitigate and bridge the gap articulated in the previous paragraph (Fox et al., 2016).

Moreover, the literature reviewed revealed that mental health providers' unique experiences and perceptions fostered the role of empathy for male IPV treatments and programs (Choudhury et al., 2022; Garraway, 2023; Giordano, 2022). Issues facing male IPV victims, including the risk of suicide, and mental health fitness, were a grave public concern (Lim et al., 2015; MacLeod, 2019; Mossière et al., 2018). Hence, understanding these issues is critical for mental health providers to implement suitable recovery programs for the male IPV victim population.

Findings in Context of the Theoretical Framework

Empathic simulation theory guided this "mental health professionals' experiences with and perceptions of the role of empathy while working with male IPV victims" study (Edwards & Dardis, 2020; Di Napoli, 2019; LaMotte, 2019, 2018). Also, scholars' studies including Ainsworth & Bowlby (1991), Bowlby (1982), Bretherton (1992), Pollard and Cantos (2021), Yuspendi et al. (2018), and Voges et al. (2019) findings revealed that attachment theory impacted IPV couples' psychological and physical relationships. The collaboration of these two theoretical frameworks fits well for exploring this research design. The study presented and showed the process for advancing scientific knowledge for the human services in the specialization of social work and community services.

Bui and Pasalich (2021) asserted that earlier research supported attachment anxiety and attachment avoidance theory to explain adult attachment insecurity. Thus, the authors suggested that attachment anxiety collaborates with fear of abandonment, promotes conflict escalation, and describes proximity-seeking behavior toward a partner. Also, attachment avoidance examined fear of intimacy, affected escalation, and adopted a self-reliant behavior (Bui & Pasalich, 2021; Gewirtz-Meydan & Finzi-Dottan, 2021).

In contrast, Gabbay, Lafontaine, and Lafontaine (2017) indicated that the established significance of attachment theory promoted support for mental health clinicians. Thus, these providers understood heterosexual IPV conflict outcomes. Furthermore, Ulloa and Hammett's (2016) empirical study found that more petite, empathic men were likelier to perpetrate IPV and be victimized. Also, women whose male partners were less empathic were more likely to perpetrate IPV and be victimized. Ulloa and Hammett's (2016) findings attributed the associations between empathy and diverse types of IPV as psychological, physical, sexual, and injury. Thus, empathy levels play a significant role in deciding the aggressive behaviors of men and their partners (Ulloa & Hammett, 2016).

On the other hand, the empathic simulation theory's historical perspective is embedded in Berrol's (2016) empirical research, which found the earliest publication on the theory. This discovery dates back to 1998 when Gallese and Goldman coauthored an article introducing mirror neurons to the empathic simulation theory of mind-reading. The research subjects were macaque monkeys, and then the authors extended the successful findings to human neurobiological responses (Berrol, 2016). Gallese and Goldman (1998) explored, discovered, and pioneered an interactive phenomenon revealing that identical sets of neurons can be activated. The neuron activation evolves when an individual witnesses another performing a movement like the one engaged in the action (de Waal et al., 2017). Significantly, later studies affirmed the activation of this mirror-matching mechanism concerning a stimulus outside the self, about another, or interpersonal (Hartmann et al., 2021; Phipps et al., 2018). The catalyst might be the visual observation of motor actions or facial expressions of emotions compared to joy, disgust, fear, compassion, and anger (Berrol, 2016; Gallese & Goldman, 1998).

Thus, unlike the attachment theory, the empathic simulation theory was the most suitable for this study to use generic qualitative methods. The collaboration of these models was used to explore and understand counselors' empathic role experiences with and beliefs about male IPV victims' experiences of victimization and seeking recovery support.

Findings in Context of the Previous Literature

In addition, the current literature reviewed revealed limited empirical studies on mental health providers' empathy experiences about male IPV victims' experiences (Huntley et al., 2019; MacLeod, 2019; McCarrick et al., 2016). The studies of Dim (2021), Huntley (2019), and Mayanja et al. (2023), relative to the findings of this current study, revealed a dearth of literature and information on the challenges and barriers associated with masculinity ego (e.g., "I am a man; I do not need help."). The data collected from the 10 respondents showed the holistic inquiry outcomes of the study (Harris et al., 2021).

The findings of this research study depicted that mental health professionals have little information, knowledge, beliefs, and experiences of the role of empathy while working with males who experienced IPV psychological distress, depression, and anxiety (Dim, 2021; Huntley et al., 2019; Scott-Storey et al., 2023). Sociocultural taboos practiced in the heterosexual families couple's cohort community may hinder male victims of intimate partner violence from seeking recovery support. The research results of this study indicated that semi-structured interview protocol was the data collection process. I utilized the data to answer the research question related to mental health professionals' experiences with and perceptions of the role of empathy while working with male IPV victims (Economou et al., 2020; Higginbottom et al., 2016; Mahamid et al., 2022; Naweed et al., 2022; Pope et al., 2023;

Roncero et al., 2022). This research problem is significant for IPV sexual abuse, social support, and spiritual prevention programs (Jung et al., 2019). The "World Health Organization (WHO) defined IPV as a continuum of abuse to include homicide, minor and severe physical assault, sexual assault, and psychological abuse (e.g., threats, intimidation, coercion, and harassment) by a current or former partner or spouse" (World Health Organization, 2013, cited in Nakalyowa-Luggya et al., 2022, p. 20,502). For Nakalyowa-Luggya et al. (2022), "IPV is a global public/community health issue, impacting individuals as well as societies worldwide" (p. 20,502). In collaboration with the previous authors, mental health service providers expressed compassion/empathy to support males who have experienced IPV abuse to mitigate coping barriers of (a) masculinity, (b) shame, (c) sociocultural stigma, (d) help-seeking, and (e) negative adverse mental health effects (Carlson et al., 2019, 2018; Crane & Easton, 2017; Harvey et al., 2018; McGinn et al., 2016; Romero-Martínez et al., 2019; Romero-Martínez et al., 2016; Watson, 2019).

Brooks et al. (2022) reported that male IPV victims' mental health concerns included fear, anxiety, victimization, and harm to their cognitive health. Mental health service providers understanding these empathic mental health experiences may develop and promote intervention strategies to foster a more positive impact on male IPV victims' experiences with sexual maltreatment and domestic violence levels of distress, depression, and emotions (Kimber et al., 2015; Ridings et al., 2017). Ridings et al. (2017) argued that social support and family resources are two pivotal empathic protective factors in buffering against IPV-risk families' homes. Besides, all the study's 10 respondents in Chapter 4 reported that emotional empathy is what someone else feels; thus, "experience sharing" is an effective stimulus that involves moral reasoning, positive social behavior, social and emotional adequacy, and mood behavior control.

Discussion of Results

This section shows the research question to interpret the study results, the meaning, and the practical and theoretical implications. This interpretation indicates an insightful understanding of the study's collaborative generic qualitative 10 respondents interviewed data constant inductive thematic analysis, synthesis alignment constructive association of the topic and primary question (Davis et al., 2020; Kagoyire et al., 2023; Percy et al., 2015; Pomey et al., 2015; Tripathi et al., 2022). The following six thematic findings contributed by addressing and aligning with the primary question. The six main themes that emerged from the inductive thematic data analysis consisted of the following:

> (a) experiences with empathy working with male IPV victims, (b) male masculinity ego issue "I am a man; I don't need help," (c) challenges working with male IPV victims, (d) perpetrators' victimization and abuse, (e) advice and training impact on mental health professionals, (f) changes in mental health professionals' experiences and effects that affect the ability to empathize.

These six themes are presented in Chapter 4, Table 2. The data thematic analysis provided comprehensive, holistic feelings and experiences of the 10 (n=10) research study professional respondents. The study results showed that the 10 mental health professional respondents who participated in the study agreed with previous authors such as Economou et al. (2020), Gateri et al. (2021), Hemmings et al. (2022), Mahamid et al. (2022), and Sattar et al. (2022) to address empathy experiences and perception concerns through the lens of male IPV survivors' masculinity ego, male victimization, and female perpetrators' behaviors (e.g., stalking, verbal abuse, and power controlling).

San-Martín et al. (2017) described empathy in patient care as a cognitive attribute that involves understanding the patient's experiences, concerns, and perspectives. Nevertheless, the 10 respondents and other researchers affirmed that empathy is associated with masculinity stigma. This sociocultural stigma constrains men's ego from seeking help and legal redress (Dim, 2021; Huntley et al., 2019). Instead, they use indirect criteria methods of reporting to friends, family members, and even self-blame (Lelaurain et al., 2018; Mwayuli et al., 2019). Some of the participants described empathy for clients' treatment from the perspective of (a) lack of disclosures, (b) female perpetrator's behaviors, (c) domestic violence escalation, (d) cultural dynamics, (e) spirituality, (f) social shame, and finally, (g) social and cultural stigma.

Male IPV Masculinity Ego Issue "I am a man; I don't need help" (Theme 2) analysis revealed that female perpetrator's behaviors and domestic violence escalation take a lot longer for male IPV victims to cope with the healing treatment protocol/process. The findings from the research indicated that the social stigma and masculinity ego barriers were critical dynamics that hindered male IPV victims from seeking help for their spouses' victimization. All 10 contributors agreed with previous authors that an improved understanding of these clients can lead to improved delivery of multidisciplinary social services (LaFrance et al., 2019; Rogers et al., 2023). These male IPV victims' experiences with empathy may provide mental health professionals with essential information for family advocacy, support groups, and treatment programs (Ogbe et al., 2020; Micklitz et al., 2023; Machado et al., 2017).

According to the 10 contributors, semi-structured interview data collection revealed that societies do not always accept and realize how men experience the effects of adverse IPV phenomena sensations. These respondents described empathy through the lens of masculinity ego, cognitive concerns, spirituality, and taboos that aligned and explained Theme 2. Thus, the findings from the study highlighted the improved understanding of male IPV victims and added knowledge for the delivery of multidisciplinary social services (LaFrance et al., 2019; Rogers et al., 2023).

Findings and Conclusion

The findings from the study indicated scholarly literature reviewed that included Dardis et al. (2021), Ermer et al. (2022), and Hailemariam et al. (2022). The 10 respondents addressed empathy through the lens of emotional victimization, mental health burdens, and perpetrators' aggressive violent reactions abuse that aligned with Themes 3 and 4 presented (Dardis et al., 2021; Ermer et al., 2022; Hailemariam et al., 2022; Hamberger et al., 2019; Romero-Martínez et al., 2019; van der Meij et al., 2022). Also, the World Health Organization (2018) reported that CPTSD experiences present the aftermath of a person (e.g., a male IPV victim) who has experienced a series of extreme perpetual stalking abusive behaviors.

During the literature review process, I found that the attachment perspective impact was associated with frustrated heterosexual couples' behaviors in IPV dysfunctional ways that precipitated psychological (e.g., emotional) and physical abuse (e.g., stalking) (Doumas et al., 2008; Pollard & Cantos, 2021). For example, as cited in Pollard and Cantos (2021), Doumas et al. (2008) asserted that an avoidant male partner with an anxious female partner was associated with both male and female IPV victimization. Duomas et al. (2008) and Gezinski (2022) argued that clinical implications included attachment avoidance relative incongruity concerning heterosexual partners' sexual adverse effectual needs and detachment in the couple's relationship. Hence, interpersonal anger (e.g., women's high attachment anxiety) may be attributed to a perceived partner who is dysfunctional and unsatisfied.

Previous authors such as Coyle et al. (2019), Burns et al. (2022), Levitt (2020), and Negus and Groble (2021) research study revealed that changes in mental health professional experience and training impacted their ability to empathize, fit, and deepen holistic understanding of ability to work with male IPV victimization. Compared with the previous authors, the research findings indicated that the 10 contributors' input was consistent with Themes 5 and 6, changes in mental health professionals' experiences that affected their ability to empathize and train other providers. These professionalisms signify a lasting impact on counselors' knowledge and understanding of empathic role experiences and feelings about male IPV victims' victimization experiences and recovery-seeking treatment support (Cao et al., 2020; El Sayed et al., 2022; Mihalache, 2019; Purvis et al., 2022; Waalkes et al., 2023).

Above all, study findings seemed to indicate that respondents' beliefs reinforced the individualistic bias in which domestic abuse advocates focused on reporting abuse against women within a framework that does not account for men (MacLeod, 2019; Mossière et al., 2018). I agreed with earlier authors and researchers such as Anastasiou et al. (2021), Depraetere et al. (2020, 2018), and Yohannes et al. (2023) that research results about male victimization and perpetration have shown confusion that requires further research studies on counselors' experiences working with the male IPV victims' population. Hence, the previous scholars, contributors' responses, and the study findings indicated how this research study filled the limited information gap in the human services discipline. The participants' descriptions provided significant information that may serve as a foundation for the unique perspective of mental health service providers' role in empathy experiences of male IPV victims' mental health issues (Saan et al., 2022; Showalter & McCloskey, 2021).

Limitations

Numerous limitations concerning the methodology designed have affected these research findings. The first case was that the qualitative method was the best approach for this study because it indicated semi-structured, open-ended interviews for focus groups, field observations, written materials, and inductive processes. The inquirer could also construct social and historical data into analytical patterns (Coccia, 2020; Tavares et al., 2016). Researchers use qualitative methods when the research question concerns respondents' experiences and beliefs, while quantitative methods are suitable for testing a hypothesized relationship between variables (Creswell, 2019; Creswell, 2018; Percy et al., 2015). Holtrop et al. (2018) stated that qualitative methods promote understanding why and how researchers' results describe different data themes and patterns. However, on the contrary, considering the potency of this qualitative framework compared to describing the causality of this research on men's IPV victimization showed that future quantitative scholars should learn the validity and reliability of this study (Augsburger & Maercker, 2020; Bhattacharyya & Verma, 2020; Tomaz et al., 2022).

Many commentators and academics asserted that generic qualitative studies gain from the established methodologies while supporting flexibility, thus fostering support for researchers whose studies do not lend to a particular established method (Josilowski, 2019; Jose & Novaco, 2016; Mjøsund et al., 2017; Percy et al., 2015; Roy et al., 2020). For example, Percy et al. (2015) made an argument about the vitality of generic qualitative inquiry for empirical studies. Hence, Percy et al. (2015) asserted that those prior researchers accounted for subjective opinions, attitudes, beliefs, and experiences of the external environment. These psychological problems cannot be quantified; thus, they need qualitative methods such as the generic qualitative approach, which is proper for mixed methods studies (Creswell, 1995; Percy et al., 2015). In addition, as Kahlke (2014) and Renate (2018) cited, Caelli et al. (2003) suggested that generic is the best fit for subjective studies because it could blend existing criteria design into a new method and keep the distinctiveness of the original approach. Overall, generic qualitative studies are attractive because they may collaborate the strengths, techniques, and procedures for sustainable, flexible outcomes (Franzen et al., 2017; Gizaw et al., 2017; Storhaug et al., 2017; Saldivar et al., 2019).

However, the generic qualitative design mixes other methodologies to contradict the research framework (Renate, 2018). Other critics contended that generic qualitative approaches lack robustness and guidance to researchers (Klein & Milner, 2019; Noyes et al., 2018; Pound et al., 2016; Coghi & Harris, 2020;

Mawn et al., 2016). For Bellamy et al. (2016), the critical concern about generic framework pitfalls was the paucity of literature on how to do it well. Largely, generic qualitative was charged with "method slurring" (Kahlke, 2014, pp. 44–45), meaning mixing the standard methodologies violated the data-collection standard operating protocol.

In addition, another significant limitation of the generic qualitative research approach used to explore the research question was a paucity of literature about administering it well. The validity of generic research design as a qualitative method seemed debatable (Bellamy et al., 2016). Renate (2018) defines the generic qualitative framework learners' approach as "those who object to a standard established method" (p. 37). Furthermore, unlike the generic qualitative approach that defiantly showed obscurity, the phenomenology framework process indicated the phrase "lived experiences" of individuals experiencing a phenomenon that revealed itself eventually (Arrey et al., 2019; Giandinoto & Edward, 2015). Ultimately, phenomenological analysis shows how individuals experience phenomena, feelings, and thoughts. Nonetheless, generic inquiry proponents Percy et al. (2015) and van der Aa et al. (2020) refuted their critics in collaboration, contending that the generic inquiry design was well fitted for this current study because it is flexible, creative, contriving, and inventive. According to the theoretically vague perspective, Burelomova et al. (2018) suggested that theoretical frameworks for studying IPV appeared comprehensive and complicated, with an absence of empirical viability findings. Thus, a restricted and limited theoretical stance might prevent a variety of exploratory insights for understanding the current topic: mental health providers' experiences and feelings of the role of empathy while working with clients who experience IPV (Augsburger et al., 2019; Vandewalle et al., 2016).

Finally, another critical limitation was developing and framing the interview questions due to little preexisting literature on the role of empathy in the treatment of male IPV survivors. Also, I found the data-collection process, transcription, and transcript protocols time-consuming, daunting, and stressful (Fu et al., 2019; Morgan et al., 2023). Nonetheless, generally, the current study seemed to provide a foundation for future studies regarding mental health providers' experiences and feelings about the role of empathy while working with clients who experience IPV. Also, the study information might have provided and established relevant understanding and data for future research work.

Implications for Policy or Practice

Theoretical Implications

These generic qualitative research findings did not reveal a new theory in the study (Ahmed & Nebeker, 2021; Ferguson, 2023; Kostere & Kostere, 2022, 2021). However, this research study showed empathic stimulation theory (EST) to enhance mental health providers' coping support programs (Okeke-Ihejirika et al., 2022; Castillo et al., 2021) dynamics. These programs might foster positive relationships with providers and their male IPV victims' recovery treatment process (Flasch et al., 2020). The study's results indicated that mental health providers used empathy to connect a strong affinity with clients to make them feel that they were being heard through the lens of words and service support needs (Blackburn & Bulsara, 2019; Patten, 2022).

This research study was guided by the EST framework to support the design and describe the research question (Bollmer et al., 2020; Fisher et al., 2021). Also, earlier authors such as Mayfield et al. (2015), Roy (2020), and Yue et al. (2021) argued that empirical studies indicated that empathic theory fosters organizational leadership motivation. This study's research results indicated that EST stimulates shared responsibility for opinions and beliefs as well as sharing the emotional state (Friedman et al., 2018; Mackenzie & Sorial, 2022; Mystakidis & Lympouridis, 2023). According to the research findings, counselors created programs to normalize the emotional anguish experienced by male victims of intimate partner violence by allowing compassion and supportive behavior. This was achieved by seeking a cognitive capacity to recognize another person's internal states, including thoughts and feelings (Xiao et al., 2016).

Radzvilavicius et al. (2019) found that the "vitality of empathy was critical for sustaining community collective consciousness" (p. 1). Moudatsou et al. (2020) articulated that empathy is critical to the social care professions and professionals. Moudatsou et al. (2020) noted how mental health providers may be supported with continuous and personal development education programs and supervision sessions that allow them to develop empathetic role skills to care for their male IPV victims' intervention recovery programs. The current study findings indicated how mental health professionals and organizations develop sustainable training programs for healthcare and social work professionals. These professionals empower institutional support and networking practices to increase awareness of male IPV victims' issues (Procentese et al., 2019). Radzvilavicius et al. (2019) posited "that a capacity for empathy is a crucial component for sustaining collaborations in societies" (p. 1).

Practical Implications

From a mental health perspective, this study's practical implication was significant to stakeholders such as African American males, IPV victims, human services professionals, social and community services specialization learners, social workers, and public policymakers. Angelidis et al. (2019) and Gangos (2019) asserted that clinicians and learners are concerned about IPV victims' low self-esteem, emotion, and anxiety outcomes. Nonetheless, mental health counselors' empathic experiences and understandings of male IPV victims' emotional, sexual, and physical experiences could develop community psychosocial rehabilitation clinics for IPV-related treatments (O'Dea et al., 2021; Watson, 2019). For instance, psychotherapists were more effective than the average population in regulating negative emotions (Kotera et al., 2021; Muir et al., 2019). Duquette (2017) suggested that mental health counselors receptive to patients' distress and down-regulating negative emotions (e.g., anxiety and depression) are essential for psychotherapists to provide practical help and sustain their well-being.

The mental health counselor's community psychosocial rehabilitation clinics could create a therapeutic context to diagnose comprehensive assessment to foster male IPV victims' recovery treatment planning (Mackowiak & Scoglio, 2018). This information implication equips mental health counselors with empathy while working with male IPV victims to develop intervention programs to bridge family bonds (Di Napoli et al., 2019; Gibson et al., 2015). This therapeutic context focus could change how mental health providers are trained to treat this marginalized population (Kendall et al., 2020).

In a study by Huan et al. (2022) and Neal and Edwards (2017), IPV survivors often reported some positive outcomes through their partner's engagement in counseling programs. However, the program's therapeutic process results seemed unsustainable with negative feedback (Rugkåsa et al., 2020; Holter et al., 2019). This study's results showed how mental health providers are trained to treat male IPV victims (Smith-Clapham et al., 2023). Focusing on using empathy effectively and avoiding judgment can improve the treatment of the male IPV population cohort (Satyanarayana & Krishnamachari, 2022). These implications are relevant to stakeholders such as researchers, policymakers (e.g., legislators), counselors, social workers, counselor learners, and human services professionals who affect this study population with programs and treatment services support (Hash et al., 2017).

Recommendations for Further Research

Recommendations Developed Directly from the Data

The research study indicated how the purposive and snowball sampling approach showed the prospecting of eligible licensed mental health provider populations to explore the research question. A generic qualitative research approach of the meaning, understanding, and uncomplicated thematic data-collection protocol and analysis sampling was proper for this study. Concerning the inductive thematic analysis, six main themes emerged consisting of (a) experiences with empathy working with IPV victims, (b) male masculinity ego issue, "I am a man; I do not need help," (c) challenges working with male IPV victims, (d) female perpetrators' victimization and abuse, (e) advice and training impact on mental health professionals, and finally, (f) changes in mental health professionals' experiences and effects that affect the ability to empathize. The findings of these themes indicated barriers that affected mental health professionals' treatment program intolerance/biases. The study results showed barriers that required future research to include: (a) sociocultural taboos and biases stigmatized female perpetration, (b) male masculinity victimization, and (c) implications of practitioners' empathic experiences with male IPV victims' dearth of disclosures for seeking help and treatment.

Hine et al. (2022), Huntley et al. (2019), and Watson (2019) contributions showed that (a) fear, shame, and denial of disclosure, (b) commitment to relationship, (c) poverty, (d) manipulation and isolation, (e) serious injuries, (f) humiliation, and (g) coercive control are significant factors that can hinder male IPV victims' recovery treatment. The current study's data analysis findings showed how meaningful masculinity, compared to societal culture, can affect heterosexual male IPV survivors' cohort mental, emotional, psychological, and physical behaviors and well-being. Future research may focus on how to mollify/mitigate heterosexual marriages and female aggression physically perpetrating and victimizing their male spouses.

Recommendation Derived from Study Limitations

Concerning methodological limitations on proving the internal generalizability of the trustworthiness of the empathic generic qualitative, I recommend a quantitative analysis for future research studies focusing on overcoming the generic non-random purposive inductive sampling procedure that shows the limited 10 respondents. The quantitative method shows the sizeable random sample rigor of the generic qualitative method framework for trustworthiness (e.g., transferability, dependability, and confirmability) of the current study's findings and data interpretation information documentation (Gibson, 2017; Tobin & Begley, 2004).

Through the lens of qualitative method framework design, this research study showed a generic qualitative design to support the research question (Al-Eisawi, 2022; Akram et al., 2023; Ellis & Hart, 2023). A detailed review of this generic qualitative research indicated that the meaning, understanding, and uncomplicated thematic procedure for sampling data collection and analysis were proper for this study (Kahlke, 2018; Liu, 2016; Percy et al., 2015). Thus, this research showed that future research on counselors' empathic role in subjective opinions, attitudes, and beliefs about their experiences and feelings of their male IPV clients is imperative/crucial (Percy et al., 2015).

A contrasting generic qualitative design with hermeneutic interpretative phenomenological analysis (IPA) indicated the reliability and trustworthiness of this research aftermath. IPA is a critical qualitative method approach that contributes to the subjectivity of the studied experiences (Ferreira, 2021, 2019). Thus, this opposed IPA design showed the experiences of empathy among mental health providers working with male victims of intimate partner violence. These experiences indicated practitioners and mental health professionals' feeling of understanding of sexual maltreatment and domestic violence levels of distress, anxiety, and emotions that are subject to future scientific research premises (Carlson et al., 2019, 2018; Harvey et al., 2018; McGinn et al., 2016; Watson, 2019).

Nonetheless, Liao et al. (2021) and Yeomans (2016) argued that the IPA framework needs to be revised because the researcher consciously tries to reduce the research preconceptions to understand the biases of the new study. The phenomenological qualitative framework data insight analysis indicated an understanding of the whole and discriminative units (Mjøsund et al., 2017). This phenomenological protocol shows a sense of the whole that has been realized for the researcher to reread the data to delineate each transition into meaningful outcomes (Caputo, 2019; Stapleton & Pattison, 2015). Hence, Percy et al. (2015) suggests that since phenomenology studies cannot measure people's subjective opinions such as attitudes, beliefs, and experiences, researchers should consider a more generic qualitative inquiry approach suitable for this current study design.

While investigating from a generic qualitative perspective, I learned about respondents' thoughts, perspectives, opinions, and attitudes about a topic and their experiences (Percy et al., 2015). Hence, the study is significant in showing the research gap in understanding mental health service providers' role in empathy experiences of male IPV victims' mental health problems. The dearth of literature findings on male IPV survivors' transformation indicated the crucial demand for future empirical research on mental health providers' empathy experiences about male IPV victims' emotional and physical experiences (Huntley et al., 2019; MacLeod, 2019; McCarrick et al., 2016).

Recommendation Based on Delimitations

The study findings indicated that therapeutic providers may use empathy to develop preventive treatment programs, professional training, and research to support professionals working with male IPV victims (Ulloa & Hammett, 2016; Wörmann et al., 2021). However, previous researchers lacked qualitative studies exploring and interpreting male IPV survivors' victimization issues (Machado et al., 2017; Spraque et al., 2017). The Henry Kaiser Family

Foundation (2021) analysis reported that approximately 119 million Americans (HKFF, 2021) exist in mental health professionals' shortage areas, and only 26.9% of the need is being met. Thus, the estimated demand for mental health professionals has increased during the COVID-19 pandemic period (HKFF, 2021).

Recommendations based on the small sample/participants of 10 semi-structured interviews data collected, the study findings, and researchers such as Augsburger et al. (2019) and Vandewalle et al. (2016) studies' outcomes revealed evidence to support future research endeavors. This study's findings showed necessary theoretical knowledge about how counselors might use empathy to treat a population that is not widely understood. "Theory is critical for practice because it helps make sense of the complex array of factors involved in IPV, including individual, interpersonal, and social factors" (Meyer & Frost, 2019, p. 33). Furthermore, theory shows the practitioners what to look for in assessing risk and guides them in acting (Meyer & Frost, 2019). Research findings on male victimization indicated uncertainty and a dearth of help-seeking reporting behaviors, suggesting further qualitative research associated with the experiences of providers working with the male IPV victim cohort (Dim, 2020; Barrett et al., 2020). Based on the study's findings about the paucity of community information on male IPV victims, I implore future researchers to focus on the IPV phenomenon relative to the research topic: mental health professionals' experiences with and perceptions of the role of empathy while working with IPV victims (Bates et al., 2020; Hardesty & Ogolsky, 2020; McCarrick et al., 2016; Bui, 2021; Ulloa & Hammett, 2016; Velotti, 2020; Zosky, 2016).

Recommendations to Investigate Issues Not Supported by the Data but Relevant to the Research Problem

In addition, from other issues' perspectives, this study indicated and showed the process of advancing scientific knowledge of counseling for the experiences of mental health practitioners working with male victims of intimate partner violence (Bent-Goodly, 2007; Kulkarni & Kulkarni, 2019; McGinn et al. 2016;

Silander et al., 2020; Wood et al., 2020). A theory is essential for guiding and directing the research process through observation, description, explanation, prediction, and intervention protocol (Meyer & Frost, 2019). This study did not create a general theory to support, conceptualize, explore, and respond to the research topic (Antabe et al., 2022; Blue, 2019; Meighan, 2022). However, the findings indicated empathic simulation theory, which showed the most proper and best-fit design for this study. For example, Bui and Pasalich (2021) premised that earlier research supported attachment anxiety and attachment avoidance theory to explain attachment insecurity among adults. The authors suggested that attachment anxiety collaborates with fear of abandonment, promotes conflict escalation, and describes proximity-seeking behavior toward a partner. Also, attachment avoidance examines fear of intimacy, affects escalation, and adopts self-reliant behavior (Bui & Pasalich, 2021; Gewirtz-Meydan & Finzi-Dottan, 2021). Thus, it was pivotal for researchers to inquire into the nature of this IPV phenomenon to arouse community consciousness, moral reasoning, positive social behaviors, and emotional vitality (Burelomova et al., 2018; Romero-Martinez et al., 2019; Suleimenova & Ivanova, 2018). This study conclusively indicated a need for more future scholarly work on the current topic relative to mental health providers' experiences with and feelings of the role of empathy while working with clients who experience IPV victims' emotions, anger, distress, and anxiety. This research study seemed sustainable to fill the paucity of literature, resources, and public legislative gap for the IPV phenomenon (Augsburger et al., 2019; Dim, 2020; Vandewalle et al., 2016).

Conclusion

In general, notwithstanding the study's research problem addressed in Chapter 1, Chapter 5 accomplished two fundamental objectives consisting of (a) interpreting the results through the lens of existing findings in the human services field and (b) recommending directives for future study. Thus, the fundamental research problem and the implications that the study answered were a lack of information and resources (e.g., public policies) about mental health providers' experiences with empathy when working with male IPV victims' experiences (Di Napoli et al., 2019; Lindsay, 2022; Wilson et al., 2021). The research study was significant because it showed the gap in understanding mental health service providers' role in empathy experiences of male IPV victims' mental health problems recommended for future scientific research studies (Hamdani et al., 2021).

Besides, research findings about male victimization remained uncertain. A dearth of help-seeking reporting and disclosure behaviors suggested a further need for qualitative research associated with the providers' experiences while working with the male IPV victim population (Dim, 2020; Barrett et al., 2020; Hardesty & Ogolsky, 2020; Park, 2021). This current study's findings showed the awareness of female perpetration of physical, sexual, and psychological abuse (Arnocky & Vaillancourt, 2014; Dim, 2020; Park, 2021). The sociocultural stigma seems to reinforce and belittle male IPV victims (Arnocky & Vaillancourt, 2014; Dim, 2020; Park, 2021).

Generally, I suggest that future researchers explore barriers inhibiting male IPV victims from seeking education and training to mitigate the female aggressive perpetration victimization phenomenon (Bates, 2020, 2019; Bui & Pasalich, 2021; Hardesty & Ogolsky, 2020; Ulloa & Hammett, 2016; Velotti, 2020; Zosky, 2016). I hope the findings of this study provide a pivotal catalyst that impels policy legislatures and social system advocacy stakeholders to inform various researchers across the globe of the deleterious effects of IPV experiences and their adverse impact on male victims (Balogun et al., 2015; Dim, 2021; Park, 2021; Taylor et al., 2022).

Aafjes-van Doorn, K., & Barber, J. P. (2023). Professional training and supervision after graduation: Is it worthwhile? In L. G. Castonguay, C. E. Hill, Louis G. Castonguay & Clara E. Hill (Eds.), *Becoming better psychotherapists* (p. 55–82). *American Psychological Association*. https://doi.org/10.1037/0000364-004

Abadie, R., Fisher, C., & Dombrowski, K. (2021). "He is under oath": Privacy and confidentiality views among people who inject drugs enrolled in a study of social networks and human immunodeficiency virus/Hepatitis C virus risk. *Journal of Empirical Research on Human Research Ethics, 16*(3), 304–311. https://doi.org/10.1177/15562646211004411

Abudulai, F., Pichon, M., Buller, A. M., Scott, J., & Sharma, V. (2022). Displacement, polygyny, romantic jealousy, and intimate partner violence: A qualitative study among Somali refugees in Ethiopia. *International Journal of Environmental Research and Public Health, 19*(9), 5757. https://doi.org/10.3390/ijerph19095757

Abassary, C., & Goodrich, K. M. (2014). Attending crisis-based supervision for counselors: The care model of crisis-based management. *The Clinical Supervisor, 33*(1), 63–81. https://doi.org/10.080/07325223.2014.918006

Abay, S., Addissie, A., Davey, G., Farsides, B., & Addissie, T. (2016). Rapid Ethical Assessment on

References

Informed Consent Content and Procedure in Hintalo-Wajirat, Northern Ethiopia: A Qualitative Study. *PLoS One, 11*(6) http://dx.doi.org.library.capella.edu/10.1371/journal.pone.0157056

Abi Khalil, P., Honein-Abou Haidar, G., El Achi, D., Al-Hakim, L., Tamim, H., & Akl, E. A. (2022). Views of medical residents on a research training program: A qualitative study. *PloS One, 17*(1), e0261583. https://doi.org/10.1371/journal.pone.0261583

Abrams, M. P., Salzman, J., Espina Rey, A., & Daly, K. (2022). Impact of providing peer support on medical students' empathy, self-efficacy, and mental health stigma. *International Journal of Environmental Research and Public Health, 19*(9), 5135. https://doi.org/10.3390/ijerph19095135

Abramo, F. C., Gambino, R., & Pulvirenti, G. (2017). Cognitive literary anthropology and neuro hermeneutics: A theoretical proposal. *Enthymema (Milano), 18*(18), 44-62. https://doi.org/10.13130/2037-2426/8353

Account of an Elizabeth Family: The Willoughbys of Wollaton by Cassandra Willoughby (1670–1735): The collections of Cassandra Willoughby, 1702. (2018). *Camden Fifth Series, 55,* 67–258. https://doi.org/10.1017/S0960116318000180

Adebayo, A., & Ackers, B. (2021). Sampling theoretically for comparison. *Electronic Journal of Business Research Methods, 19*(1), 42–56. https://doi.org/10.34190/ejbrm.19.1.2434

Adejimi, A. A., Akinyemi, O. O., Sekoni, O. O., & Fawole, O. I. (2022). Reaching out to men in ending intimate partner violence: A qualitative study among male civil servants in Ibadan, Nigeria. *International Journal of Qualitative Studies on Health and Well-being, 17*(1), 2128263–2128263. https://doi.org/10.1080/17482631.2022.2128263

Adjei, S. B. (2017). Sociocultural groundings of battered women's entrapment in an abusive marital relationship in Ghana. *Journal of*

Aggression, Maltreatment & Trauma, 26(8), 879–901. https://doi.org/10.1080/10926771.2017.1284171

Adomako, E. B., & Darkwa Baffour, F. (2021). Suffering in the hands of a loved one: The endemic to intimate partner violence and consequences on migrant female head-load carriers in Ghana. *Journal of Interpersonal Violence, 36*(21–22), NP11940–NP11967. https://doi.org/10.1177/0886260519888547

Afifi, T. O., Mota, N., Sareen, J., & MacMillan, H. L. (2017). The relationships between harsh physical punishment and child maltreatment in childhood and intimate partner violence in adulthood. *B.M.C. Public Health, 17*(1), 493. https://doi.org/10.1186/s12889-017-4359-8

Ahmed, W. S., & Nebeker, C. (2021). Assessment of research ethics education offerings of pharmacy master programs in an Arab nation compared to top programs worldwide: A qualitative content analysis. *PloS One, 16*(2), e0238755. https://doi.org/10.1371/journal.pone.0238755

Ahrens, C. E., Dworkin, E. R., & Hart, A. C. (2021). Social reactions of intimate partner violence survivors: A qualitative validation of crucial constructs from the social reaction's questionnaire. *Psychology of Women Quarterly, 45*(1), 37–49. https://doi.org/10.1177/0361684320975663

Ainsworth, M. D. S., & Bowlby, J. (1991). An ethological approach to personality development. *American Psychologist, 46*, 331–34.

Aiyenigba, A. O., Weeks, A. D., & Rahman, A. (2019). Managing psychological trauma of infertility. *African Journal of Reproductive Health, 23*(2), 76–91. https://doi.org/10.29063/ajrh2019/v23i2.8

Aksnes, D. W., Langfeldt, L., & Wouters, P. (2019). Citations, citation indicators, and research quality: An overview of basic concepts and theories. *Sage Open, 9*(1), 215824401982957. https://doi.org/10.1177/2158244019829575

References

Akram, O. K., Franco, D. J., & Lee, A. (2023). Undergraduate and graduate students' challenges: A qualitative study with ONDAS framework across multiple disciplines and innovative research methodologies. *Qualitative Report, 28*(10), COV4–2915. https://doi.org/10.46743/2160-3715/2023.6679

Alhalal, E., Ta'an, W., & Alhalal, H. (2021, 2019). Intimate partner violence in Saudi Arabia: A systematic review. *SAGE Publications.* https://doi.org/10.1177/1524838019867156

Alahari, U. (2017). Supporting socio-emotional competence and psychological well-being of school psychologists through mindfulness practice. *Contemporary School Psychology, 21*(4), 369–379. https://doi.org/10.1007/s40688-017-0154-x

Alahmad, G. (2018). Informed consent in pediatric oncology: A systematic review of qualitative literature. *Cancer Control, 25*(1), 1073274818773720. https://do i.org/10.1177/1073274818773720

Albanesi, C., Tomasetto, C., & Guardabassi, V. (2021). Evaluating interventions with victims of intimate partner violence: A community psychology approach. *B.M.C. Women's Health, 21*, 1–15. http://doi.org.library.capella.edu/10.1186/s12905-021-01268-7

Al-Baghdadi, M., Green, R., Durham, J., Steele, J., & Araujo-Soares, V. (2019). Decision-making in managing T.M.J. disc displacement without reduction: A qualitative study. *Journal of Dentistry, 91*, 103223. https://doi.org/10.1016/j.jdent.2019.103223

Alebachew Bayih, W., Minuye Birhan, B., Yeshambel Alemu, A., & Oei, J. L. (2020). The burden of traditional neonatal uvulectomy among admissions to neonatal intensive care units, north-central Ethiopia, 2019: A triangulated cross-sectional study. *PloS One, 15*(7), e0234866. https://doi.org/10.1371/journal.pone.0234866

Alexa-Stratulat, T., Neagu, M., Neagu, A., Alexa, I. D., & Ioan, B. G. (2018). Consent for taking part in clinical trials—is it informed? *Developing World Bioethics, 18*(3), 299–306. https://doi.org/10.1111/dewb.12199

Al-Eisawi, D. (2022). A design framework for a novice using grounded theory method and coding in qualitative research: Organizational absorptive ability and knowledge management. *International Journal of Qualitative Methods, 21*, 160940692211135. https://doi.org/10.1177/16094069221113551

Alkaraki, A. K., Khabour, O. F., Alzoubi, K. H., Al-Ebbini, L. M. K., & Altaany, Z. (2020). Informed consent form challenges for genetic research in Jordan. *Journal of Multidisciplinary Healthcare, 13*, 235–239. https://doi.org/10.2147/JMDH.S243669

Al-Modallal, H. (2016). Childhood maltreatment in college women: effect on severe physical partner violence. *Journal of Family Violence, 31*(5), 607–615. https://doi.org/10.1007/s10896-016-9797-z

Alonso, V., Santos, J. V., Pinto, M., Ferreira, J., Lema, I., Lopes, F., & Freitas, A. (2020). Health records as the basis of clinical coding: Is the quality adequate? A qualitative study of medical coders' feelings. *Health Information Management, 49*(1), 28–37. https://doi.org/10.1177/1833358319826351

Alshammari, K. F., McGarry, J., & Higginbottom, G. M. A. (2018). Nurse education and understanding related to domestic violence and abuse against women: An integrative literature review. *Nursing Open, 5*(3), 237–253. https://doi.org/10.1002/nop2.133

Alsawalqa, R. O., & Alrawashdeh, M. N. (2022). The role of patriarchal structure and gender stereotypes in cyber dating abuse: A qualitative examination of male perpetrators experiences. *The British Journal of Sociology, 73*(3), 587–606. https://doi.org/10.1111/1468-4446.12946

Alsawalqa, R. O. (2023). A qualitative study to investigate male victims' experiences of female-perpetrated domestic abuse in Jordan. *Current Psychology (New Brunswick, N.J.), 42*(7), 5505–5520. https://doi.org/10.1007/s12144-021-01905-2

References

Alsufyani, M. H., Alghoribi, M. H., Bin Salman, T. O., Alrabie, A. F., Alotaibi, I. S., Kharbosh, A. M., Alsheikh, M. Y., Alshahrani, A. M., & Fathelrahman, A. I. (2023). Generic substitutions and therapeutic interchanges in hospital pharmacies: A qualitative study from western *Saudi Arabia. Healthcare (Basel), 11*(13), 1893. https://doi.org/10.3390/healthcare11131893

Al'Uqdah, S. N., Maxwell, C., & Hill, N. (2016). Intimate partner violence in the African American community: Risk, theory, and interventions. *Journal of Family Violence, 31*(7), 877–884. https://doi.org/10.1007/s10896-016-9819-x

Alven, L., Wilke, D. J., & Spinelli, C. (2019). "Getting everyone on the same page": Child welfare workers' collaboration challenges on intimate partner violence cases. *Journal of Family Violence, 34*(1), 21–31. https://doi.org/10.1007/s10896-018-0002-4

America's Health Rankings analysis of U.S. HHS, Centers for Medicare & Medicaid Services, National Plan and Provider Enumeration System, United Health Foundation, *AmericasHealthRankings.org*, accessed 2022.

Anastasiou, E., Liebling, H., Webster, M., & MacCallum, F. (2021). The experiences and views of service providers on the mental health and well-being services for Syrian refugees in Coventry and Warwickshire. *European Journal of Psychology Open, 80*(4), 165–177. https://doi.org/10.1024/2673-8627/a000017

Anderson, E. E. (2014). Ethical considerations in collecting health survey data. In T. P. Johnson (Ed.), *Health survey methods* (487–511). John Wiley & Sons, Inc. https://doi.org/10.1002/9781118594629.ch19

Angelidis, A., Solis, E., Lautenbach, F., van der Does, W., & Putman, P. (2019). I am going to fail. Acute cognitive performance anxiety increases threat interference and impairs W.M.'s performance. *PloS One, 14*(2), e0210824. https://doi.org/10.1371/journal.pone.0210824

Annion, M., Ojasoo, M., Ernits, Ü., & Puusepp, K. (2023). Emotional coping of nursing students during mental health nursing simulation training. *Proceedings of the Estonian Academy of Sciences, 72*(3), 212–219. https://doi.org/10.3176/proc.2023.3.03

Antabe, R., Robinson, K., Husbands, W., Miller, D., Harriot, A., Johnson, K., Wong, J. P., Poon, M. K., Kirya, J. W., & James, C. (2022). "You have to make it cool": How heterosexual black men in Toronto, Canada, conceptualize policy and programs to address HIV and promote health. *PloS One, 17*(12), e0278600. https://doi.org/10.1371/journal.pone.0278600

Appel, L., Lewis, S., Kisonas, E., & Recknagel, J. (2022). ARCHIVE: Experiences conducting an online workshop teaching intergenerational participants to create virtual reality films about their lives during the COVID-19 pandemic. *Educational Gerontology, 48*(7), 305–330. https://doi.org/10.1080/03601277.2022.2039848

APNA 30th annual conference, October 19–22, 2016, Hartford, Connecticut. (2017). *Journal of the American Psychiatric Nurses Association, 23*(4), 289–318. https://doi.org/10.1177/1078390317715029

Apolinario-Hagen, J., Vehreschild, V., & Alkoudmani, R. M. (2017). Current views and perspectives on E-mental health: An exploratory survey study for understanding public attitudes toward internet-based psychotherapy in Germany. *JMIR Mental Health, 4*(1), e8. https://doi.org/10.2196/mental.6375

Aragbuwa, A. (2021). A standard reading of selected online readers' comments on domestic violence against men in Nigeria. *Men and Masculinities, 24*(3), 451–467. https://doi.org/10.1177/1097184X19898875

Arnocky, S., & Vaillancourt, T. (2014). Sex differences in response to victimization by an intimate partner: More stigmatization and less help-seeking among males. *Journal of Aggression, Maltreatment & Trauma, 23*(7), 705–724. https://doi.org/10.1080/10926771.2014.933465

References

Arrey, S. K., Kirshbaum, M. N., & Finn, V. (2019). In search of care strategies for distressed people with communication difficulties and a learning disability in palliative care settings: The lived experiences of registered learning disability nurses and palliative care professionals. *Journal of Research in Nursing, 24*(6), 386–400. https://doi.org/10.1177/1744987118764532

Arroyo, K., Lundahl, B., Butters, R., Vanderloo, M., & Wood, D. S. (2017). Short-term interventions for survivors of intimate partner violence: A systematic review and meta-analysis. *Trauma, Violence & Abuse, 18*(2), 155–171. https://doi.org/10.1177/1524838015602736

Artioli, G., Deiana, L., De Vincenzo, F., Raucci, M., Amaducci, G., Bassi, M. C., Di Leo, S., Hayter, M., & Ghirotto, L. (2021). Health professionals and students' experiences of reflective writing in learning: A qualitative meta-synthesis. *BMC Medical Education, 21*(1), 1–394. https://doi.org/10.1186/s12909-021-02831-4

Asad, S., & Chreim, S. (2016). Peer support providers' role experiences on interprofessional mental health care teams: A qualitative study. *Community Mental Health Journal, 52*(7), 767–774. https://doi.org/10.1007/s10597-015-9970-5

Asaoka, H., Koido, Y., Kawashima, Y., Ikeda, M., Miyamoto, Y., & Nishi, D. (2021). Longitudinal change of psychological distress among healthcare professionals with and without psychological first aid training experience during the COVID-19 pandemic. *International Journal of Environmental Research and Public Health, 18*(23), 12474. https://doi.org/10.3390/ijerph182312474

Asiimwe, R., Lesch, E., Karume, M., & Blow, A. J. (2021). Expanding our international reach: Trends in developing systemic family therapy training and implementation in Africa. *Journal of Marital and Family Therapy, 47*(4), 815–830. https://doi.org/10.1111/jmft.12514

Atance-Pereira, D., Zamarro-Arranz, M. L., Velarde-García, J. F., Huertas-Hoyas, E., Cachón-Pérez, J. M., Parás-Bravo, P., & Palacios-Ceña, D. (2020). Perspectives of victims of gender violence. *Journal of Psychosocial Nursing and Mental Health Services, 58*(6), 30–39. https://doi.org/10.3928/02793695-20200319-01

Atif, M., Sehar, A., Malik, I., Mushtaq, I., Ahmad, N., & Babar, Z. (2021). What impact do medicine shortages have on patients? A qualitative study exploring patients' experience and views of healthcare professionals. *BMC Health Services Research, 21*(1), 1–827. https://doi.org/10.1186/s12913-021-06812-7

Atzil-Slonim, D., Bar-Kalifa, E., Fisher, H., Lazarus, G., Hasson-Ohayon, I., Lutz, W., Rubel, J., & Rafaeli, E. (2019). Therapists' empathic accuracy toward their clients' emotions. *Journal of Consulting and Clinical Psychology, 87*(1), 33–45. https://doi.org/10.1037/ccp0000354

Auchter, B., & Backes, B. L. (2013). NIJ's program of domestic violence research: Collaborative efforts to build knowledge guided by safety for victims and accountability of perpetrators. *Violence Against Women, 19*(6), 713–736. https://doi.org/10.1177/1077801213494703

Audette, L. M., Hammond, M. S., & Rochester, N. K. (2020, 2019). Methodological issues with coding participants in anonymous psychological longitudinal studies. *Educational and Psychological Measurement, 80*(1), 163–185. https://doi.org/10.1177/0013164419843576

Augsburger, M., Basler, K., & Maercker, A. (2019). Is there a female cycle of violence after exposure to childhood maltreatment? A meta-analysis. *Psychological Medicine, 49*(11), 1776–1786. https://doi.org/10.1017/S0033291719000680

Augsburger, M., & Maercker, A. (2020). Associations between trauma exposure, posttraumatic stress disorder, and aggression perpetrated by women. A meta-analysis. *Clinical Psychology (New York, N.Y.), 27*(1). https://doi.org/10.1037/h0101759

Awenat, Y. F., Peters, S., Gooding, P. A., Pratt, D., Huggett, C., Harris, K., Armitage, C. J., & Haddock, G. (2019). Qualitative analysis of ward staff experiences during research of a novel suicide-prevention psychological therapy for psychiatric inpatients: Understanding the barriers and facilitators. *PloS One, 14*(9), e0222482. https://doi.org/10.1371/journal.pone.0222482

Babchuk, L. R. (2018). Food's ceramic pot source of cadmium intoxication the human 8body. *Fìzika ì Hìmìâ Tverdogo Tìla 18*(3), 354–357. https://doi.org/10.15330/pcss.18.3.354-357

Bacchus, L. J., Alkaiyat, A., Shaheen, A., Alkhayyat, A. S., Owda, H., Halaseh, R., Jeries, I., Feder, G., Sandouka, R., & Colombini, M. (2021). Adaptive work in the primary health care response to domestic violence in occupied Palestinian territory: A qualitative evaluation using extended normalization process theory. *BMC Family Practice, 22*(1), 3. https://doi.org/10.1186/s12875-020-01338-z

Badu, E., O'Brien, A. P., & Mitchell, R. (2019). An integrative review on methodological considerations in mental health research—design, sampling, data collection procedure, and quality assurance. *Archives of Public Health, 77*(1), 1–37. https://doi.org/10.1186/s13690-019-0363-z

Bagwell-Gray, M. E., Messing, J. T., & Baldwin-White, A. (2015). Intimate partner sexual violence: A review of terms, definitions, and prevalence. *Trauma, Violence & Abuse, 16*(3), 316–335. https://doi.org/10.1177/1524838014557290

Baird, S. L., Alaggia, R., & Jenney, A. (2021). "Like opening up old wounds": Conceptualizing intersectional trauma among survivors of intimate partner violence. *Journal of Interpersonal Violence, 36*(17–18), 8118–8141. https://doi.org/10.1177/0886260519848788

Baird, S. L., Tarshis, S., & Messenger, C. (2022). The use of neuroscience in intimate partner violence (IPV) interventions: A scoping review. *Clinical Social Work Journal, 50*(2), 194–206. https://doi.org/10.1007/s10615-022-00840-4

Bailey, B. (2021). Women's psychological aggression toward an intimate male partner: Between the impulsive and the instrumental. *Journal of Interpersonal Violence, 36*(11–12), NP6526–NP6546. https://doi.org/10.1177/0886260518815138

Bain, L. E. (2017). Ethics approval: Responsibilities of journal editors, authors, and research ethics committees. *The Pan African Medical Journal, 28*, 200. https://doi.org/10.11604/pamj.2017.28.200.14170

Balogun, M. O., & John-Akinola, Y. O. (2015). A qualitative study of intimate partner violence among women in Nigeria. *Journal of Interpersonal Violence, 30*(14), 2410–2427. https://doi.org/10.1177/0886260514553112

Bagshaw, A. T. M., Horwood, L. J., Fergusson, D. M., Gemmell, N. J., & Kennedy, M. A. (2017). Microsatellite polymorphisms are associated with human behavioral and psychological phenotypes, including a gene-environment interaction. *B.M.C. Medical Genetics, 18*(1), 12. https://doi.org/10.1186/s12881-017-0374-y

Bandara, W., Furtmueller, E., Gorbacheva, E., Miskon, S., & Beekhuyzen, J. (2015). Achieving rigor in literature reviews: Insights from qualitative data analysis and tool-support. *Communications of the Association for Information Systems, 37*, 8. https://doi.org/10.17705/1CAIS.03708

Banfield, L. E. (2019). Fostering spiritual resilience and vitality in formerly incarcerated persons of African American descent. *The Journal of Pastoral Care & Counseling, 73*(4), 222–231. https://doi.org/10.1177/1542305019886532

Band-Winterstein, T., & Freund, A. (2018). "Walking between the raindrops": Intimate partner violence in the ultra-orthodox society in Israel from social workers' perspective. *Journal of Interpersonal Violence, 33*(19), 3001–3024. https://doi.org/10.1177/0886260516633218

Banyard, V. L., Edwards, K. M., Moschella, E. A., & Seavey, K. M. (2019). "Everybody is close-knit": Disconnections between helping victims of intimate partner violence and, more generally, helping in rural communities. *Violence Against Women, 25*(3), 337–358. https://doi.org/10.1177/1077801218768714

Bardus, M., El Rassi, R., Chahrour, M., Akl, E. W., Raslan, A. S., Meho, L. I., & Akl, E. A. (2020). The use of social media to increase the impact of health research: Systematic review. *Journal of Medical Internet Research, 22*(7), e15607. https://doi.org/10.2196/15607

Barker, S. L., Maguire, N., Bishop, F. L., & Stopa, L. L. (2019). Expert viewpoints of peer support for people experiencing homelessness: A Q sort study. *Psychological Services, 16*(3), 402–414. https://doi.org/10.1037/ser0000258

Baksh, B. (2018). To bracket or not to bracket: Reflections of a novice qualitative researcher. *Reflections: Narratives of professional helping, 24*(3), 45–55. Retrieved from http://library.capella.edu/login?qurl=https%3A%2F%2Fwww.proquest.com%2Fdocview%2F2133763174%3Faccountid%3D27965

Barkhuizen, M. (2015). Police reaction to the male victim of domestic violence in South Africa: Case study analysis. *Police Practice & Research: An International Journal, 16*(4), 291–302. doi:10.1080/15614263.2015.1038025

Bakkalbasioglu, E. (2020). How to access elites when textbook methods fail? Challenges of purposive sampling and advantages of using interviewees as "Fixers." *The Qualitative Report, 25*(3), COV9. https://doi.org/10.46743/2160-3715/2020.3976

Barrett, B. J., Peirone, A., & Cheung, C. H. (2020). Help-seeking experiences of survivors of intimate partner violence in Canada: The role of gender, violence severity, and social belonging. *Journal of Family Violence, 35*(1), 15–28. https://doi.org/10.1007/s10896-019-00086-8

Barry, J. A., Kingerlee, R., Seager, M., & Sullivan, L. (2019). In Barry J. A., Kingerlee R., Seager M., and Sullivan L. (Eds.), *The Palgrave Handbook of Male Psychology and Mental Health (1st ed.).* Springer International. https://doi.org/10.1007/978-3-030-04384-1

Bartholomew, T. T., Gundel, B. E., Kang, E., Joy, E. E., Maldonado-Aguiñiga, S., Robbins, K. A., & Li, H. (2021). Integrating cultural beliefs about illness in counseling with refugees: A phenomenological study. *Journal of Cross-Cultural Psychology, 52*(8–9), 705–725. https://doi.org/10.1177/00220221211038374

Barton, E., Thominet, L., Boeder, R., & Primeau, S. (2018). Do community members have a compelling voice in the ethical deliberation of a behavioral institutional review board? *Journal of Business and Technical Communication, 32*(2), 154–197. https://doi.org/10.1177/1050651917746460

Baškarada, S., & Koronios, A. (2018). A philosophical discussion of qualitative, quantitative, and mixed methods research in social science. *Qualitative Research Journal, 18*(1), 2–21. https://doi.org/10.1108/QRJ-D-17-00042

Basile, K. C., Smith, S. G., Liu, Y., Lowe, A., Gilmore, A. K., Khatiwada, S., & Kresnow, M. (2021). Victim and perpetrator characteristics in alcohol/drug-involved sexual violence victimization in the U.S. *Drug and Alcohol Dependence, 226*, 108839. https://doi.org/10.1016/j.drugalcdep.2021.108839

Bates, E. A., & Carthy, N. L. (2020). "She convinced me I had Alzheimer's": Experiences of intimate partner violence in older men. *Psychology of Men & Masculinity, 21*(4), 675–685. https://doi.org/10.1037/men0000280

Bates, E. A., & Taylor, J. C. (2019). *Intimate partner violence: New perspectives in research and practice (1st ed.)*. Milton: Routledge. https://doi.org/10.4324/9781315169842

Bates, E. A., Graham-Kevan, N., & Archer, J. (2014). Testing predictions from the male control theory of men's partner violence. *Aggressive Behavior, 40*(1), 42–55. https://doi.org/10.1002/ab.21499

Bates, E. A. (2020, 2019). "No One Would Ever Believe Me": An exploration of the impact of intimate partner violence victimization on men. *Psychology of Men & Masculinity, 21*(4), 497–507. https://doi.org/10.1037/men0000206

Bean, A. R. (2021). Surviving COVID-19 (increased domestic violence, marginalized communities, and innovative solutions). *Journal of Family Strengths, 21*(2).

Beechay, S. (2019). If I go, there will be trouble. If I stay, there will be double: Revenge porn, domestic violence, and family offenses. *Family Court Review, 57*(4), 539–553. https://doi.org/10.1111/fcre.12447

Bechtoldt, M. N., Beersma, B., & van Kleef, G. A. (2019). When (not) to empathize: The differential effects of combined emotion recognition and empathic concern on client satisfaction across professions. *Motivation and Emotion, 43*(1), 112–129. https://doi.org/10.1007/s11031-018-9725-z

Bedi, R. P., & Pradhan, K. (2023). Differences between Canadian Psychological Association nonmember and member counseling psychologists. *The Counseling Psychologist, 51*(2), 180–209. https://doi.org/10.1177/00110000221136218

Bellamy, K., Ostini, R., Martini, N., & Kairuz, T. (2016). Looking to understand: Using generic qualitative research to explore access to medicines and pharmacy services among resettled refugees. *International Journal of Clinical Pharmacy, 38*(3), 671–675. https://doi.org/10.1007/s11096-016-0261-1

Bellamy, K., Ostini, R., Martini, N., & Kairuz, T. (2017). Perspectives of resettled African refugees on accessing medicines and pharmacy services in Queensland, Australia. The *International Journal of Pharmacy Practice, 25*(5), 358–364. https://doi.org/10.1111/ijpp.12324

Bellesheim, K. R. (2016). Ethical challenges and legal issues for mental health professionals working with family caregivers of individuals with serious mental illness. *Ethics & Behavior, 26*(7), 607–620. https://doi.org/10.1080/10508422.2015.1130097

Belmont Report (1979). The Belmont Report: Ethical principles and guidelines for the protection of human subjects of research. Retrieved December 12, 2005, from http://ohsr.od.nih.gov/guidelines/belmont.html.

Benebo, F. O., Schumann, B., & Vaezghasemi, M. (2018). Intimate partner violence against women in Nigeria: A multilevel study investigating the effect of women's status and community norms. *BMC Women's Health, 18*(1), 136. https://doi.org/10.1186/s12905-018-0628-7

Bender, A. K. (2017). Ethics, methods, and measures in intimate partner violence research: The field's current state. *Violence Against Women, 23*(11), 1382–1413. https://doi.org/10.1177/1077801216658977

Bennett, V. E., Godfrey, D. A., Snead, A. L., Kehoe, C. M., Bastardas-Albero, A., & Babcock, J. C. (2020). Couples and family interventions for intimate partner aggression: A comprehensive review. *Partner Abuse, 11*(3), 292–317. https://doi.org/10.1891/PA-2020-0011

Bent-Goodley, T. B. (2004). Feelings of domestic violence: A dialogue with African American women. *Health & Social Work, 29*(4), 307–316. https://doi.org/10.1093/hsw/29.4.307

Bent-Goodley, T. B. (2007). Health Disparities and violence against women: Why and how cultural and societal influences matter. *Trauma, Violence & Abuse, 8*(2), 90–104. https://doi.org/10.1177/1524838007301160

Berger, J. L., Douglas, E. M., & Hines, D. A. (2016). Legal and administrative partner aggression affects the mental health of male victims and their children. *Aggressive Behavior, 42*(4), 346–361. https://doi.org/10.1002/ab.21630

Bergman, J. (2020, 2019). Intersectionality: A means for addressing the needs of children with mental health issues engaged with the family law and criminal justice systems. *Windsor Yearbook of Access to Justice, 36,* 115–137. https://doi.org/10.22329/wyaj.v36i0.6415

Berland, L., & Crucet, K. (2016). Epistemological trade-offs: Accounting for context when evaluating epistemological student engagement sophistication in scientific practices. *Science Education, 100*(1), 5–29. https://doi.org/10.1002/sce.21196

Bernardi, D. A., & Steyn, F. (2019). A model for female-perpetrated domestic violence. *Victims & Offenders, 14*(4), 441–461. https://doi.org/10.1080/15564886.2019.1602573

Berenguera, A., Mata-Cases, M., Mauricio, D., Rubinat, E., Franch-Nadal, J., Mollo-Inesta, A., & Bolibar, B. (2020). Understanding the physical, social, and emotional experiences of people with uncontrolled type 2 diabetes: A qualitative study (original research). *Patient Preference and Adherence, 2323.*

Berrol, C. (2016). Reflections on Dance/Movement therapy and interpersonal neurobiology: The first 50 years. *American Journal of Dance Therapy, 38*(2), 303–310. https://doi.org/10.1007/s10465-016-9227-z

Berry, O. O., Fitelson, E., & Monk, C. (2020). Recognizing and addressing domestic violence: Issues for psychiatrists. *The Psychiatric Times, 37*(2), 35.

Bessaha, M., Persaud, U., Asfe, R., & Muñoz-Laboy, M. (2023). Community-based providers' perspectives on addressing loneliness and mental health services for migrant youth and emerging adults. *Journal of Social Service Research, 49*(1), 93–104. https://doi.org/10.1080/01488376.2022.2164640

Best, P., Gil-Rodriguez, E., Manktelow, R., & Taylor, B. J. (2016). Seeking help from everyone and no one: Conceptualizing the online help-seeking process among adolescent males. *Qualitative Health Research, 26*(8), 1067–1077. https://doi.org/10.1177/1049732316648128

Bhayana, C., Gupta, V., & Sharda, K. (2021). The role of shared leadership in managing conflicts in multigenerational teams: A research framework. *Business Perspectives and Research, 9*(2), 252–268. https://doi.org/10.1177/2278533720964928

Bhatia, P., & Soletti, A. B. (2019). Hushed voices: Views and experiences of older women on partner abuse in later life. *Ageing International, 44*(1), 41–56. https://doi.org/10.1007/s12126-018-9331-0

Bhattacharyya, S. S., & Verma, S. (2020). Firm–civil society organizational collaborations in the context of corporate social responsibility (CSR) initiatives; development of collaboration typology. *World Journal of Entrepreneurship, Management and Sustainable Development, 16*(4), 359–375. https://doi.org/10.1108/WJEMSD-12-2019-0101

Bindels, E., Verberg, C., Scherpbier, A., Heeneman, S., & Lombarts, K. (2018). Reflection revisited: A qualitative study is how physicians conceptualize and experience meditation professionally. *B.M.C. Medical Education, 18*(1), 105. https://doi.org/10.1186/s12909-018-1218-y

Birch, S. A. J., Severson, R. L., & Baimel, A. (2020). Children's understanding of when a person's confidence and hesitancy are cues to their credibility. *PloS One, 15*(1), e0227026. https://doi.org/10.1371/journal.pone.0227026

Bird, S. M., Sohrabi, H. R., Sutton, T. A., Weinborn, M., Rainey-Smith, S. R., Brown, B., Patterson, L., Taddei, K., Gupta, V., Carruthers, M., Lenzo, N., Knuckey, N., Bucks, R. S., Verdile, G., & Martins, R. N. (2016). Cerebral amyloid-β accumulation and deposition following traumatic brain injury—A narrative review and meta-analysis of animal studies. *Neuroscience and Biobehavioral Reviews, 64*, 215–228. https://doi.org/10.1016/j.neubiorev.2016.01.004

Birkley, E. L., Eckhardt, C. I., & Dykstra, R. E. (2016). Posttraumatic stress disorder symptoms, intimate partner violence, and relationship functioning: A meta-analytic review. *Journal of Traumatic Stress, 29*(5), 397–405. https://doi.org/10.1002/jts.22129

References

Bjørkvold, T., & Blikstad-Balas, M. (2018). Students as researchers: What and why seventh-grade students choose to write when investigating their research question. *Science Education (Salem, Mass.), 102*(2), 304–341. https://doi.org/10.1002/sce.21324

Blake, K. R., Hopkins, R. E., Sprunger, J. G., Eckhardt, C. I., & Denson, T. F. (2018). Relationship quality and cognitive reappraisal moderate the effects of negative urgency on behavioral inclinations toward aggression and intimate partner violence. *Psychology of Violence, 8*(2), 218–228. https://doi.org/10.1037/vio0000121

Blackmore, C., Johnson-Warrington, V. L., Williams, J. E., Apps, L. D., Young, H. M., Bourne, C. L., & Singh, S. J. (2017). Develop a training program to support healthcare professionals in delivering the SPACE for COPD self-management program. *International Journal of Chronic Obstructive Pulmonary Disease, 12,* 1669–1681. https://doi.org/10.2147/COPD.S127504

Blackburn, P., & Bulsara, C. (2019). "You either need help . . . you feel you don't need help . . . or you don't feel worthy of asking for it:" receptivity to bereavement support. *Palliative & Supportive Care, 17*(2), 172–185. https://doi.org/10.1017/S1478951517001122

Blue, S. (2019). Institutional rhythms: Combining practice theory and rhythm analysis to conceptualize processes of institutionalization. *Time & Society, 28*(3), 922–950. https://doi.org/10.1177/0961463X17702165

Bollmer, G., & Guinness, K. (2020). Empathy and nausea: Virtual reality and Jordan Wolfson's actual violence. *Journal of Visual Culture, 19*(1), 28–46. https://doi.org/10.1177/1470412920906261

Bornheimer, L. A., Li Verdugo, J., Holzworth, J., Smith, F. N., & Himle, J. A. (2022). Mental health provider perspectives of the COVID-19 pandemic impact on service delivery: A focus on challenges in remote engagement, suicide risk assessment, and treatment of psychosis. *BMC Health Services Research, 22*(1), 718. https://doi.org/10.1186/s12913-022-08106-y

Bomsta, H., & Sullivan, C. M. (2018). IPV survivors' feelings of how a flexible funding housing intervention affected their children. *Journal of Family Violence, 33*(6), 371–380. https://doi.org/10.1007/s10896-018-9972-5

Bonagura, A. G., & Widom, C. S. (2023). Child maltreatment and psychiatric disorders increase the risk of stalking victimization. *Journal of Interpersonal Violence, 38*(1–2), 60–83. https://doi.org/10.1177/08862605221078889

Booth, A., Noyes, J., Flemming, K., Gerhardus, A., Wahlster, P., van der Wilt, Gert Jan, Mozygemba, K., Refollow, P., Sacchini, D., Tummers, M., & Rehfuess, E. (2018). The structured method review found seven (RETREAT) criteria for selecting qualitative evidence synthesis approaches. *Journal of Clinical Epidemiology, 99*, 41–52. https://doi.org/10.1016/j.jclinepi.2018.03.003

Bornheimer, L. A., Li Verdugo, J., Holzworth, J., Smith, F. N., & Himle, J. A. (2022). Mental health provider perspectives of the COVID-19 pandemic impact on service delivery: A focus on challenges in remote engagement, suicide risk assessment, and treatment of psychosis. *BMC Health Services Research, 22*(1), 718. https://doi.org/10.1186/s12913-022-08106-y

Bouchard, J., & Wong, J. S. (2021). Pathways to engagement: An exploratory qualitative analysis of factors easing Men's engagement in IPV intervention programs. *Violence Against Women, 27*(14), 2642–2663. https://doi.org/10.1177/1077801220981144

Bouwman, R., de Graaff, B., de Beurs, D., van de Bovenkamp, H., Leistikow, I., & Friele, R. (2018). Involving patients and families in analyzing suicides, suicide attempts, and other sentinel events in mental healthcare: A qualitative study in the Netherlands. International *Journal of Environmental Research and Public Health, 15*(6), 1104. https://doi.org/10.3390/ijerph15061104

Bowen Murray, M. D. (1978). *Family therapy in clinical practice:* Jason Aronson, 565 pages. New York City.

Bowen, G. A. (2008). Naturalistic inquiry and the saturation concept: A research note. *Qualitative Research: QR, 8*(1), 137–152. https://doi.org/10.1177/1468794107085301

Bowers, D. B., & Seashore, S. B. (1966). Predicting organizational effectiveness with a four-factor theory of leadership. *Administrative Science Quarterly, 11*(2), 247–256.

Bowland, S., Edmond, T., & Fallot, R. D. (2012). Evaluation of a spiritually focused intervention with older trauma survivors. *Social Work, 57,* 73–82. http://dx.doi.org/10.1093/sw/swr001

Bowlby J. (1998). Developmental psychiatry comes of age. *Am J Psychiatry, 145*(1), 1–10. https://doi: 10.1176/ajp.145.1.1. pmid: 3276225.

Bowlby, J. (1969). *Attachment and loss: Volume 1 (Attachment)*. Basic Books.

Bowlby, J. (1982). *Attachment and loss (Vol. I): Attachment (2nd ed.)*. New York, NY: Basic Books.

Boyda, D., & McFeeters, D. (2015). Childhood maltreatment and social functioning in adults with sub-clinical psychosis. *Psychiatry Research, 226*(1), 376–382. https://doi.org/10.1016/j.psychres.2015.01.023

Bracewell, K., Hargreaves, P., & Stanley, N. (2022). The consequences of the COVID-19 lockdown on stalking victimization. *Journal of Family Violence, 37*(6), 951–957. https://doi.org/10.1007/s10896-020-00201-0

Brassard, A., Charbachi, N., Claing, A., Godbout, N., Savard, C., Lafontaine, M., & Péloquin, K. (2022). Childhood sexual abuse, dyadic empathy, and intimate partner violence among men seeking psychological help. *Journal of Interpersonal Violence, 37*(23–24), NP22114–NP22134. https://doi.org/10.1177/08862605211069690

Bradley, B. D., Jung, T., Tandon-Verma, A., Khoury, B., Chan, T. C. Y., & Cheng, Y. (2017). Operations research in global health: A scoping review focusing on the themes of health equity and impact. *Health Research Policy and Systems, 15*(1), 32. https://doi.org/10.1186/s12961-017-0187-7

Bragard, E., Fisher, C. B., & Curtis, B. L. (2020). "They know what they are getting into:" Researchers confront the benefits and challenges of online recruitment for HIV research. *Ethics & Behavior, 30*(7), 481–495. https://doi.org/10.1080/10508422.2019.1692663

Braun, V., & Clarke, V. (2006). Using thematic analysis in psychology. *Qualitative Research in Psychology, 3*, 77–101.

Braun, P., Schwientek, A., Guthardt, L., Loerbroks, A., & Apolinário-Hagen, J. (2022). How to raise awareness about electronic mental health services among prospective healthcare providers: A qualitative study on information preferences. *European Psychiatry, 65*(S1), S292. https://doi.org/10.1192/j.eurpsy.2022.745

Breeze, B., & Jollymore, G. (2017). Understanding solicitation: Beyond the binary variable of being asked or not being asked. *International Journal of Nonprofit and Voluntary Sector Marketing, 22*(4), n/a. https://doi.org/10.1002/nvsm.1607

Breland, J. Y., Donalson, R., Dinh, J. V., & Maguen, S. (2018, 2017). Trauma exposure and disordered eating: A qualitative study. *Women & Health, 58*(2), 160–174. https://doi.org/10.1080/03630242.2017.1282398

Bretherton, I. (1992). The Origins of Attachment Theory: John Bowlby and Mary Ainsworth. *Developmental Psychology, 28*(5), 759. https://library.capella.edu/login?url=https://www.proquest.com/scholarly-journals/origins-attachment-theory-john-bowlby-mary/docview/224545271/se-2

Brinkmann, S., & Kvale, S. (2015). *Interviews: Learning the craft of qualitative research interviewing (3rd ed.).* Sage Publication.

Bronte, G., Cosi, D. M., Magri, C., Frassoldati, A., Crinò, L., & Calabrò, L. (2023). Immune checkpoint inhibitors in "Special" NSCLC populations: A practical approach? *International Journal of Molecular Sciences, 24*(16), 12622. https://doi.org/10.3390/ijms241612622

Brooks, C., Martin, S., Broda, L., & Poudrier, J. (2020). "How many silences are there?" Men's experience of victimization in intimate partner relationships. *Journal of Interpersonal Violence, 35*(23–24), 5390–5413. https://doi.org/10.1177/0886260517719905

Brooks, D., Wirtz, A., Celentano, D., Beyrer, C., Arrington-Sanders, R., & Hailey-Fair, K. (2021,2020). Gaps in science and evidence-based interventions to respond to intimate partner violence among black, gay, and bisexual men in the U.S.: A call for an intersectional social justice approach. *Sexuality & Culture, 25*(1), 306–317. https://doi.org/10.1007/s12119-020-09769-7

Brooks, N., Petherick, W., Kannan, A., Stapleton, P., & Davidson, S. (2021). Understanding female-perpetrated stalking. *Journal of Threat Assessment and Management, 8*(3), 65–76. https://doi.org/10.1037/tam0000162

Brooks, C., Martin, S., Broda, L., & Poudrier, J. (2020). "How many silences are there?" Men's experience of victimization in intimate partner relationships. *Journal of Interpersonal Violence, 35*(23–24), 5390–5413. https://doi.org/10.1177/0886260517719905

Brown, N. (2018). Exploring the lived experience of fibromyalgia using creative data collection methods. *Cogent Social Sciences, 4*(1), 1447759. https://doi.org/10.1080/23311886.2018.1447759

Brown, S. S. G., Dams-O'Connor, K., Watson, E., Balchandani, P., & Feldman, R. E. (2021*). Case report: An MRI (Magnetic Resonance Imaging) traumatic brain injury longitudinal case study at 7 teslas: Pre- and post-injury structural network and volumetric reorganization and recovery. (No. 12).* https://doi.org/10.3389/fneur.2021.631330

Bryant-Davis, T., & Wong, E. C. (2013). Faith to move mountains: Religious coping, spirituality, and interpersonal trauma recovery. *The American Psychologist, 68*(8), 675–684. https://doi.org/10.1037/a0034380

Bryngeirsdottir, H. S., & Halldorsdottir, S. (2022). Fourteen main obstacles on the journey to post-traumatic growth experienced by female survivors of intimate partner violence: "It was all so confusing." *International Journal of Environmental Research and Public Health, 19*(9), 5377. https://doi.org/10.3390/ijerph19095377

Bryson, K., Wilkinson, C., Kuah, S., Matthews, G., & Turnbull, D. (2017). A pilot exploratory investigation on pregnant women's views about Stan fetal monitoring technology. *B.M.C. Pregnancy and Childbirth, 17*(1), 446. https://doi.org/10.1186/s12884-017-1598-8

Buchanan, A., & Powell, R. (2017). De-moralization as emancipation: Liberty, progress, and the evolution of invalid moral norms. *Social Philosophy & Policy, 34*(2), 108–135. https://doi.org/10.1017/S0265052517000231

Bui, N. H., & Pasalich, D. S. (2021). Insecure attachment, maladaptive personality traits, and the perpetuation of in-person and cyber psychological abuse. *Journal of Interpersonal Violence, 36*(5–6), 2117–2139. https://doi.org/10.1177/0886260518760332

Buonomo, I., Santoro, P. E., Benevene, P., Borrelli, I., Angelini, G., Fiorilli, C., Gualano, M. R., & Moscato, U. (2022). Buffering the effects of burnout on healthcare professionals' health—the mediating role of compassionate relationships at work in the COVID era. *International Journal of Environmental Research and Public Health, 19*(15), 8966. https://doi.org/10.3390/ijerph19158966

Burelomova, A. S., Gulina, M. A., & Tikhomandritskaya, O. A. (2018). Intimate partner violence: An overview of the existing theories, conceptual frameworks, and definitions. *Psychology in Russia: Ultramodern, 11*(3), 128–144. https://doi.org/10.11621/pir.2018.0309

Burns, S. C., Kogan, C. S., Heyman, R. E., Foran, H. M., Smith Slep, A. M., Dominguez-Martinez, T., Grenier, J., Matsumoto, C., & Reed, G. M. (2022). Exploring mental health professionals' experiences of intimate partner violence–related training: Results from a global survey. *Journal of Interpersonal Violence, 35*(23–24), 5390–5413. https://doi.org/10.1177/0886260520908020

References

Burris, C. T., Schrage, K. M., & Rempel, J. K. (2016). No country for girly men: High instrumentality men express empathic concern when caring is "manly." *Motivation and Emotion, 40*(2), 278–289. https://doi.org/10.1007/s11031-015-9525-7

Burnell, R., Umanath, S., & Garry, M. (2023). Collective memories serve similar functions to autobiographical memories. *Memory (Hove), 31*(3), 316–327. https://doi.org/10.1080/09658211.2022.215480

Butina, M., Campbell, S., & Miller, W. (2015). Conducting qualitative research introduction. *Clinical Laboratory Science, 28*(3), 186–189. https://doi.org/10.29074/ascls.28.3.186

Butters, R. P., Droubay, B. A., Seawright, J. L., Tollefson, D. R., Lundahl, B., & Whitaker, L. (2020). Intimate partner violence perpetrator treatment: Tailoring interventions to individual needs. *Clinical Social Work Journal, 49*(3), 391–404. https://doi.org/10.1007/s10615-020-00763-y

Brooks, C., Martin, S., Broda, L., & Poudrier, J. (2020). "How many silences are there?" Men's experience of victimization in intimate partner relationships. *Journal of Interpersonal Violence, 35*(23–24), 5390–5413. https://doi.org/10.1177/0886260517719905

Bryngeirsdottir, H. S., & Halldorsdottir, S. (2022). "I'm a winner, not a victim": The facilitating factors of post-traumatic growth among women who have suffered intimate partner violence. *International Journal of Environmental Research and Public Health, 19*(3), 1342. https://doi.org/10.3390/ijerph19031342

Caelli K., Ray L., & Mill J. (2003). "Clear as mud": Toward greater clarity in generic qualitative research. *International Journal of Qualitative Methods, 2*(2), 1–24.

Cage, J., Kobulsky, J. M., McKinney, S. J., Holmes, M. R., Berg, K. A., Bender, A. E., & Kemmerer, A. (2022). The effect of exposure to intimate partner violence on Children's academic functioning: A systematic review of the literature. *Journal of Family Violence, 37*(8), 1337–1352. https://doi.org/10.1007/s10896-021-00314-0

Calvete, E., Corral, S., & Estévez, A. (2008). Coping as a mediator and moderator between intimate partner violence and symptoms of anxiety and depression. *Violence Against Women, 14*, 886–904. https://doi.org/10.177/1077801208320907

Camfield, L. (2019). Rigor and ethics in big-team qualitative data: Experiences from research in international development. *The American Behavioral Scientist (Beverly Hills), 63*(5), 604–621. https://doi.org/10.1177/0002764218784636

Campbell, R. D., Dennis, M. K., Lopez, K., Matthew, R., & Choi, Y. J. (2021). Qualitative research in communities of color: Challenges, strategies, and lessons. *Journal of the Society for Social Work and Research, 12*(1), 177–200. https://doi.org/10.1086/713408

Campbell, R., Goodman-Williams, R., & Javorka, M. (2019). A trauma-informed approach to sexual violence research ethics and open science. *Journal of Interpersonal Violence, 34*(23–24), 4765–4793. https://doi.org/10.1177/0886260519871530

Campoverde, F., de Las Casas, M., & Blitchtein-Winicki, D. (2022). Is there an association between being a victim of physical violence by an intimate partner and binge drinking in men and women? Secondary analysis of a national study, Peru 2020. *International Journal of Environmental Research and Public Health, 19*(21), 14403. https://doi.org/10.3390/ijerph192114403

Canto, J. M., Vallejo-Martín, M., Perles, F., & San Martín, J. (2020). The influence of ideological variables in denying violence against women: The role of sexism and social dominance orientation in Spanish. *International Journal of Environmental Research and Public Health, 17*(14), 4934. https://doi.org/10.3390/ijerph17144934

Cao, H., Li, X., Li, X., Ward, L., Xie, Z., Hu, H., Zhang, Y., & Liu, J. (2020). Factors influencing participant compliance in acupuncture trials: An in-depth interview study. *PloS One, 15*(4), e0231780. https://doi.org/10.1371/journal.pone.0231780

References

Capella University (2023). *Doctoral Dissertation Guidebook.* Retrieved from campustools.capella.edu.

Capella University (2024). *Qualitative Dissertation Chapter Guide.* Retrieved from campustools.capella.edu.

Capella University (2018). *Qualitative Chapter Guide.* Retrieved from campustools.capella.edu.

Capella University (2023). *Qualitative Dissertation Template.* Retrieved from campustools.capella.edu.

Capella University (2019). *Research Philosophy and Assumptions.* Retrieved from campustools.capella.edu.

Capella University (2020). *Programs of Research.*

Caputo, A. (2019). Psychodynamic insights from narratives of people with amyotrophic lateral sclerosis: A qualitative phenomenological study. *Mediterranean Journal of Clinical Psychology, 7*(2). https://doi.org/10.6092/2282-1619/2019.7.2009

Carcary, M. (2020). The research audit trail: Methodological guidance for application in practice. *Electronic Journal of Business Research Methods, 18*(2), 166–177. https://doi.org/10.34190/JBRM.18.2.008

Cardinale, E. M., & Marsh, A. A. (2015). Impact of psychopathy on moral judgments about causing fear and physical harm. *PloS One, 10*(5), e0125708. https://doi.org/10.1371/journal.pone.0125708

Cardone, R. (2019). Empathetic British feminists at the crossroads of colonialism and self-determination. *International Journal of Sociology and Social Policy, 39*(1/2), 84–97. https://doi.org/10.1108/IJSSP-04-2018-0058

Carlson, J., Voith, L., Brown, J. C., & Holmes, M. (2019, 2018). Viewing children's exposure to intimate partner violence through a developmental, social-ecological, and survivor lens: The field's current state, challenges, and future directions. *Violence Against Women, 25*(1), 6–28. doi:10.1177/1077801218816187

Carroll, R. P., & Prickett, S. (1998). *The Bible: Authorized King James version*. Oxford University Press Incorporated. https://doi.org/10.1093/actrade/9780199535941.book.1

Carraro, A., Gobbi, E., Stanton, R., Santi, G., & Rosenbaum, S. (2023). Psychometric properties of the Italian version of the emic-hp (exercise in mental illness questionnaire-health professionals' version) to investigate health professionals' views of exercise for the treatment of mental illness. *Clinical Neuropsychiatry, 20*(1), 55–60. https://doi.org/10.36131/cnfioritieditore20230107

Carthy, N., Best, D., & Divers, A. (2023). The process of leaving abuse: Midlife and older male experiences of female-perpetrated intimate partner violence. *Journal of Interpersonal Violence, 38*(17-18), 10409–10432. https://doi.org/10.1177/08862605231173431

Cascardi, M., Jouriles, E. N., & Temple, J. R. (2020). Distinct and overlapping correlates of psychological and physical partner violence perpetration. *Journal of Interpersonal Violence, 35*(13–14), 2375–2398. https://doi.org/10.1177/0886260517702492

Castillo, Y. A., Rinehart, K., Fischer, J., & Weber, W. (2021). Strategies and barriers to work behavior change: Perceptions of prevocational rehabilitation professionals. *Journal of Applied Rehabilitation Counseling, 52*(3), 213–231. https://doi.org/10.1891/JARC-D-20-00012

Castro, D. R., Kluger, A. N., & Itzchakov, G. (2016). Does the avoidance-attachment style attenuate the benefits of being listened to? *European Journal of Social Psychology, 46*(6), 762–775. https://doi.org/10.1002/ejsp.2185

Cavallaro, J. L., & Sridhar, M. (2020). Reducing bias in human rights fact-finding: The potential of the clinical simulation model to overcome ethical, practical, and cultural tensions in "Foreign" contexts. *Human Rights Quarterly, 42*(2), 488–512. https://doi.org/10.1353/hrq.2020.0016

References

Cavanaugh, M. M., Solomon, P., & Gelles, R. J. (2011). The dialectical psychoeducational workshop (DPEW): The conceptual framework and curriculum for a preventative intervention for males at risk for IPV. *Violence Against Women, 17*(8), 970–989. https://doi.org/10.1177/1077801211414266

Chan, E. A., Tsang, P. L., Chang, S. S. Y., Wong, F. Y., & Lam, W. (2019). A qualitative study of nurses' perspectives on communication with patients in busy oncology wards. *PloS One, 14*(10), e0224178. https://doi.org/10.1371/journal.pone.0224178

Chatterji, S., Stern, E., Dunkle, K., & Heise, L. (2020). Community activism as a strategy to reduce intimate partner violence (IPV) in rural Rwanda: Results of a community randomized trial. *Journal of Global Health, 10*(1), 010406. https://doi.org/10.7189/jogh.10.010406

Chen, H., Liu, C., Cao, X., Hong, B., Huang, D., Liu, C., & Chiou, W. (2021). Effects of loving-kindness meditation on doctors' mindfulness, empathy, and communication skills. *International Journal of Environmental Research and Public Health, 18*(8), 4033. https://doi.org/10.3390/ijerph18084033

Chen, S., Krupa, T., Lysaght, R., McCay, E., & Piat, M. (2014). Development of a recovery education program for inpatient mental health providers. *Psychiatric Rehabilitation Journal, 37*(4), 329–332. https://doi.org/10.1037/prj0000082

Chepuka, L., Taegtmeyer, M., Chorwe-Sungani, G., Mambulasa, J., Chirwa, E., & Tolhurst, R. (2014). Feelings of the mental health impact of intimate partner violence and health service responses in Malawi. *Global Health Action, 7*(1), 24816. https://doi.org/10.3402/gha.v7.24816

Cheung, J. C. (2016). An exploration of social workers' role in remunerative vocational training: Caring, controlling, or contractual? *Qualitative Social Work: Q.S.W.: Research and Practice, 15*(2), 231–246. https://doi.org/10.1177/1473325015588122

Cheung, K. L., ten Klooster, P. M., Smit, C., de Vries, H., & Pieterse, M. E. (2017). The impact of non-response bias due to sampling in public health studies: A comparison of voluntary versus mandatory recruitment in a Dutch national survey on adolescent health. *BMC Public Health, 17*(1), 276. https://doi.org/10.1186/s12889-017-4189-8

Cheung, J. C. (2022). Responses to COVID-19 in major social work journals: A systematic review of empirical studies, comments, and editorials. *Research on Social Work Practice, 32*(2), 168–185. https://doi.org/10.1177/10497315211046846

Cheung, S. P., & Huang, C. (2022). Adolescent dating and relationship quality: The role of exposure to intimate partner violence in early childhood. *Journal of Social and Personal Relationships, 39*(6), 1717–1738. https://doi.org/10.1177/02654075211062947

Chiba, R., Umeda, M., Goto, K., Miyamoto, Y., Yamaguchi, S., & Kawakami, N. (2017). The property of the Japanese version of the recovery knowledge inventory (RKI) among mental health service providers: A cross-sectional study. *International Journal of Mental Health Systems, 11*(1), 71. https://doi.org/10.1186/s13033-017-0178-7

Chiba, R., Umeda, M., Goto, K., Miyamoto, Y., Yamaguchi, S., & Kawakami, N. (2018). Correction to: The property of the Japanese version of the recovery knowledge inventory (RKI) among mental health service providers: A cross-sectional study. *International Journal of Mental Health Systems, 12*(1), 34. https://doi.org/10.1186/s13033-018-0214-2

Childress, S., Shrestha, N., Kenensarieva, K., Urbaeva, J., & Schrag, R. V. (2024). The role of culture in the justification and perpetuation of domestic violence: The perspective service providers in Kyrgyzstan. *Violence Against Women, 30*(5), 1198–1225. https://doi.org/10.1177/10778012231186814

Chioneso, N. A., Hunter, C. D., Gobin, R. L., McNeil Smith, S., Mendenhall, R., & Neville, H. A. (2020). Community healing and resistance through storytelling: A framework to address racial trauma in African communities. *Journal of Black Psychology, 46*(2–3), 95–121. https://doi.org/10.1177/0095798420929468

Cho, H., Shamrova, D., Han, J., & Levchenko, P. (2020). Patterns of intimate partner violence victimization and survivors' help-seeking. *Journal of Interpersonal Violence, 35*(21–22), 4558–4582. https://doi.org/10.1177/0886260517715027

Choi, A. W. M. (2020). Validation of the scale for assessing the psychological vulnerability and its association with the health of intimate partner violence victims in the Chinese young adult population. *PloS One, 15*(7), e0235761. https://doi.org/10.1371/journal.pone.0235761

Chopin, J., Beauregard, E., & Paquette, S. (2023). Sexual victimization involving solo female offenders: A crime script approach. *Crime and Delinquency, 69*(12), 2531–2560. https://doi.org/10.1177/00111287211061717

Choudhury, S., Yeh, P. G., & Markham, C. M. (2022). Coping with adverse childhood experiences during the COVID-19 pandemic: Perceptions of mental health service providers. *Frontiers in Psychology, 13,* 975300. https://doi.org/10.3389/fpsyg.2022.975300

Chwang, E. (2014). Shared vulnerabilities in research. *American Journal of Bioethics, 14*(12), 3–11. https://doi.org/10.1080/15265161.2014.964872

Cimino, A. N., Yi, G., Patch, M., Alter, Y., Campbell, J. C., Gundersen, K. K., Tang, J. T., Tsuyuki, K., & Stockman, J. K. (2019). The effect of intimate partner violence and probable traumatic brain injury on mental health outcomes for black women. *Journal of Aggression, Maltreatment & Trauma, 28*(6), 714–731. https://doi.org/10.1080/10926771.2019.1587657

Cislaghi, B., & Heise, L. (2018). Theory and practice of social norms interventions: Eight common pitfalls. *Globalization and Health, 14*(1), 83. https://doi.org/10.1186/s12992-018-0398-x

Clark, A. M., & Sousa, B. J. (2018). The mental health of people doing qualitative research: Getting serious about risks and remedies. *International Journal of Qualitative Methods, 17*(1), 160940691878724. https://doi.org/10.1177/1609406918787244

Clarke, K., Holt, A., Norris, C., & Nel, P. W. (2017). Adolescent-to-parent violence and abuse, such as Parents' management of tension and ambiguity. An interpretative phenomenological analysis. *Child & Family Social Work, 22*(4), 1423–1430. https://doi.org/10.1111/cfs.12363

Cloutier, C., & Ravasi, D. (2021). Using tables to enhance trustworthiness in qualitative research. *Strategic Organization, 19*(1), 113–133. https://doi.org/10.1177/1476127020979329

Cloyes, K. G., Rosenkranz, S. J., Berry, P. H., Supiano, K. P., Routt, M., Shannon-Dorcy, K., & Llanque, S. M. (2016). Essential elements of an effective prison hospice program. *American Journal of Hospice & Palliative Medicine, 33*(4), 390–402. https://doi.org/10.1177/1049909115574491

Coccia, M. (2020). Properties of the evolution of scientific fields: An inductive study in applied sciences. *Journal of Social and Administrative Sciences, 7*(1), 24. https://doi.org/10.1453/jsas.v7i1.2016

Cockburn, J., O'Donoghue, S., Taylor, C., Mukherjee, J. R., Douwes, E., Rouget, M., Slotow, R., Mukherjee, S., Boon, R., & Roberts, D. (2016). Evaluating the outcomes and processes of a research-action partnership: The need for continuous reflective evaluation. *Bothalia, 46*(2), 1–16. https://doi.org/10.4102/abc.v46i2.2154

Cole, B. P., & Davidson, M. M. (2019). Exploring men's feelings about male depression. *Psychology of Men & Masculinity, 20*(4), 459–466. https://doi.org/10.1037/men0000176

References

Cofie, N. (2020). A multilevel analysis of contextual risk factors for intimate partner violence in Ghana. *International Review of Victimology, 26*(1), 50–78. https://doi.org/10.1177/0269758018799030

Cogan, C. M., Paquet, C. B., Lee, J. Y., Miller, K. E., Crowley, M. D., & Davis, J. L. (2021). Differentiating the symptoms of posttraumatic stress disorder and bipolar disorders in adults: Using a trauma-informed assessment approach. *Clinical Psychology and Psychotherapy, 28*(1), 251–260. https://doi.org/10.1002/cpp.2504

Coghi, F., & Harris, R. J. (2020). A large deviation perspective on ratio observables in reset processes: Robustness of rate functions. *Journal of Statistical Physics, 179*(1), 131–154. https://doi.org/10.1007/s10955-020-02513-3

Colizzi, M., Ruggeri, M., & Lasalvia, A. (2020). Should we be concerned about stigma and discrimination in people at risk for psychosis? A systematic review. *Psychological Medicine, 50*(5), 705–726. https://doi.org/10.1017/S0033291720000148

Collier, A., & Wyer, M. (2016). Researching reflexively with patients and families: Two studies using video-reflexive ethnography to collaborate with patients and families in patient safety research. *Qualitative Health Research, 26*(7), 979–993. https://doi.org/10.1177/1049732315618937

Compaoré, R., Brizuela, V., Khisa, A. M., Gómez, A. L., Baguiya, A., Bonet, M., Thorson, A., Gitau, E., & Kouanda, S. (2021). 'We always find things to learn from.' Lessons from the implementation of the global maternal sepsis study on research ability: A qualitative study. *B.M.C. Health Services Research, 21*(1), 208. https://doi.org/10.1186/s12913-021-06195-9

Connelly, L. M. (2014). Ethical Considerations in Research Studies. *Medsurg Nursing, 23*(1), 54–55. http://library.capella.edu/login?qurl=https%3A%2F%2Fwww.proquest.com%2 Fscholarly-journals%2Fethical-considerations-research-studies%2Fdocview% 2F1506150659%2Fse-2%3Faccountid%3D27965

Conrad, C. F., & Serlin, R. C. (2011). Approaching rigor in applied qualitative research. In Clifton Conrad, C. F. Conrad, Ronald Serlin & R. C. Serlin (Eds.), *The Sage Handbook for education research* (2nd ed., 263). Sage Incorporated. https://doi.org/10.4135/9781483351377.n17

Contractor, A. A., Brown, L. A., & Weiss, N. H. (2018). Relation between lifespan polytrauma typologies and post-trauma mental health. *Comprehensive Psychiatry, 80*, 202–213. https://doi.org/10.1016/j.comppsych.2017.10.005

Cooper, C., Booth, A., Varley-Campbell, J., Britten, N., & Garside, R. (2018). Defining the process of literature searching in systematic reviews: A literature review of guidance and supporting studies. *B.M.C. Medical Research Methodology, 18*(1), 85. https://doi.org/10.1186/s12874-018-0545-3

Cooper, R. (2016). Decoding coding via the coding manual for qualitative researchers by Johnny Saldana. *Qualitative Report*. https://doi.org/10.46743/2160-3715/2009.2856

Cooper, Donald R., and Schindler, Pamela S. (2008). *Business Research Method* (10th ed). Boston: McGraw Hill Education.

Correa da Cunha, H., Farrell, C., Andersson, S., Amal, M., & Floriani, D. E. (2022). Toward a more in-depth measurement of cultural distance: A re-evaluation of the underlying assumptions. *International Journal of Cross-Cultural Management: CCM, 22*(1), 157–188. https://doi.org/10.1177/14705958221089192

Corbin, J., & Strauss, A. (2008). *Basics of Qualitative Research: Techniques and Procedures for Developing Grounded Theory* (3rd ed.). Sage.

Corbin J., & Strauss, A. (2015). Basics of Qualitative Research: Techniques and Procedures for Developing Grounded Theory (4th ed.). Sage.

Corbally, M. (2015). Accounting for intimate partner violence: A biographical analysis of narrative strategies used by men experiencing IPV from their female partners. *Journal of Interpersonal Violence, 30*(17), 3112–3132. https://doi.org/10.1177/0886260514554429

Costa, B., & Dewaele, J. (2019). The talking cure—building the core skills and the confidence of counselors and psychotherapists to work effectively with multilingual patients through training and supervision. *Counseling and Psychotherapy Research, 19*(3), 231–240. https://doi.org/10.1002/capr.12187

Costa, E. C. V., & Gomes, S. C. (2018). Social support and self-esteem moderate the relationship between intimate partner violence and depression and anxiety symptoms among Portuguese women. *Journal of Family Violence, 33*(5), 355–368. https://doi.org/10.1007/s10896-018-9962-7

Costa, M., Barré, T., Coste, M., Yaya, I., Berenger, C., Tanti, M., Cutarella, C., Mora, M., Poloméni, P., Maynard, M., Teuma, D., Bazin, M., Maradan, G., Roux, P., & Carrieri, P. M. (2020). Screening and care for alcohol use disorder in France: Expectations, barriers, and levers using a mixed-methods approach. *B.M.C. Public Health, 20*(1), 358–358. https://doi.org/10.1186/s12889-020-08495-x

Cotter, C. A., O'Neill, M. K., Stevens, M. N., Sanders, P. G., & Henninger, J. (2023). Counseling with male clients: The case for relational resilience approach. *American Journal of Men's Health, 17*(3), 15579883231179328. https://doi.org/10.1177/15579883231179328

Cotti, C., Foster, J., Haley, M. R., & Rawski, S. L. (2020). Duluth versus cognitive behavioral therapy: A natural field experiment on intimate partner violence diversion programs. *Journal of Experimental Psychology. Applied, 26*(2), 384–395. https://doi.org/10.1037/xap0000249

Cowlishaw, S., Freijah, I., Kartal, D., Sbisa, A., Mulligan, A., Notarianni, M., Couineau, A., Forbes, D., O'Donnell, M., Phelps, A., Iverson, K. M., Heber, A., O'Dwyer, C., Smith, P., & Hosseini, F. (2022).

Intimate partner violence (IPV) in military and veteran populations: A systematic review of population-based surveys and population screening studies. *International Journal of Environmental Research and Public Health, 19*(14), 8853. https://doi.org/10.3390/ijerph19148853

Coxon, A., McBain, H., Pavlova, N., Rowlands, H., & Mulligan, K. (2020). Are diabetes self-management programs for the general diabetes population effective for people with severe mental illness? A systematic review. *B.M.C. Psychiatry, 20*(1), 386–386. https://doi.org/10.1186/s12888-020-02779-7

Coyle, L., Hanna, D., Dyer, K. F. W., Read, J., Curran, D., & Shannon, C. (2019). Does trauma-related training relate to, or impact, mental health professionals' frequency of asking about or detecting trauma history? Systematic literature reviews. *Psychological Trauma, 11*(7), 802–809. https://doi.org/10.1037/tra0000434

Crane, C. A., & Easton, C. J. (2017). Integrated treatment options for male perpetrators of intimate partner violence: Integrated treatments for partner violence. *Drug and Alcohol Review, 36*(1), 24–33. https://doi.org/10.1111/dar.12496

Creswell, J. W. (2013). *Qualitative inquiry & research design: Choosing among five approaches* (3rd ed.). Sage.

Creswell, J. W., & Guetterman, T. C. (2019). *The Academic Research Design for planning, conducting, and evaluating quantitative and qualitative research* (6th ed.). Pearson.

Creswell, J. W., & Poth, C. N. (2018). *Qualitative inquiry and research design: Choosing among five approaches* (4th ed.). Sage.

Creswell, J., Codlin, A. J., Andre, E., Micek, M. A., Bedru, A., Carter, E. J., & Ditiu, L. (2014). The early programmatic implementation of expert mtb/rif testing results in nine countries. *B.M.C. Infectious Diseases, 14*(1), 2-2. https://doi.org/10.1186/1471-2334-14-2

Creswell, J. W. (2013). *Qualitative inquiry & research design: Choosing among five approaches* (3rd ed.). Sage.

Creswell, J. (2008). *Research design: Qualitative, quantitative, and mixed methods approach.* (3rd ed.). Sage.

Creswell, J. (2003). *Research design: Qualitative, quantitative, and mixed methods approach.* (2nd ed.). Sage.

Creswell, J. (1995). *Research design: Qualitative, quantitative approaches.* Sage.

Crim, K. R. (1970). The new English Bible. *The Bible Translator, 21*(3), 149–154. https://doi.org/10.1177/000608447002100308

Crivatu, I. M., Horvath, M. A. H., & Massey, K. (2023). *The impacts of working with victims of sexual violence: A rapid evidence assessment.* Sage. https://doi.org/10.1177/15248380211016024

Cunningham-Williams, R. M., Wideman, E., & Fields, L. (2019). Ph.D. student development: A conceptual model for research-intensive social work Ph.D. programs. *Journal of Evidence-Based Social Work, 16*(3), 278–293. https://doi.org/10.1080/26408066.2019.1588820

Cutillo-Schmitter, T. A., Mascara, E. B., Wynne, P., Martin, P., Sliner, B. J., Cunningham, F., & Bigdeli, S. P. (1996). Exemplars from an acute care geriatric psychiatry unit. *Journal of Gerontological Nursing, 22*(4), 13–27. https://doi.org/10.3928/0098-9134-19960401-05

Dabrowska, A., & Boduszek, D. (2017, 2016). Child abuse and neglect profiles and their psychosocial consequences in a large sample of incarcerated males. *Child Abuse & Neglect, 65,* 266–277. https://doi.org/10.1016/j.chiabu.2016.12.003

Daniel, B. K. (2019). Using the TACT framework to learn the principles of rigor in qualitative research. *Electronic Journal of Business Research Methods, 17*(3), 118–129. https://doi.org/10.34190/JBRM.17.3.002

Dagi, T. F. (2017). Seven ethical issues are affecting neurosurgeons in the context of health care reform. *Neurosurgery, 80*(4S), S83–S91. https://doi.org/10.1093/neuros/nyx017

Dako-Gyeke, P., Addo-Lartey, A. A., Ogum Alangea, D., Sikweyiya, Y., Chirwa, E. D., Coker-Appiah, D., & Adanu, R. M. K. (2019). Small small quarrels bring about happiness or love in the relationships': Exploring community beliefs and gendered norms contributing to male perpetrated intimate partner violence in the central region of Ghana. *PloS One, 14*(11), e0225296. https://doi.org/10.1371/journal.pone.0225296

Dardis, C. M., Davin, K. R., Lietzau, S. B., & Gidycz, C. A. (2021). Disclosing unwanted pursuit victimization: Indirect effects of negative reactions on PTSD symptomatology among undergraduate women. *Journal of Interpersonal Violence, 36*(21–22), 10431–10453. https://doi.org/10.1177/0886260519884696

Davidson, R. D., & Beck, C. J. A. (2017). Using couple-level patterns of intimate partner violence to predict divorce outcomes. *Psychology, Public Policy, and Law, 23*(1), 85–95. https://doi.org/10.1037/law0000106

Davis, J. D., Miles, G. M., & Quinley III, J. H. (2019). It is the same, but different. *International Journal of Sociology and Social Policy, 39*(7/8), 550–573. https://doi.org/10.1108/ijssp-01-2019-0022

Davis, M., & Jonson-Reid, M. (2020). The dual use of religious faith in intimate partner abuse perpetration: Perspectives of Latino men in a parish-based intervention program. *Social Work and Christianity, 47*(4), 71–95. https://doi.org/10.34043/swc.v4713.109

Davis, K. C., Masters, N. T., Casey, E., Kajumulo, K. F., Norris, J., & George, W. H. (2018). How childhood maltreatment profiles of male victims predict adult perpetration and psychosocial functioning. *Journal of Interpersonal Violence, 33*(6), 915–937. https://doi.org/10.1177/0886260515613345

References

Davis, C., Baty, B. J., Hippman, C., Trepanier, A., & Erby, L. (2020). Genetic counselors with advanced skills: II. A new career trajectory framework. *Journal of Genetic Counseling, 29*(5), 771–785. https://doi.org/10.1002/jgc4.1204

Davis, G. E. (2023). Reacting to non-prototypical victims: Blame, empathy, and willingness to label sexual assaults of men and sexual minority victims. *Journal of Interpersonal Violence, 38*(11–12), 7457–7484. https://doi.org/10.1177/08862605221145709

Day, A., & Bowen, E. (2015). Offending competency and coercive control in intimate partner violence. *Aggression and Violent Behavior, 20,* 62–71. https://doi.org/10.1016/j.avb.2014.12.004

Debowska, A., & Boduszek, D. (2017). Child abuse and neglect profiles and their psychosocial consequences in a large sample of incarcerated males. *Child Abuse & Neglect, 65,* 266–277. https://doi.org/10.1016/j.chiabu.2016.12.003

de Jong, K., Ariti, C., van der Kam, S., Mooren, T., Shanks, L., Pintaldi, G., & Kleber, R. (2016). Monitoring and evaluating psychosocial intervention outcomes in humanitarian aid. *PloS One, 11*(6), e0157474. https://doi.org/10.1371/journal.pone.0157474

Dekel, B., & Abrahams, N. (2023). "I'm not the mother I wanted to be": Understanding the increased responsibility, decreased control, and double level of intentionality experienced by abused mothers. *PloS One, 18*(6), e0287749. https://doi.org/10.1371/journal.pone.0287749

Dekel, R., Shaked, O., Ben-Porat, A., & Itzhaky, H. (2020). Physical and mental health interrelations: Self-rated health, depression, and PTSD among female IPV survivors. *Violence Against Women, 26*(3–4), 379–394. https://doi.org/10.1177/1077801219832916

Dekel, B., Abrahams, N., & Andipatin, M. (2019). Exploring the intersection between violence against women and children from the perspective of parents convicted of child homicide. *Journal of Family Violence, 34*(1), 9–20. https://doi.org/10.1007/s10896-018-9964-5

Denner, J., Meyer, B., & Bean, S. (2005). Young women's leadership alliance: Youth-adult partnerships in an all-female after-school program. *Journal of Community Psychology, 33*(1), 87–100

Depraetere, J., Vandeviver, C., Beken, T. V., & Keygnaert, I. (2020, 2018). Big Boys do not cry: A critical interpretive synthesis of male sexual victimization. Sage. https://doi.org/10.1177/1524838018816979

Dezso, F., Birkás, B., Vizin, G., Váncsa, S., Szőcs, H., Erőss, A., Lex, D., Gede, N., Molnar, Z., Hegyi, P., & Csathó, Á. (2022). Examining the mental health adversity among healthcare providers during the two waves of the COVID-19 pandemic: Results from a cross-sectional, survey-based study. *BMJ Open, 12*(8), e059493. https://doi.org/10.1136/bmjopen-2021-059493

Dery, I., Akurugu, C. A., & Baataar, C. (2022). Community leaders' beliefs of and responses to intimate partner violence in northwestern Ghana. *PloS One, 17*(3), e0262870. https://doi.org/10.1371/journal.pone.0262870

Devlin, A. M., & Wight, D. (2018). Developing a new drug recovery community in the U.K.: A qualitative study of the transferability of intervention from San Partigiano, Italy, to Scotland. *The Lancet (British Edition), 392,* S29. https://doi.org/10.1016/S0140-6736(18)32155-X

Devine, L., Parke, S., Harrington, L., & Makouar, N. (2022). "Psy" expert evidence in the family courts: The potential for corpus-assisted analysis. *Language and Law, 9*(1), 92–119. https://doi.org/10.21747/21833745/lanlaw/9_1a5

de Waal FBM, Preston SD. (2017). Mammalian empathy: Behavioral manifestations and neural basis. *Nat Rev Neurosci. 2017 Aug, 18*(8), 498–509. doi: 10.1038/nrn.2017.72. Epub 2017 Jun 29. PMID: 28655877.

De Waard, E. J., & Kalkman, J. P. (2022). Synthesizing extreme context studies in project management journals: Introducing a time-based project management typology. *International Journal of Managing*

Projects in Business, 15(5), 886–912. https://doi.org/10.1108/IJMPB-08-2021-0227

Dewidar, A. E., Gado, E., Gemeay, E., & Sabra, A. (2022). Effect of training program about compassion on professional quality of life of mental health nurses. International Egyptian *Journal of Nursing Sciences and Research, 2*(2), 81–97. https://doi.org/10.21608/ejnsr.2022.212300

Dheensa, S., McLindon, E., Spencer, C., Pereira, S., Shrestha, S., Emsley, E., & Gregory, A. (2023). *Healthcare professionals' experiences of domestic violence and abuse: A meta-analysis of prevalence and systematic review of risk markers and consequences.* Sage. https://doi.org/10.1177/15248380211061771

Dichter, M. E., Sorrentino, A. E., Haywood, T. N., Tuepker, A., Newell, S., Cusack, M., & True, G. (2019). Women's participation in research on intimate partner violence: Findings on recruitment, retention, and participants' experiences. *Women's Health Issues, 29*(5), 440–446. https://doi.org/10.1016/j.whi.2019.03.007

Dichter, M. E., Chatterjee, A., Protasiuk, E., & Newman, B. S. (2022). "I'd go from a mountain top and tell my story": Perspectives of survivors of intimate partner violence on storytelling for social change. *Violence Against Women, 28*(6–7), 1708–1720. https://doi.org/10.1177/10778012211024267

Di Napoli, I., Procentese, F., Carnevale, S., Esposito, C., & Arcidiacono, C. (2019). Ending intimate partner violence (IPV) and finding men at stake: An ecological approach. *International Journal of Environmental Research and Public Health, 16*(9), 1652. https://doi.org/10.3390/ijerph16091652

Di Napoli, I., Carnevale, S., Esposito, C., Block, R., Arcidiacono, C., & Procentese, F. (2020). "Kept in Check": Representations and feelings of social and health professionals facing intimate partner violence (IPV). *International Journal of Environmental Research and Public Health, 17*(21), 7910. https://doi.org/10.3390/ijerph17217910

Dim, E. E., & Lysova, A. (2022). Male victims' experiences with and beliefs of the criminal justice response to intimate partner abuse. *Journal of Interpersonal Violence, 37*(15–16), NP13067–NP13091. https://doi.org/10.1177/08862605211001476

Dim, E. E. (2020). Ethnoregional dynamics of intimate partner violence against women in Nigeria. Sage. https://doi.org/10.1177/1524838018801335

Dim, E. E. (2021). Experiences of physical and psychological violence against male victims in Canada: A qualitative study. *International Journal of Offender Therapy and Comparative Criminology, 65*(9), 1029–1054. https://doi.org/10.1177/0306624X20911898

Dim, E. E., & Elabor-Idemudia, P. (2018). Prevalence and predictors of psychological violence against male victims in intimate relationships in Canada. *Journal of Aggression, Maltreatment & Trauma, 27*, 846–866.

Dlamini, S., & Makhaye, M. (2023). Community policing as a panacea for gender-based violence impasse. *African Journal of Gender, Society & Development, 12*(2), 7–29. https://doi.org/10.31920/2634-3622/2023/v12n2a1

Doig, C. J., Page, S. A., McKee, J. L., & Moore, E. E. . . . Kirkpatrick, A. W. Closed or open after laparotomy (COOL) after Source Control for Severe Complicated Intra-Abdominal Sepsis Investigators. (2019). Ethical considerations in conducting surgical research in severe complicated intra-abdominal sepsis. *World Journal of Emergency Surgery, 14*(1), 39. https://doi.org/10.1186/s13017-019-0259-9

Dodaj, A., Sesar, K., & Šimić, N. (2020). Impulsivity and empathy in dating violence among a sample of college females. *Behavioral Sciences, 10*(7), 117. https://doi.org/10.3390/bs10070117

Dokkedahl, S., Kristensen, T. R., Murphy, S., & Elklit, A. (2021). The complex trauma of psychological violence: Cross-sectional findings from a cohort of four Danish women shelters. *European Journal of*

Psychotraumatology, 12(1), 1863580.
https://doi.org/10.1080/20008198.2020.1863580

Dong, K., Jameel, B., & Gagliardi, A. R. (2022). How is patient-centered care conceptualized in obstetrical health? Comparison of themes from concept analyses in obstetrical health- and patient-centered care. Health Expectations: *An International Journal of Public Participation in Health Care and Health Policy, 25*(3), 823–839. https://doi.org/10.1111/hex.13434

Doumas, D. M., Pearson, C. L., Elgin, J. E., & McKinley, L. L. (2008). Adult attachment as a risk factor for intimate partner violence: The "Mispairing" of partners' attachment styles. *Journal of Interpersonal Violence, 23*(5), 616–634. https://doi.org/10.1177/0886260507313526

Downie, S., Kanya, I., Madden, K., Bhandari, M., & Jariwala, A. C. (2021). Intimate partner violence (IPV) in male and female orthopedic trauma patients: A multicenter, cross-sectional prevalence study. *BMJ Open, 11*(8), e046164. https://doi.org/10.1136/bmjopen-2020-046164

Donovan, J. L., Rooshenas, L., Jepson, M., Elliott, D., Wade, J., Avery, K., Mills, N., Wilson, C., Paramasivan, S., & Blazeby, J. M. (2016). Optimizing recruitment and informed consent in randomized controlled trials: Developing and implementing quintet recruitment intervention. *Trials, 17*(1), 283. https://doi.org/10.1186/s13063-016-1391-4

Doyle, J. L. (2020). Experiences of intimate partner violence: The role of psychological, economic, physical, and sexual violence. *Women's Studies International Forum, 80*, 102370. https://doi.org/10.1016/j.wsif.2020.102370

Doyle, J. L., & McWilliams, M. (2020). What difference does peace make? Intimate partner violence and violent conflict in Northern Ireland. *Violence Against Women, 26*(2), 139–163. https://doi.org/10.1177/1077801219832902

Drury, A., Sheila, P., & Anne-Marie, B. (2023). Adapting the pillar integration process for theory development: The theoretical model of healthcare factors influencing quality of life in cancer survivorship. *Journal of Mixed Methods Research, 17*(3), 264–287. https://doi.org/10.1177/15586898221134730

Duchaine, C. S., Aubé, K., Gilbert-Ouimet, M., Vézina, M., Ndjaboué, R., Massamba, V., . . . & Brisson, C. (2020). Psychosocial stressors at work and the risk of sickness absence due to a diagnosed mental disorder: a systematic review and meta-analysis. *Jama Psychiatry, 77*(8), 842–851.

Dumesnil, H., Apostolidis, T., & Verger, P. (2018). General practitioners' opinions about psychotherapy and their relationships with mental health professionals in managing major depression: A qualitative survey. *PloS One, 13*(1), e0190565. https://doi.org/10.1371/journal.pone.0190565

Duquette, P. (2017). Increasing our insular world view: Interoception and psychopathology for psychotherapists. *Frontiers in Neuroscience, 11,* 135. https://doi.org/10.3389/fnins.2017.00135

Dyar, C., Feinstein, B. A., Zimmerman, A. R., Newcomb, M. E., Mustanski, B., & Whitton, S. W. (2020). Dimensions of sexual orientation and rates of intimate partner violence among young sexual minority individuals assigned female at birth: The role of perceived partner jealousy. *Psychology of Violence, 10*(4), 411–421. https://doi.org/10.1037/vio0000275

Dziewa, A., & Glowacz, F. (2022). I was getting out from intimate partner violence: Dynamics and processes. A qualitative analysis of female and male victims' narratives. *Journal of Family Violence, 37*(4), 643–656. https://doi.org/10.1007/s10896-020-00245-2

Easterbrooks, M. A., Katz, R. C., Kotake, C., Stelmach, N. P., & Chaudhuri, J. H. (2018). Intimate partner violence in the first two years of life: Implications for toddlers' behavior regulation. *Journal of Interpersonal Violence, 33*(7), 1192–1214. doi:10.11770886260515614562

References

Ebenau, A. F., Dijkstra, B. A. G., Huurne, C. T., Hasselaar, G. J., Vissers, K. C. P., & Groot, C. M. (2020). Palliative care for patients with substance use disorder and multiple problems: A qualitative study on healthcare professionals' experiences, volunteers and experts-by-experience. *BMC Palliative Care, 19*(1), 8. https://doi.org/10.1186/s12904-019-0502-x

Eckhardt, M., Carlfjord, S., Faresjö, T., Crespo-Burgos, A., Forsberg, B. C., & Falk, M. (2019). Universal health coverage in marginalized populations: A qualitative evaluation of a health reform implementation in rural Ecuador: The Journal of Health Care Organization, Provision, and Financing. *Inquiry, 56*. Retrieved from https://doi.org/10.org.library.capella.edu/10.1177/0046958019880699.

Eckstein, J. J. (2016). IPV stigma and its social management: The roles of relationship-type, abuse-type, and victims' sex. *Journal of Family Violence, 31*(2), 215–225. https://doi.org/10.1007/s10896-015-9752-4

Economou, M., Peppou, L. E., Kontoangelos, K., Palli, A., Tsaliagkou, I., Legaki, E., Gournellis, R., & Papageorgiou, C. (2020). Mental health professionals' attitudes to severe mental illness and its correlates in psychiatric hospitals of Attica: The role of workers' empathy. *Community Mental Health Journal, 56*(4), 614–625. https://doi.org/10.1007/s10597-019-00521-6

Ee, J., Stenfert Kroese, B., & Rose, J. (2022). *Experiences of mental health professionals providing services to adults with intellectual disabilities and mental health problems: A systematic review and meta-synthesis of qualitative research studies.* Sage. https://doi.org/10.1177/17446295211016182

Edelaar, L., Nikiphorou, E., Fragoulis, G. E., Iagnocco, A., Haines, C., Bakkers, M., Barbosa, L., Cikes, N., Ndosi, M., Primdahl, J., Prior, Y., Pchelnikova, P., Ritschl, V., Schäfer, V. S., Smucrova, H., Storrønning, I., Testa, M., Wiek, D., & Vliet Vlieland, Theodora P. M. (2020). 2019 EULAR recommendations for the generic core competencies of health professionals in rheumatology. *Annals of the Rheumatic Diseases, 79*(1), 53–60. https://doi.org/10.1136/annrheumdis-2019-215803

Edmonds, W. A., & Kennedy, T. D. (2017). *An applied guide to research designs quantitative, qualitative, and mixed methods.* Sage.

Edwards, K. M., & Dardis, C. M. (2020). Disclosure recipients' social reactions to victims' disclosures of intimate partner violence. *Journal of Interpersonal Violence, 35*(1–2), 53–76. https://doi.org/10.1177/0886260516681155

Eiroa-Orosa, F. J., & García-Mieres, H. (2019). A systematic review and meta-analysis of recovery educational interventions for mental health professionals. *Administration and Policy in Mental Health and Mental Health Services Research, 46*(6), 724–752. https://doi.org/10.1007/s10488-019-00956-9

Eksin, C., Shamma, J. S., & Weitz, J. S. (2017). Disease dynamics in a stochastic network game: A little empathy goes a long way in averting outbreaks. *Scientific Reports, 7*(1), 44122. https://doi.org/10.1038/srep44122)

Elliott, M., & Ragsdale, J. M. (2020). Mental health professionals with mental illnesses: A qualitative interview study. *American Journal of Orthopsychiatry, 90*(6), 677–686. https://doi.org/10.1037/ort0000499

Ellis, J., & Hart, D. (2023). Strengthening the choice for a generic qualitative research design. *Qualitative Report, 28*(6), 1759–1768. https://doi.org/10.46743/2160-3715/2023.5474

eLenzi, D., eTrentini, C., eTambelli, R., & ePantano, P. (2015). Neural basis of attachment-caregiving systems interaction: Insights from neuroimaging. *Frontiers in Psychology, 6.* https://doi.org/10.3389/fpsyg.2015.01241

El-Kotob, R., Pagcanlungan, J. R., Craven, B. C., Sherrington, C., Mourtzakis, M., & Giangregorio, L. (2022). Researchers' perspectives on adverse event reporting in resistance training trials: A qualitative study. *Applied Physiology, Nutrition, and Metabolism, 47*(9), 893–902. https://doi.org/10.1139/apnm-2022-0012

References

El Sayed, S. A., DeShay, R. A., Davis, J. B., Knox, K. N., & Kerley, K. R. (2022). A blue step forward: An exploratory study of law enforcement beliefs of intimate partner violence in the Southern United States. *Journal of Interpersonal Violence, 37*(9–10), NP6514–NP6534. https://doi.org/10.1177/0886260520966675

Ellis, J. L., & Hart, D. L. (2023). Strengthening the choice for a generic qualitative research design. *Qualitative Report, 28*(6), 1759–1768. https://doi.org/10.46743/2160-3715/2023.5474

Elliott, M., & Ragsdale, J. M. (2020). Mental health professionals with mental illnesses: A qualitative interview study. *American Journal of Orthopsychiatry, 90*(6), 677–686. https://doi.org/10.1037/ort0000499

Elliott, L., Golub, A., Bennett, A., & Guarino, H. (2015). PTSD and cannabis-related coping among recent veterans in New York City. *Contemporary Drug Problems, 42*(1), 60–76. https://doi.org/10.1177/0091450915570309

Emelianchik-Key, K., Glass, B., & Labarta, A. C. (2023). Teen dating violence: Examining counseling students' responses to gendered vignettes. *The Professional Counselor (Greensboro, N.C.), 13*(2), 98–112. https://doi.org/10.15241/kek.13.2.98

Emezue, C. N., & Udmuangpia, T. (2022). Authentic empathy and the role of victim service providers in (de)stigmatizing male sexual victimization. *Journal of Interpersonal Violence, 37*(7–8), NP3832–NP3855. https://doi.org/10.1177/0886260520948150

Entilli, L., & Cipolletta, S. (2017). When the woman gets violent: The construction of domestic abuse experience from heterosexual men's perspective. *Journal of Clinical Nursing, 26*(15–16), 2328–2341. https://doi.org/10.1111/jocn.13500

Ermer, A. E., Roach, A. L., Coleman, M., & Ganong, L. (2022). Attitudes about forgiveness and leaving a relationship: The context of relationship aggression. *Journal of Interpersonal Violence, 37*(13–14), NP11964–NP11990. https://doi.org/10.1177/0886260521997437

Erdem, G., & Safi, O. A. (2018). The cultural lens approach to Bowen family systems theory: Contributions of family change theory: Bowen family systems and family change. *Journal of Family Theory & Review, 10*(2), 469–483. https://doi.org/10.1111/jftr.12258

Espinoza, R. C., & Warner, D. (2016). Where do we go from here? Examining intimate partner violence by bringing male victims, female perpetrators, and psychological sciences into the fold. Journal of Family Violence, 31(8), 959-966. https://doi.org/10.1007/s10896-016-9881-4

Ess, C. M. (2017). Can we say anything ethical about digital religion? Philosophical and methodological considerations. *New Media & Society, 19*(1), 34–42. https://doi.org/10.1177/1461444816649914

Esterov, D., Yin, Z., Persaud, T., Shan, X., Murphy, M. C., Ehman, R. L., Huston, J., & Brown, A. W. (2024). Association between anatomic and clinical indicators of injury severity after moderate-severe traumatic brain injury: A pilot study using multiparametric magnetic resonance imaging. *Neurotrauma Reports, 5*(1), 232–242. https://doi.org/10.1089/Neur.2023.0122

Ethicist, P. (2018). Practical ethicist: What is "Understandable" language? *Journal of Empirical Research on Human Research Ethics, 13*(4), 368–370. https://doi.org/10.1177/1556264618786589

Evans, M., Malpass, A., Agnew-Davies, R., & Feder, G. (2018). Women's experiences of a randomized controlled trial of a specialist psychological advocacy intervention following domestic violence: A nested qualitative study. *PloS One, 13*(11), e0193077. https://doi.org/10.1371/journal.pone.0193077

Evans-Lacko, S., Aguilar-Gaxiola, S., Al-Hamzawi, A., Alonso, J., Benjet, C., Bruffaerts, R., Chiu, W. T., Florescu, S., de Girolamo, G., Gureje, O., Haro, J. M., He, Y., Hu, C., Karam, E. G., Kawakami, N., Lee, S., Lund, C., Kovess-Masfety, V., Levinson, D., Navarro-Mateu, F., Pennell, B. E., Sampson, N. A., Scott, K. M., Tachimori, H., Ten Have, M., Viana, M. C., Williams, D. R., Wojtyniak, B. J., Zarkov, Z., Kessler, R. C., Chatterji, S., Thornicroft, G. (2018). Socio-economic variations in the mental health treatment gap for people with anxiety, mood, and substance use disorders: results from the WHO World Mental Health (WMH) surveys. *Psychol Med. 2018 Jul, 48*(9), 1560–1571. doi 10.1017/S0033291717003336. Epub 2017 Nov 27. PMID: 29173244; PMCID: PMC6878971.

Everett, J. A. C., Faber, N. S., & Crockett, M. (2015). Preferences and beliefs in ingroup favoritism. *Frontiers in Behavioral Neuroscience, 9*, 15. https://doi.org/10.3389/fnbeh.2015.00015

Expósito-Álvarez, C., Santirso, F. A., Gilchrist, G., Gracia, E., & Lila, M. (2023). Participants in court-mandated intervention programs for intimate partner violence perpetrators with substance use problems: A systematic review of specific risk factors. *Intervención Psicosocial, 32*(2), 89–108. https://doi.org/10.5093/pi2023a7

Ezell, J. M. (2021). *Understanding the situational context for interpersonal violence: A review of individual-level attitudes, attributions, and triggers.* Sage Publications. https://doi.org/10.1177/1524838019869100

Fagerlund, M., Houtsonen, J., Notko, M., & Husso, M. (2022). Conceptualizing violence in close relationships: Discrepancies between police conceptions and the letter of the law in Finland. *European Journal on Criminal Policy and Research, 28*(1), 37–56. https://doi.org/10.1007/s10610-020-09448-1

Falcone, M. A., & Meynen, T. (2019). An investigation of the knowledge of intimate partner violence among clinical staff working with male substance misusers. *Advances in Dual Diagnosis, 12*(3), 105–116. https://doi.org/10.1108/ADD-02-2019-0001

Falgares, G., Marchetti, D., Manna, G., Musso, P., Oasi, O., Kopala-Sibley, D. C., . . . Verrocchio, M. C. (2018). Childhood maltreatment, pathological personality dimensions, and suicide risk in young adults. *Frontiers in Psychology, 9*, 806. https://doi.org/10.3389/2018.00806

Falkenström, E., Ohlsson, J., & Höglund, A. T. (2016). Developing ethical competence in healthcare management. *The Journal of Workplace Learning, 28*(1), 17–32. https://doi.org/10.1108/JWL-04-2015-0033

Fang, X., Zhao, W., Zhang, C. (2020). Methodology for credibility assessment of historical global LUCC datasets. *Sci. China Earth Sci., 63*, 1013–1025. https://doi.org/10.1007/s11430-019-9555-3

Fauchon, C., Faillenot, I., Quesada, C., Meunier, D., Chouchou, F., Garcia-Larrea, L., & Peyron, R. (2019). Brain activity sustains the modulation of pain by empathetic comments. *Scientific Reports, 9*(1), 8398. https://doi.org/10.1038/s41598-019-44879-9

Feyaerts, G., Deguerry, M., Deboosere, P., & De Spiegelaere, M. (2017). Analysis of the decision-support function of policy assessment in real-world policymaking in poverty and social inequalities. Case study on migrant integration policies in the Brussels-capital region. *Environmental Impact Assessment Review, 67*, 40–48. https://doi.org/10.1016/j.eiar.2017.08.007

Fearon, E., Bourne, A., Tenza, S., Palanee-Phillips, T., Kabuti, R., Weatherburn, P., Nutland, W., Kimani, J., & Smith, A. D. (2020). Online socializing among men who have sex with men and transgender people in Nairobi and Johannesburg and implications for public health–related research and health promotion: An analysis of qualitative and respondent-driven sampling survey data. *Journal of the International Aids Society, 23*(S6), 25603. https://doi.org/10.1002/jia2.25603

Feddersen, H., Søndergaard, J., Andersen, L., Munksgaard, B., & Primdahl, J. (2022). Barriers and facilitators for coherent rehabilitation among people with inflammatory arthritis—a qualitative interview study. *BMC Health Services Research, 22*(1), 1–1347. https://doi.org/10.1186/s12913-022-08773-x

Fedina, L., Nam, B., Jun, H., Shah, R., Von Mach, T., Bright, C. L., & DeVylder, J. (2021). Moderating effects of resilience on depression, psychological distress, and suicidal ideation associated with interpersonal violence. *Journal of Interpersonal Violence, 36*(3–4), NP1335–NP1358. https://doi.org/10.1177/0886260517746183

Fedrigo, L., Cerantola, M., Frésard, C. E., & Masdonati, J. (2023). Refugees' meaning of work: A qualitative investigation of work purposes and expectations. *Journal of Career Development, 50*(1), 52–68. https://doi.org/10.1177/08948453211066343

FeldmanHall, O., Dalgleish, T., Evans, D., & Mobbs, D. (2015). Empathic concern drives costly altruism. *NeuroImage, 105*, 347–356. https://doi.org/10.1016/j.neuroimage.2014.10.043

Ferguson, T. (2023). Reflecting on students' reflections: Exploring students' experiences to enhance course delivery. *Qualitative Report, 28*(4), 1193–1209. https://doi.org/10.46743/2160-3715/2023.5868

Fernández, D., Vigo, D., Sampson, N. A., Hwang, I., Aguilar-Gaxiola, S., Al-Hamzawi, A. O., Alonso, J., Andrade, L. H., Bromet, E. J., de Girolamo, G., de Jonge, P., Florescu, S., Gureje, O., Hinkov, H., Hu, C., Karam, E. G., Karam, G., Kawakami, N., Kiejna, A., . . . Haro, J. M. (2021). Patterns of care and dropout rates from outpatient mental healthcare in low-, middle-, and high-income countries from the World Health Organization's World Mental Health Survey Initiative. *Psychological Medicine, 51*(12), 2104–2116. https://doi.org/10.1017/S0033291720000884

Ferreira, J. (2021, 2019). Migrant women victims of intimate partner violence and the criminal justice system in Portugal. *Journal of Interpersonal Violence, 36*(13–14), NP6767–NP6802. https://doi.org/10.1177/0886260518820709

Ferreira, E., Figueiredo, A. S., & Santos, A. (2023). Understanding the emotional impact and coping strategies of professionals working with domestic violence victims. *Social Sciences (Basel), 12*(9), 525. https://doi.org/10.3390/socsci12090525

Ferranti, D., Lorenzo, D., Munoz-Rojas, D., & Gonzalez-Guarda, R. M. (2018). Health education needs of intimate partner violence survivors: Perspectives from female survivors and social service providers. *Public Health Nursing, 35*(2), 118–125. https://doi.org/10.1111/phn.12374

Feyaerts, D., Benner, M., van Cranenbroek, B., van der Heijden, Olivier W. H., Joosten, I., & van der Molen, Renate G. (2017). Human uterine lymphocytes acquire a more experienced and tolerogenic phenotype during pregnancy. *Scientific Reports, 7*(1), 2884–10. https://doi.org/10.1038/s41598-017-03191-0

Field, N. (2018, 2005). In Field N. (Ed.), *Ten lectures on psychotherapy and spirituality (1st ed.)*. Taylor and Francis. https://doi.org/10.4324/9780429480928

Fisher, A. K., Lee, N. Y., Digby, P. K., & Allen, S. C. (2021). BSW students' descriptions of an experiential exercise on intimate partner violence. *Journal of Teaching in Social Work, 41*(3), 290–313. https://doi.org/10.1080/08841233.2021.1926402

Fitzpatrick, S., & Hewett, N. (2018). What works in inclusion health: An overview of effective interventions for marginalized and excluded populations. *The Lancet, 391*(10117), 266–280. https://doi.org/10.1016/S0140-6736(17)31959-1

Flasch, P., Murray, C. E., & Crowe, A. (2017). Overcoming abuse: A phenomenological investigation of the journey to recovery from past intimate partner violence. *Journal of Interpersonal Violence, 32*(22), 3373–3401. https://doi.org/10.1177/0886260515599161

Flasch, P., Fall, K., Stice, B., Easley, R., Murray, C., & Crowe, A. (2019;2020;). Messages to new survivors by longer-term survivors of intimate partner violence. *Journal of Family Violence, 35*(1), 29–41. https://doi.org/10.1007/s10896-019-00078-8

Flasch, P., Fall, K., Stice, B., Easley, R., Murray, C., & Crowe, A. (2020). Messages to new survivors by longer-term survivors of intimate partner violence. *Journal of Family Violence, 35*(1), 29–41. https://doi.org/10.1007/s10896-019-00078-8

References

Fletcher, J. M., Savage, R., & Vaughn, S. (2021). A commentary on Bowers (2020) and the role of phonics instruction in reading. *Educational Psychology Review, 33*(3), 1249–1274. https://doi.org/10.1007/s10648-020-09580-8

Fleischack, A., Macleod, C., & Böhmke, W. (2020). The conundrums of counseling women in violent intimate partner relationships in South Africa: Implications for practice. *International Journal for the Advancement of Counselling, 42*(1), 65–80. https://doi.org/10.1007/s10447-019-09384-8

Flores-Camacho, A. L., Castillo-Verdejo, D. L., & Penagos-Corzo, J. C. (2022). Development and validation of a brief scale of vengeful tendencies (BSVT-11) in a Mexican sample. *Behavioral Sciences, 12*(7), 215. https://doi.org/10.3390/bs12070215

Flynn, K. E., Kliems, H., Saoji, N., Svenson, J., & Cox, E. D. (2018). Content validity of the promise® pediatric family relationships measures for children with chronic illness. *Health and Quality of Life Outcomes, 16*(1), 203. https://doi.org/10.1186/s12955-018-1030-8

Fitzgerald, M. & Freud, S. (2017, 1908). Why did Sigmund Freud refuse to see Pierre Janet? Origins of psychoanalysis: Janet, Freud, or both? *History of Psychiatry, 28*(3), 358–364. https://doi.org/10.1177/0957154X17709747

Field, S., Onah, M., van Heyningen, T., & Honikman, S. (2018). Domestic and intimate partner violence among pregnant women in a low resource setting in South Africa: A facility-based, mixed-methods study. *B.M.C. Women's Health, 18*(1), 119. https://doi.org/10.1186/s12905-018-0612-2

Fong, V. C., Hawes, D., & Allen, J. L. (2017, 2019). A systematic review of risk and protective factors for externalizing problems in children exposed to intimate partner violence. *Trauma, Violence & Abuse, 20*(2), 149–167. https://doi.org/10.1177/1524838017692383

Fisher, A. K., Lee, N. Y., Digby, P. K., & Allen, S. C. (2021). BSW students' descriptions of an experiential exercise on intimate partner violence. *Journal of Teaching in Social Work, 41*(3), 290–313. https://doi.org/10.1080/08841233.2021.1926402

France, E. F., Cunningham, M., Ring, N., Uny, I., Duncan, E. A., Jepson, R. G., Maxwell, M., Roberts, R. J., Turley, R. L., Booth, A., Britten, N., Flemming, K., Gallagher, I., Garside, R., Hannes, K., Lewin, S., Noblit, G. W., Pope, C., Thomas, J., . . . Noyes, J. (2019). Improving reporting of meta-ethnography: The eMERGe reporting guidance. Journal of Advanced Nursing, 75(5), 1126-1139. https://doi.org/10.1111/jan.13809

Frohmader, T. J., Lin, F., & Chaboyer, W. P. (2017). Nurse mentor beliefs in delivering a home-based cardiac rehabilitation program to support patients living in rural areas: An interpretive study. *Nurse Education in Practice, 24,* 77–83. https://doi.org/10.1016/j.nepr.2017.04.002

Forsdike, K., O'Connor, M., Castle, D., & Hegarty, K. (2019). Exploring Australian psychiatrists' and psychiatric trainees' knowledge, attitudes, and preparedness in responding to adults experiencing domestic violence. *Australasian Psychiatry: Bulletin of the Royal Australian and New Zealand College of Psychiatrists, 27*(1), 64–68. https://doi.org/10.1177/1039856218789778

Foster, K. N., & McCloughen, A. J. (2020). Emotionally intelligent strategies students use to manage challenging interactions with patients and families: A qualitative inquiry. *Nurse Education in Practice, 43,* 102743. https://doi.org/10.1016/j.nepr.2020.102743

Foye, U., Stuart, R., Trevillion, K., Oram, S., Allen, D., Broeckelmann, E., Jeffreys, S., Jeynes, T., Crawford, M. J., Moran, P., McNicholas, S., Billings, J., Dale, O., Simpson, A., & Johnson, S. (2022). Clinician views on best practice community care for people with complex emotional needs and how it can be achieved: A qualitative study. *BMC Psychiatry, 22*(1), 72. https://doi.org/10.1186/s12888-022-03711-x

Fox, K. A., Nobles, M. R., & Fisher, B. S. (2016). A multi-theoretical framework to assess gendered stalking victimization: The utility of self-control, social learning, and control balance theories. *Justice Quarterly, 33*(2), 319–347. https://doi.org/10.1080/07418825.2014.902985

Fox, J. M., Reilly, J. L., Kosson, D. S., Brown, A., Hanlon, R. E., & Brook, M. (2020). Differentiating perpetrators of intimate partner violence from other violent offenders using a statistical learning model: The role of cognition and life history variables. *Journal of Interpersonal Violence, 8*(8) 6260520918567–886260520918567. https://doi.org/10.1177/0886260520918567

France, E. F., Cunningham, M., Ring, N., Uny, I., Duncan, E. A., Jepson, R. G., Maxwell, M., Roberts, R. J., Turley, R. L., Booth, A., Britten, N., Flemming, K., Gallagher, I., Garside, R., Hannes, K., Lewin, S., Noblit, G. W., Pope, C., Thomas, J., . . . Noyes, J. (2019). Improving reporting of meta-ethnography: The appear reporting guidance. *Journal of Advanced Nursing, 75*(5), 1126–1139. https://doi.org/10.1111/jan.13809

Franzen, S. R. P., Chandler, C., & Lang, T. (2017). Health research ability development in low and middle-income countries: Reality or rhetoric? A systematic meta-narrative review of the qualitative literature. *BMJ Open, 7*(1), e012332. https://doi.org/10.1136/bmjopen-2016-012332

Frawley, T., Meehan, A., & De Brún, A. (2018). Impact of organizational change for leaders in mental health. *Journal of Health Organization and Management, 32*(8), 980–1001. https://doi.org/10.1108/JHOM-08-2018-0220

Frazer, E., Mitchell, R. A., Nesbitt, L. S., Williams, M., Mitchell, E. P., Williams, R. A., & Browne, D. (2018). The violence epidemic in the African American community: A call by the National Medical Association for comprehensive reform. *Journal of the National Medical Association, 110*(1), 4–15. https://doi.org/10.1016/j.jnma.2017.08.009

Friedman, V. J., Arieli, D., & Aboud-Armali, O. (2018). Facilitating emotional reappraisal in conflict transformation. *Conflict Resolution Quarterly, 35*(4), 351–366. https://doi.org/10.1002/crq.21210

Fridberg, H., Wallin, L., Tistad, M., Sahlgrenska akademin, Göteborgs universities, Gothenburg University, Institution för vårdvetenskap och hälsa, Institute of Health and Care Sciences, & Sahlgrenska Academy. (2021). The innovation characteristics of person-centered care as perceived by healthcare professionals: An interview study employing a deductive-inductive content analysis guided by the joined framework for implementation research. *BMC Health Services Research, 21*(1), 1–904. https://doi.org/10.1186/s12913-021-06942-y

Frohmader, T. J., Lin, F., & Chaboyer, W. P. (2017). Nurse mentor beliefs in delivering a home-based cardiac rehabilitation program to support patients living in rural areas: An interpretive study. *Nurse Education in Practice, 24*, 77–83. https://doi.org/10.1016/j.nepr.2017.04.002

Furtak, E. M., & Penuel, W. R. (2019). Coming to terms: Addressing the persistence of "hands-on" and other reform terminology in the era of science as practice. *Science Education, 103*(1), 167–186. https://doi.org/10.1002/sce.21488

Fu, S., Chang, P. L., Friesen, M. L., Teakle, N. L., Tarone, A. M., & Sze, S. (2019). Naming similar transcripts in a related organism from de Bruijn graphs of RNA-seq data, with applications to studying salt and waterlogging tolerance in melilotus. *BMC Genomics, 20*(Suppl 5), 425. https://doi.org/10.1186/s12864-019-5702-5

Gabbay, N., & Lafontaine, M. (2017). Understanding the relationship between attachment, caregiving, and same-sex intimate partner violence. *Journal of Family Violence, 32*(3), 291–304. https://doi.org/10.1007/s10896-016-9897-9

Gage, A. N., & Lease, S. H. (2021, 2018). An exploration of the link between masculinity and endorsement of IPV myths in American men. *Journal of Interpersonal Violence, 36*(13–14), 6145–6165. https://doi.org/10.1177/0886260518818430

Galan-Cisneros, P. A., Hildebrandt, E. J., Vasquez, J., & Gomez, R. J. (2023). The new normal that never happened: Faculty and students navigating through a collective and shared trauma. *Reflections: Narratives of Professional Helping, 29*(1), 8–25.

Galasinski, D. (2017). Discourses of men's suicide notes: A qualitative analysis. *Bloomsbury Academic.* https://doi.org/10.5040/9781350005761

Gallese, V. & Goldman, A. Mirror neurons and the simulation theory of mind-reading. (1998). *Trends Cognit. Sci. 2,* 493–501. https://doi.org/10.1016/S1364-6613(98)01262-5.

Galletly, C., Clark, L., McFarlane, A., Searle, A., Sawyer, M., Sim, M., Baghurst, P., & van Hooff, M. (2016). A longitudinal cohort study includes childhood lead exposure, childhood trauma, substance use, and subclinical psychotic experiences. *Psychiatry Research, 239,* 54–61. https://doi.org/10.1016/j.psychres.2016.02.066

Gangos, C. J., Nega, C., & Apergi, F. (2019). Adaptation and psychometric evaluation of the children's knowledge of abuse questionnaire (CKAQ-RIII) in Greek elementary school children. *Journal of Child Sexual Abuse, 28*(2), 222–239. https://doi.org/10.1080/10538712.2018.1538175

Garland, T. S., Policastro, C., Branch, K. A., & Henderson, B. B. (2019). Bruised and battered: Reinforcing intimate partner violence in comic books. *Feminist Criminology, 14*(5), 584–611. https://doi.org/10.1177/1557085118772093

Garraway, C. (2023). A time for reflection: Exploring the unique feelings and experiences of black patients with mental health issues at the end of life. *CANNT Journal, 33*(1), 142.

Gashaw, B. T., Schei, B., Solbraekke, K. N., & Magnus, J. H. (2020). Ethiopian health care workers' insights into and responses to intimate partner violence in pregnancy—A qualitative study. *International Journal of Environmental Research and Public Health, 17*(10), 3745. https://doi.org/10.3390/ijerph17103745

Gateri, A. M., Ondicho, T. G., Karimi, E., & Department of Community Medicine and Global Health, University of Oslo. (2021). Correlates of domestic violence against men: Qualitative insights from Kenya. *African Journal of Gender, Society & Development, 10*(3), 87–111. https://doi.org/10.31920/2634-3622/2021/v10n3a5

Geddes, A., Parker, C., & Scott, S. (2018). When the snowball does not roll and the use of 'horizontal' networking in qualitative social research. *International Journal of Social Research Methodology, 21*(3), 347–358. https://doi.org/10.1080/13645579.2017.1406219

Gellini, H., & Marczak, M. (2022). Evaluation of service providers' experiences and views on the mental health and wellbeing services for Syrian refugees in Warwickshire. *Clinical Psychology Forum (Leicester, England: 2005), 1*(355), 39–46. https://doi.org/10.53841/bpscpf.2022.1.355.39

Gentles, S. J., Charles, C., Ploeg, J., & McKibbon, K. A. (2015). Sampling in Qualitative Research: Insights from an Overview of the Methods Literature. *The Qualitative Report, 20*(11), 1772–1789. http://library.capella.edu/login?qurl=https%3A%2F%2Fwww.proquest.com%2Fscholarlyjournals%2Fsampling-qualitative-research-insights-overview%2Fdocview%2F1750038029%2Fse-2%3Faccountid%3D27965

Geoffrion, S., Morselli, C., & Guay, S. (2016). Rethinking compassion fatigue through the lens of professional identity: The case of child-protection workers. *Trauma, Violence & Abuse, 17*(3), 270–283. https://doi.org/10.1177/1524838015584362

Gerhardt, U., Breitschwerdt, R., & Thomas, O. (2017). Engineering sustainable mental health: The role of action research. *AI & Society, 32*(3), 339–357. https://doi.org/10.1007/s00146-015-0640-5

References

Gewirtz-Meydan, A., & Finzi-Dottan, R. (2021). Psychological abuse as a mediator between insecure attachment orientations and relationship satisfaction. *Family Relations, 70*(2), 498–513. https://doi.org/10.1111/fare.12490

Gezinski, L. B. (2022). "It's kind of hit and miss with them": A qualitative investigation of police response to intimate partner violence in a mandatory arrest state. *Journal of Family Violence, 37*(1), 99–111. https://doi.org/10.1007/s10896-020-00227-4

Gheyoh Ndzi, E., & Holmes, A. (2022). Examining the relationship between paternal mental health and informal support networks: Reflections on the impact of the COVID-19 pandemic. *International Journal of Environmental Research and Public Health, 19*(19), 12751. https://doi.org/10.3390/ijerph191912751

Giardino, E. R., & Hickey, J. V. (2020). Doctor of Nursing Practice Students' Perceptions of professional change through the DNP program. *Journal of Professional Nursing, 36*(6), 595–603. https://doi.org/10.1016/j.profnurs.2020.08.012

Giandinoto, J., & Edward, K. (2015). The phenomenon of co-morbid physical and mental illness in acute medical care: The lived experience of Australian health professionals. *B.M.C. Research Notes, 8*(1), 295. https://doi.org/10.1186/s13104-015-1264-z

Giannuzzi, V., Felisi, M., Bonifazi, D., Devlieger, H., Papanikolaou, G., Ragab, L., Fattoum, S., Tempesta, B., Reggiardo, G., & Ceci, A. (2021). Ethical and procedural issues for applying researcher-driven multi-national pediatric clinical trials in and outside the European Union: The challenging experience of the deep project. *B.M.C. Medical Ethics, 22*(1), 49. https://doi.org/10.1186/s12910-021-00618-2

Giannetta, N., Villa, G., Pennestrì, F., Sala, R., Mordacci, R., & Manara, D. F. (2021). Ethical problems and moral distress in primary care: A scoping review. *International Journal of Environmental Research and Public Health, 18*(14), 7565. https://doi.org/10.3390/ijerph18147565

Gibbs, A., Dunkle, K., & Jewkes, R. (2018). Emotional and economic intimate partner violence as critical drivers of depression and suicidal ideation: A cross-sectional study among young women in South Africa's informal settlements. *PloS One, 13*(4). https://doi.org/10.1371/journal.pone.0194885

Gibson, C., Callands, T. A., Magriples, U., Divney, A., & Kershaw, T. (2015). Intimate partner violence, power, and equity among adolescent parents: Relation to child outcomes and parenting. *Maternal and Child Health Journal, 19*(1), 188-195. https://doi.org/10.1007/s10995-014-1509-9

Gibson, C. B. (2017). Elaboration, generalization, triangulation, and interpretation: Enhancing the value of mixed method research. *Organizational Research Methods, 20*(2), 193–223. https://doi.org/10.1177/1094428116639133

Gies, S. V., Healy, E., Green, B., & Bobnis, A. (2020). From villain to victim. *Criminology & Public Policy, 19*(2), 389–408. https://doi.org/10.1111/1745-9133.12497

Gilbert, A. W., Jones, J., Stokes, M., & May, C. R. (2021). A qualitative study is the factors influencing patient preferences for virtual consultations in an orthopedic rehabilitation setting. *B.M.J. Open, 11*(2), e041038. https://doi.org/10.1136/bmjopen-2020-041038

Gilchrist, G., Munoz, J. T., & Easton, C. J. (2015). Should we reconsider anger management when addressing physical intimate partner violence perpetration by alcohol-abusing males? A systematic review. *Aggression and Violent Behavior, 25*, 124–132. https://doi.org/10.1016/j.avb.2015.07.008

Gill, C., Campbell, M. A., & Ballucci, D. (2021). Police officers' definitions and understandings of intimate partner violence in New Brunswick, Canada. *Police Journal, 94*(1), 20–39. https://doi.org/10.1177/0032258X19876974

Giorgi, A. (1997). The phenomenological method's theory, practice, and evaluation as a qualitative research procedure. *Journal of*

Phenomenological Psychology, 28(2), 235–260. https://doi.org/10.1163/156916297X00103

Gillum, T. L., Doucette, M., Mwanza, M., & Munala, L. (2018). Exploring Kenyan Women's Perceptions of intimate partner violence. *Journal of Interpersonal Violence, 33*(13), 2130–2154. https://doi.org/10.1177/0886260515622842

Gilmore, A. K., & Flanagan, J. C. (2019, 2020). Acute mental health symptoms among individuals receiving a sexual assault medical forensic exam: The role of earlier intimate partner violence victimization. *Archives of Women's Mental Health, 23*(1), 81–89. https://doi.org/10.1007/s00737-019-0947-1

Giorgi, A. (1997). The phenomenological method's theory, practice, and evaluation as a qualitative research procedure. *Journal of Phenomenological Psychology, 28*(2), 235–260. doi:10.1163/156916297X00103

Giorgi, A. (2009). *The Descriptive Phenomenological Method in Psychology: A Modified Husserlian Approach.* Duquesne University.

Giordano, P. C. (2022). Some cognitive transformations about the dynamics of resistance. *Criminology & Public Policy, 21*(4), 787–809. https://doi.org/10.1111/1745-9133.12609

Girme, Y. U., Overall, N. C., Simpson, J. A., & Fletcher, G. J. O. (2015). "All or nothing": Attachment avoidance and the curvilinear effects of partner support. *Journal of Personality and Social Psychology, 108*(3), 450–475. https://doi.org/10.1037/a0038866

Gizaw, A. A., Bygstad, B., & Nielsen, P. (2017). Open gentrification. *Information Systems Journal, 27*(5), 619–642. https://doi.org/10.1111/isj.12112

Godfrey, D. A., Kehoe, C. M., Bastardas-Albero, A., & Babcock, J. C. (2020). Empathy mediates the relations between working memory and the perpetration of intimate partner violence and aggression. *Behavioral Sciences, 10*(3), 63. https://doi.org/10.3390/bs10030063

Gogo, S., & Musonda, I. (2022). Using the exploratory sequential approach in mixed-method research: A case of contextual top leadership interventions in construction H&S. *International Journal of Environmental Research and Public Health, 19*(12), 7276. https://doi.org/10.3390/ijerph19127276

Goldenberg, A. J., Maschke, K. J., Joffe, S., Botkin, J. R., Rothwell, E., Murray, T. H., Anderson, R., Deming, N., Rosenthal, B. F., & Rivera, S. M. (2015). I.R.B. practices and policies about the secondary research use of biospecimens. *B.M.C. Medical Ethics, 16*(1), 32. https://doi.org/10.1186/s12910-015-0020-1

Gölge, Z. B., Özgeldi, E. B., & Akdemir, S. (2021). Female perpetrators of sexual abuse. *Psikiyatride Güncel Yaklaşimlar, 13*(3), 524–536. https://doi.org/10.18863/pgy.822224

Gone, J. P., & Kirmayer, L. J. (2020). Advancing indigenous mental health research: Ethical, conceptual and methodological challenges. *Transcultural Psychiatry, 57*(2), 235–249. https://doi.org/10.1177/1363461520923151

Gonzalez, M. M. (2016). The Coding Manual for Qualitative Research: A Review. *The Qualitative Report, 21*(8), 1546–1548. https://doi.org/10.46743/2160-3715/2016.2561

Goodman, S., & Walker, K. (2016). 'Some I do not remember and some I do': Memory talk in intimate partner violence accounts. *Discourse Studies, 18*(4), 375–392. https://doi.org/10.1177/1461445616647884

Goodman-Scott, E., Carlisle, R., Clark, M., & Burgess, M. (2017, 2016). A powerful tool: A phenomenological study of school counselors' experiences with social stories. *Professional School Counseling, 20*(1), 25–35. https://doi.org/10.5330/1096-2409-20.1.25

Goodman, L. A., Bennett Cattaneo, L., Thomas, K., Woulfe, J., Chong, S. K., & Fels Smyth, K. (2015). Advancing domestic violence program evaluation: Development and validation of the measure of victim empowerment related to safety (movers). *Psychology of Violence, 5*(4), 355–366. https://doi.org/10.1037/a0038318

Goodson, A., & Hayes, B. E. (2021). Help-seeking behaviors of intimate partner violence victims: A cross-national analysis in developing nations. *Journal of Interpersonal Violence, 36*(9–10), NP4705–NP4727. https://doi.org/10.1177/0886260518794508

Good, M. & Willoughby, T. (2008). Adolescence is a sensitive period for spiritual development. *Child Development Perspectives, 2*(1), 32–37.

Gou, L. H., & Woodin, E. M. (2017). Relationship dissatisfaction as a mediator for the link between attachment insecurity and psychological aggression over the transition to parenthood. *Couple and Family Psychology, 6*(1), 1–17. https://doi.org/10.1037/cfp0000072

Gouvêa Maciel, G., Magalhães, P. C., de Sousa, L., Pinto, I. R., & Clemente, F. (2022). A scoping review on perception-based definitions and measurements of corruption. *Public Integrity, ahead-of-print*(ahead-of-print), 1–18. https://doi.org/10.1080/10999922.2022.2115235

Gracia, E., Martín-Fernández, M., Lila, M., Merlo, J., & Ivert, A. (2019). Prevalence of intimate partner violence against women in Sweden and Spain: A psychometric study of the 'Nordic paradox'. *PloS One, 14*(5), e0217015. https://doi.org/10.1371/journal.pone.0217015

Graham-Bermann, S. A., Cater, Å. K., Miller-Graff, L. E., & Howell, K. H. (2017). Adults' explanations for intimate partner violence during childhood and associated effects. *Journal of Clinical Psychology, 73*(6), 652–668. https://doi.org/10.1002/jclp.22345

Granja, C., Janssen, W., & Johansen, M. A. (2018). Factors deciding the success and failure of eHealth interventions: Systematic literature review. *Journal of Medical Internet Research, 20*(5), e10235. https://doi.org/10.2196/10235

Grandgenett, H. M., Steel, A. L., Brock, R. L., & DiLillo, D. (2022). Responding to the disclosure of sexual assault: The potential impact of victimization history and rape myth acceptance. *Journal of Interpersonal Violence, 37*(5–6), 2102–2125. https://doi.org/10.1177/0886260519898429

Gray, C., & Baisden, P. (2020). Interprofessional education for group processes in Mental/Behavioral health. *Therapeutic Recreation Journal, 54*(4), 436–452. https://doi.org/10.18666/TRJ-2020-V54-I4-10421

Grady, M. D., Levenson, J. S., & Bolder, T. (2017). Linking adverse childhood effects and attachment: A theory of etiology for sexual offending. *Trauma, Violence, & Abuse, 18*(4), 433–444. https://doi.org/10.1177/1524838015627147

Greenberg, L. S. (2021). Empathic attunement to affect. *American Psychological Association,* 115–142. https://doi.org/10.1037/0000248-006

Greene, M. C., Heise, L., Musci, R. J., Wirtz, A. L., Johnson, R., Leoutsakos, J., Wainberg, M. L., & Tol, W. A. (2021). Improving estimation of the association between alcohol use and intimate partner violence in low-income and middle-income countries. *Injury Prevention, 27*(3), 221–226. https://doi.org/10.1136/injuryprev-2019-043433

Greenman, S. J., & Matsuda, M. (2016). From early dating violence to adult intimate partner violence: Continuity and sources of resilience in adulthood. *Criminal Behaviour and Mental Health, 26*(4), 293–303. https://doi.org/10.1002/cbm.2012

Gregory, K. (2019). Lessons of a failed study: Lone research, media analysis, and bracketing limitations. *International Journal of Qualitative Methods, 18,* 160940691984245. https://doi.org/10.1177/1609406919842450

Gregory, A., Johnson, E., Feder, G., Campbell, J., Konya, J., & Perôt, C. (2022). Feelings of peer support for victim-survivors of sexual violence and abuse: An exploratory study with key stakeholders. *Journal of Interpersonal Violence, 37*(15–16), NP14036–NP14065. https://doi.org/10.1177/08862605211007931

Greshilova, I. A., Kimova, S. Z., & Dambaeva, B. B. (2020). Designing the professional development model of teachers considers the axiological imperatives of continuing education. *Euromentor Journal, 11*(1), 101–125.

Griffiths, J., Lever Taylor, B., Morant, N., Bick, D., Howard, L. M., Seneviratne, G., & Johnson, S. (2019). A qualitative comparison of experiences of specialist mother and baby units versus general psychiatric wards. *BMC Psychiatry, 19*(1), 401. https://doi.org/10.1186/s12888-019-2389-8

Guček, N. K., Selič, P., Nena K. G. & Polina S. (2018). Depression in intimate partner violence victims in Slovenia: A crippling pattern of factors found in family practice attendees. *International Journal of Environmental Research and Public Health, 15*(2), 210. https://doi.org/10.3390/ijerph15020210

Guest, G., Namey, E., & Chen, M. (2020). A simple method to assess and report thematic saturation in qualitative research. *PloS One, 15*(5), e0232076. https://doi.org/10.1371/journal.pone.0232076

Guerrero, M., MD. (2016). Firearm ownership and suicide rates among US men and women, 1981–2013. *The Journal of Emergency Medicine, 51*(3), 342. https://doi.org/10.1016/j.jemermed.2016.07.027

Gumz, A., Neubauer, K., Horstkotte, J. K., Geyer, M., Löwe, B., Murray, A. M., & Kästner, D. (2017). A bottom-up approach to assess verbal therapeutic techniques. Development of the psychodynamic interventions list (PIL). *PloS One, 12*(8), e0182949. https://doi.org/10.1371/journal.pone.0182949

Gunbayi, I. (2005). Women and men teachers' approach to leadership styles. Social Behavior & Personality: *An International Journal, 33*(7), 685–698.

Gunn, A., & Miranda Samuels, G. (2020). Promoting recovery identities among mothers with histories of addiction: Strategies of family engagement. *Family Process, 59*(1), 94–110. https://doi.org/10.1111/famp.12413

Gupta, J., & Reed, E. A. (2019). Economic and social empowerment to reduce global intimate partner violence: Disentangling the pathways. *The Lancet Global Health, 7*(10), e1304–e1305. https://doi.org/10.1016/S2214-109X(19)30372-9

Guruge, S., Ford-Gilboe, M., Varcoe, C., Jayasuriya-Illesinghe, V., Ganesan, M., Sivayogan, S., Kanthasamy, P., Shanmugalingam, P., & Vithanarachchi, H. (2017). Intimate partner violence in the postwar context: Women's experiences and community leaders' feelings in the eastern province of Sri Lanka. *PloS One, 12*(3), e0174801. https://doi.org/10.1371/journal.pone.0174801

Gutenbrunner, C., Salmon, K., & Jose, P. E. (2017, 2018). Do overgeneral autobiographical memories predict increased psychopathological symptoms in community youth? A 3-year longitudinal investigation. *Journal of Abnormal Child Psychology, 46*(2), 197–208. https://doi.org/10.1007/s10802-017-0278-5

Guzmán-González, M., Lafontaine, M., & Levesque, C. (2016). Romantic attachment and physical intimate partner violence perpetration in a Chilean sample: The mediating role of emotion regulation difficulties. *Violence and Victims, 31*(5), 854–868. https://doi.org/10.1891/0886-6708.VV-D-14-00114

Haas, Y. (2019). Developing a generic retail business model—a qualitative comparative study. *International Journal of Retail & Distribution Management, 47*(10), 1029–1056. https://doi.org/10.1108/IJRDM-10-2018-0234

Hägg-Martinell, A., Hult, H., Henriksson, P., & Kiessling, A. (2017). Medical students' opportunities to take part and learn from activities at an internal medicine ward: An ethnographic study. *B.M.J. Open, 7*(2), e013046. https://doi.org/10.1136/bmjopen-2016-013046

References

Hailemariam, M., Zlotnick, C., Taft, A., & Johnson, J. E. (2022). MOSAIC (Mothers' Advocates in the Community) for pregnant women and mothers of children under 5 with experience of intimate partner violence: A pilot randomized trial study protocol. *PloS One, 17*(5), e0267679. https://doi.org/10.1371/journal.pone.0267679

Håland, K., Lundgren, I., Lidén, E., Eri, T. S., Sahlgrenska akademin, Göteborgs universitet, Gothenburg University, Institutionen för vårdvetenskap och hälsa, Institute of Health and Care Sciences, & Sahlgrenska Academy. (2016). Fathers' experiences of being in change during pregnancy and early parenthood in a context of intimate partner violence. *International Journal of Qualitative Studies on Health and Well-being, 11*(1), 30935–10. https://doi.org/10.3402/qhw.v11.30935

Hall, C. M., Northam, H., Webster, A., & Strickland, K. (2022). Determinants of seasonal influenza vaccination hesitancy among healthcare personnel: An integrative review. *Journal of Clinical Nursing, 31*(15–16), 2112–2124. https://doi.org/10.1111/jocn.16103

Hall, J. A., Schwartz, R., & Duong, F. (2021). How do lay people define empathy? *The Journal of Social Psychology, 161*(1), 5–24. https://doi.org/10.1080/00224545.2020.1796567

Halford, W. K., & Pepping, C. A. (2019). What every therapist needs to know about couple therapy. *Behavior Change, 36*(3), 121–142. https://doi.org/10.1017/bec.2019.12

Hamadani, J. D., Hasan, M. I., Baldi, A. J., Hossain, S. J., Shiraji, S., Bhuiyan, M. S. A., Mehrin, S. F., Fisher, J., Tofail, F., Tipu, S M Mulk Uddin, Grantham-McGregor, S., Biggs, B., Braat, S., & Pasricha, S. (2020). Immediate impact of stay-at-home orders to control COVID-19 transmission on socioeconomic conditions, food insecurity, mental health, and intimate partner violence in Bangladeshi women and their families: An interrupted time series. *The Lancet Global Health, 8*(11), e1380–e1389. https://doi.org/10.1016/S2214-109X(20)30366-1

Hamberger, L. K., Barry, C., & Franco, Z. (2019). Implementing trauma-informed care in primary medical settings: Evidence-based rationale and approaches. *Journal of Aggression, Maltreatment & Trauma, 28*(4), 425–444. https://doi.org/10.1080/10926771.2019.1572399

Hamdani, S. U., Huma, Z., Suleman, N., Warraitch, A., Muzzafar, N., Farzeen, M., Minhas, F. A., Rahman, A., & Wissow, L. S. (2021). Scaling-up school mental health services in low resource public schools of rural Pakistan: The theory of change (ToC) approach. *International Journal of Mental Health Systems, 15*(1), 8. https://doi.org/10.1186/s13033-021-00435-5

Hamel, J., Cannon, C., Buttell, F., & Ferreira, R. (2020). A survey of IPV perpetrator treatment providers: Ready for evidence-based practice? *Partner Abuse, 11*(4), 387–414. https://doi.org/10.1891/PA-2020-0024

Hamm, L. M., Boluk, K. A., Black, J. M., Dai, S., & Thompson, B. (2019). The phenomenological approach to childhood cataract treatment in New Zealand using semi-structured interviews: How might we improve care provision. *B.M.J. Open, 9*(1), e024869. https://doi.org/10.1136/bmjopen-2018-024869

Hamp, A., Stamm, K., Lin, L., & Christidis, P. (2016). 2015 A.P.A. Survey of Psychology Health Service Providers: American Psychological Association Center for Workforce Studies. Retrieved from https://www.apa.org/workforce/data-tools/index.

Hannes, K., Heyvaert, M., Slegers, K., Vandenbrande, S., & Van Nuland, M. (2015). Exploring the potential for a combined standard for reporting guidelines for qualitative research: An argument Delphi approach. *International Journal of Qualitative Methods, 14*(4), 160940691561152. https://doi.org/10.1177/1609406915611528

Hardacker, C. T., Baccellieri, A., Mueller, E. R., Brubaker, L., Hutchins, G., Zhang, J. L. Y., & Hebert-Beirne, J. (2019). Bladder health experiences, feelings, and knowledge of sexual and gender minorities. *International Journal of Environmental Research and Public Health, 16*(17), 3170. https://doi.org/10.3390/ijerph1617317

Hardesty, J. L., & Ogolsky, B. G. (2020). A socio-ecological perspective on intimate partner violence research: A decade in review. *Journal of Marriage and Family, 82*(1), 454–477. https://doi.org/10.1111/jomf.12652

Hardesty, J. L., Haselschwerdt, M. L., & Crossman, K. A. (2019). Qualitative research on interpersonal violence: Guidance for early-career scholars. *Journal of Interpersonal Violence, 34*(23–24), 4794–4816. https://doi.org/10.1177/0886260519871532

Hardie, P., Darley, A., Langan, L., Lafferty, A., Jarvis, S., & Redmond, C. (2022). Interpersonal and communication skills development in general nursing preceptorship education and training programs: A scoping review. *Nurse Education in Practice, 65*, 103482. https://doi.org/10.1016/j.nepr.2022.103482

Hardin, H. K., Bender, A. E., Hermann, C. P., & Speck, B. J. (2021). An integrative review of adolescent trust in the healthcare provider relationship. *Journal of Advanced Nursing, 77*(4), 1645–1655. https://doi.org/10.1111/jan.14674

Harris, E. (2023). CDC report: Health worker mental health crisis continued in 2022. *JAMA: The Journal of the American Medical Association, 330*(20), 1945. https://doi.org/10.1001/jama.2023.21869

Harris, E. G., Fleming, D. E., & Dapko, J. L. (2021). A holistic examination of the antecedents and outcomes of frontline employee job resourcefulness. *Journal of Managerial Issues, 33*(2), 174–190.

Harrison, L., & Clark, L. (2016). Contemporary social justice issues: A focus on race and physical education in the United States. *Research Quarterly for Exercise and Sport, 87*(3), 230–241. https://doi.org/10.1080/02701367.2016.1199166

Harrits, G. S., & Møller, M. Ø. (2021). Qualitative vignette experiments: A mixed methods design. *Journal of Mixed Methods Research, 15*(4), 526–545. https://doi.org/10.1177/1558689820977607

Hartmann, H., Rütgen, M., Riva, F., & Lamm, C. (2021). Another's pain in my brain: No evidence that placebo analgesia affects the sensory-discriminative part in empathy for pain. *NeuroImage (Orlando, Fla.), 224*, 117397. https://doi.org/10.1016/j.neuroimage.2020.117397

Harkness, E. F., & Bower, P. J. (2009). On-site mental health workers delivering psychological therapy and psychosocial interventions to patients in primary care: Effects on the professional practice of primary care providers. *Cochrane Database of Systematic Reviews, 2009*(1), CD000532. https://doi.org/10.1002/14651858.CD000532.pub2

Hart, D., & Baruch, Y. (2022). The dynamics of diplomatic careers: The shift from traditional to contemporary careers. *Human Resource Management, 61*(2), 259–276. https://doi.org/10.1002/hrm.22092

Harvey, S., Lees, S., Mshana, G., Pilger, D., Hansen, C., Kapiga, S., & Watts, C. (2018). A cluster randomized controlled trial to assess the impact on intimate partner violence of a 10-session participatory gender training curriculum delivered to women taking part in a group-based microfinance loan scheme in Tanzania: Study protocol. *B.M.C. Women's Health, 18*(1), 55–55. https://doi.org/10.1186/s12905-018-0546-8

Hash, K. M., Poole, J., Floyd, M., Moore, C. D., Rogers, A. T., & Tower, L. E. (2017). Innovative experiential learning activities in aging: The experiences of four B.E.L. projects. *Journal of Teaching in Social Work, 37*(2), 156–170. https://doi.org/10.1080/08841233.2017.1300207

Hasking, P. A., Lewis, S. P., Robinson, K., Heath, N. L., & Wilson, M. S. (2019). Researching nonsuicidal self-injury in schools: Ethical considerations and recommendations. *School Psychology International, 40*(3), 217–234. https://doi.org/10.1177/0143034319827056

References

Hassani, P., Abdi, A., Jalali, R., & Salari, N. (2016). Use of intuition by critical care nurses: A phenomenological study. *Advances in Medical Education and Practice, 7*(1), 65–71. https://doi.org/10.2147/AMEP.S100324

Hattingh, H. L., Emmerton, L., Ng Cheong Tin, P., & Green, C. (2016;2015). Use of community pharmacy space to enhance privacy: A qualitative study. Health Expectations: *An International Journal of Public Participation in Health Care and Health Policy, 19*(5), 1098–1110. https://doi.org/10.1111/hex.12401

Hawgood, J., Ownsworth, T., Kõlves, K., Spence, S. H., Arensman, E., & De Leo, D. (2022). Impact of systematic tailored assessment for responding to suicidality (STARS) protocol training on mental health professionals' attitudes, perceived capabilities, knowledge, and reluctance to intervene. *Frontiers in Psychiatry, 12*, 827060. https://doi.org/10.3389/fpsyt.2021.827060

Hayes, B., Hassed, S., Chaloner, J. L., & Guy, C. (2016). Duchenne muscular dystrophy: A survey of perspectives on carrier testing and communication within the family. *Journal of Genetic Counseling, 25*(3), 443–453. https:/www.doi.org/10.1007/s10897-015-9898-5

Heard, C. P. (2023). Spirituality and occupation in living (SOiL) model: Conceptualizing occupational performance through the lens of spirituality. *The Open Journal of Occupational Therapy, 11*(3), 1–17. https://doi.org/10.15453/2168-6408.2081

Heard, E., Mutch, A., & Fitzgerald, L. (2020;2017;). *Using applied theater in primary, secondary, and tertiary prevention of intimate partner violence: A systematic review*. Sage. https://doi.org/10.1177/1524838017750157

Helou, A., Stewart, K., Ryan, K., & George, J. (2021). Pregnant women's experiences with managing hypertensive disorders of pregnancy: A qualitative study. *BMC Health Services Research, 21*(1), 1–1292. https://doi.org/10.1186/s12913-021-07320-4

Helms, C., Gardner, A., & McInnes, E. (2017). Consensus on an Australian nurse practitioner specialty framework using Delphi method: Results from the brilliant 2 study. *Journal of Advanced Nursing, 73*(2), 433–447. https://doi.org/10.1111/jan.13109

Hellemans, S., Loeys, T., Buysse, A., & De Smet, O. (2015). Prevalence and impact of intimate partner violence (IPV) among an ethnic minority population. *Journal of Interpersonal Violence, 30*(19), 3389–3418. https://doi.org/10.1177/0886260514563830

Heng, T. T. (2020). Examining the role of theory in qualitative research: A literature review of studies on Chinese international students in higher education. *Journal of International Students, 10*(4), 798–816. https://doi.org/10.32674/jis.v10i4.1571

Hennink, M. M., Kaiser, B. N., & Marconi, V. C. (2017;2016;). Code saturation versus meaning saturation: How many interviews are enough? *Qualitative Health Research, 27*(4), 591–608. https://doi.org/10.1177/1049732316665344

Henry, N., Gavey, N., & Johnson, K. (2023). Image-based sexual abuse as a means of coercive control: Victim-survivor experiences. *Violence Against Women, 29*(6–7), 1206–1226. https://doi.org/10.1177/10778012221114918

Heim, E., Kohrt, B. A., Koschorke, M., Milenova, M., & Thornicroft, G. (2018). Reducing mental health-related stigma in primary health care settings in low- and middle-income countries: A systematic review. *Epidemiology and Psychiatric Sciences, 29*, e3. https://doi.org/10.1017/S2045796018000458

Heim, E., Henderson, C., Kohrt, B. A., Koschorke, M., Milenova, M., & Thornicroft, G. (2019). Reducing mental health-related stigma among medical and nursing students in low- and middle-income countries: A systematic review. *Epidemiology and Psychiatric Sciences, 29*, e28. https://doi.org/10.1017/S2045796019000167

Hemmings, L., Heneghan, N. R., Byrd, E., Stubbs, B., & Soundy, A. (2022). Healthcare professionals' feelings and experiences of physiotherapy for people with mental illness: A protocol for a systematic review and meta-ethnography. *BMJ Open, 12*(8), e061227. https://doi.org/10.1136/bmjopen-2022-061227

Herbitter, C., Vaughan, M. D., & Pantalone, D. W. (2021). Mental health provider bias and clinical competence in addressing asexuality, consensual non-monogamy, and BDSM: A narrative review. *Sexual and Relationship Therapy, ahead-of-print*(ahead-of-print), 1–24. https://doi.org/10.1080/14681994.2021.1969547

Herlihy, B., & Corey, G. (2006). *A.C.A. ethical standards case book*. American Counseling Association.

Heron, R. L., Eisma, M. C., & Browne, K. (2022). Barriers and facilitators of showing domestic violence to the UK health service. *Journal of Family Violence, 37*(3), 533–543. https://doi.org/10.1007/s10896-020-00236-3

Heron, R. L., & Eisma, M. C. (2021). Barriers and facilitators of showing domestic violence to the healthcare service: A systematic review of qualitative research. *Health & Social Care in the Community, 29*(3), 612–630. https://doi.org/10.1111/hsc.13282

Herrman, J. W., Palen, L., Kan, M., Feinberg, M., Hill, J., Magee, E., & Haigh, K. M. (2019). Young mothers' and fathers' beliefs of relationship violence: A focus group study. *Violence Against Women, 25*(3), 274–296. https://doi.org/10.1177/1077801218780356

Hesse, C. A., Strauss, C., Shorey, R. C., Stuart, G. L., & Cornelius, T. L. (2021). Examination of the transient changes in effect resulting from participation in research addressing intimate partner violence. *Journal of Interpersonal Violence, 36*(9–10), NP5014–NP5032. https://doi.org/10.1177/0886260518795172

Heywood, I., Sammut, D., & Bradbury-Jones, C. (2019). A qualitative exploration of 'survivorship among women who have experienced domestic violence and abuse: Developing a new model. *B.M.C. Women's Health, 19*(1), 106. https://doi.org/10.1186/s12905-019-0789-z

Higginbottom, G. M., Safipour, J., Yohani, S., O'Brien, B., Mumtaz, Z., Paton, P., Chiu, Y., & Barolia, R. (2016). An ethnographic investigation of the maternity healthcare experience of immigrants in rural and urban Alberta, Canada. *BMC Pregnancy and Childbirth, 16*(1), 20. https://doi.org/10.1186/s12884-015-0773-z

Higgins, T. C., O'Malley, A. S., & Keith, R. E. (2021). Exploring and overcoming the challenges primary care practices face with care management of high-risk patients in CPC+: A mixed-methods study. *Journal of General Internal Medicine: JGIM, 36*(10), 3008–3014. https://doi.org/10.1007/s11606-020-06528-0

Hill, G., & Kemp, S. M. (2018). Uh-oh! What have we missed? A qualitative investigation into everyday insight experience. *The Journal of Creative Behavior, 52*(3), 201–211. https://doi.org/10.1002/jocb.142

Hind, K., Sian, O., Kylee, T., Johnson, S., & Howard, L. M. (2015). Recent intimate partner violence among people with chronic mental illness: Findings from a national cross-sectional survey. *The British Journal of Psychiatry, 207*(3), 207–212. http://dx.doi.org.library.capella.edu/10.1192/bjp.bp.114.144899

Hine, B., Noku, L., Bates, E. A., & Jayes, K. (2022). But who is the victim here? exploring judgments toward hypothetical bidirectional domestic violence scenarios. *Journal of Interpersonal Violence, 37*(7–8), NP5495–NP5516. https://doi.org/10.1177/0886260520917508

Hine, B., Bates, E. A., & Wallace, S. (2020). "I have guys call me and say 'I cannot be the victim of domestic abuse'": Exploring the experiences of telephone support providers for male domestic violence and abuse victims. *Journal of Interpersonal Violence,* 88626052094455–886260520944551. https://doi.org/10.1177/0886260520944551

Hoare, I., Agu, N., Falope, O., Wesley, C. A., & Coulter, M. (2022). A multiple streams framework approach to access to domestic violence services in an indigenous community. *Violence Against*

Women, 28(9), 2080–2097. https://doi.org/10.1177/10778012211030947

Hodges, S. D., & Myers, M. W. (2007). Empathy. *Encyclopedia of Social Psychology, 1,* 296–298.

Hoskins, N., & Kunkel, A. (2020). "I do not even deserve a chance": An ethnographic study of adverse childhood experiences among male perpetrators of intimate partner violence. *Qualitative Report, 25*(4), 1009–1037.

Hogan, K. F., Hegarty, J. R., Ward, T., & Dodd, L. J. (2012). Counsellors' experiences of working with male victims of female-perpetrated domestic abuse. *Counseling and Psychotherapy Research, 12*(1), 44–52. https://doi.org/10.1080/14733145.2011.630479

Hoogendijk, C., Hicks, J., & Wilderom, C. P. M. (2023). Clarifying organizational generativity: A future forming perspective for OD practitioners and researchers. *Organization Development Journal, 41*(2), 38–59.

Holter, M., Ness, O., Johansen, A., & Brendryen, H. (2019). Getting change-space: A grounded theory study of automated eHealth therapy. *Qualitative Report, 24*(7), 1636–1657. https://doi.org/10.46743/2160-3715/2019.3988

Holtrop, J. S., Rabin, B. A., & Glasgow, R. E. (2018). Qualitative approaches to use of the RE-AIM framework: Rationale and methods. *B.M.C. Health Services Research, 18*(1), 1-10. https://doi.org/10.1186/s12913-018-2938-80

Houghton, C., Murphy, K., Meehan, B., Thomas, J., Brooker, D., & Casey, D. (2017). From screening to synthesis: Using nvivo enhances transparency in qualitative evidence synthesis. *Journal of Clinical Nursing, 26*(5–6), 873–881. https://doi.org/10.1111/jocn.13443

Houston-Kolnik, J. D., Todd, N. R., & Greeson, M. R. (2019). Overcoming the "Holy hush": A qualitative examination of protestant Christian leaders' responses to intimate partner violence. *American Journal of Community Psychology, 63*(1–2), 135–152. https://doi.org/10.1002/ajcp.12278

Houston-Kolnik, J. D., & Vasquez, A. L. (2022). Cognitive interviewing: Lessons learned and recommendations for structured interviews with survivors of crime. *Journal of Family Violence, 37*(2), 325–335. https://doi.org/10.1007/s10896-020-00232-7

Howell, K. H., Barnes, S. E., Miller, L. E., & Graham-Bermann, S. A. (2016, 2014). Developmental variations in the impact of intimate partner violence exposure during childhood. *Journal of Injury and Violence Research, 8*(1), 43–57. https://doi.org/10.5249/jivr.v8i1.663

Horwitz, S. H., Benowitz, J. R., LaRussa-Trott, M., Santiago, L., Pearson, J., Skiff, D., Nichols-Hadeed, C., Stone, J. T., & Cerulli, C. (2015). Family law attorneys' beliefs and experiences with intimate partner violence: An exploratory study. *Journal of Child Custody, 12*(3–4), 231–247. https://doi.org/10.1080/15379418.2015.1090298

Huang, H., Liu, Y., & Su, Y. (2020). What is the relationship between empathy and mental health in preschool teachers: The role of teaching experience. *Frontiers in Psychology, 11*, 1366. https://doi.org/10.3389/fpsyg.2020.01366

Huang, K., Kumar, M., Cheng, S., Urcuyo, A. E., & Macharia, P. (2022). Applying technology to promote sexual and reproductive health and prevent gender-based violence for adolescents in low and middle-income countries: Digital health strategies synthesis from an umbrella review. *BMC Health Services Research, 22*(1), 1373. https://doi.org/10.1186/s12913-022-08673-0

Huard Pelletier, V., Girard, S., & Lemoyne, J. (2020). Adolescent hockey players' predispositions to adopt sport and exercise behaviors: An ecological perspective. *PloS One, 15*(2), e0228352. https://doi.org/10.1371/journal.pone.0228352

Hughes, J. F. (2017). Dreams, myths, and power. *Dreaming, 27*(2), 161–176. https://doi.org/10.1037/drm0000055

References

Hughes, K., Horwood, J. F., Clements, C., Leyland, D., & Corbett, H. J. (2016). Complications of inguinal herniotomy are comparable in term and premature infants. Hernia: The *Journal of Hernias and Abdominal Wall Surgery, 20*(4), 565–569. https://doi.org/10.1007/s10029-015-1454-6

Hui, V., & Constantino, R. E. (2021). The association between life satisfaction, emotional support, and perceived health among women who experienced intimate partner violence (IPV) was a 2007 behavioral risk factor surveillance system. *B.M.C. Public Health, 21*(1), 641. https://doi.org/10.1186/s12889-021-10665-4

Hullenaar, K. L., Rivara, F. P., Wang, J., & Zatzick, D. F. (2023). Exploring collaborative care effects on the mental and physical health of patients with and without violent victimization histories. *Journal of Interpersonal Violence, 38*(9–10), 6865–6887. https://doi.org/10.1177/08862605221138655

Hull, L. E., Lynch, K. G., & Oslin, D. W. (2019). VA primary care and mental health providers' comfort with genetic testing: Survey results from the PRIME care study. *Journal of General Internal Medicine: JGIM, 34*(6), 799–801. https://doi.org/10.1007/s11606-018-4776-0

Hulley, J., Wager, K., Gomersall, T., Bailey, L., Kirkman, G., Gibbs, G., & Jones, A. D. (2023). Continuous traumatic stress: Examining the experiences and support needs of women after separation from an abusive partner. *Journal of Interpersonal Violence, 38*(9–10), 6275–6297. https://doi.org/10.1177/08862605221132776

Hultmann, O., Möller, J., Ormhaug, S., & Broberg, A. (2014). Asking routinely about intimate partner violence in a child and adolescent psychiatric clinic: A qualitative study. *Journal of Family Violence, 29*(1), 67–78.

Huntley, A. L., Szilassy, E., Potter, L., Malpass, A., Williamson, E., & Feder, G. (2020). Help-seeking by male domestic violence and abuse victims: An example of an integrated mixed methods synthesis of systematic review evidence defining methodological terms. *BMC Health Services Research, 20*(1), 1085. https://doi.org/10.1186/s12913-020-05931-x

Huntley, A. L., Potter, L., Williamson, E., Malpass, A., Szilassy, E., & Feder, G. (2019). Help-seeking by male victims of domestic violence and abuse (D.V.A.): A systematic review and qualitative evidence synthesis. *BMJ Open, 9*(6), e021960. https://doi.org/10.1136/bmjopen-2018-021960

Hunt, K. E., Robinson, L. E., Valido, A., Espelage, D. L., & Hong, J. S. (2022). Teen dating violence victimization: Associations among peer justification, attitudes toward gender inequality, sexual activity, and peer victimization. *Journal of Interpersonal Violence, 37*(9–10), 5914–5936. https://doi.org/10.1177/08862605221085015

Husebø, A. M. L., Karlsen, B., & Husebø, S. E. (2020). Health professionals' beliefs of colorectal cancer patients' treatment burden and their supportive work to improve the burden - a qualitative study. *BMC Health Services Research, 20*(1), 661. https://doi.org/10.1186/s12913-020-05520-y

Hyett, N., Kenny, A., & Dickson-Swift, V. (2014). Methodology or method? A critical review of qualitative case study reports. *International Journal of Qualitative Studies on Health and Well-being, 9*(1), 23606. https://doi.org/10.3402/qhw.v9.23606

Ibanga, D. (2018). Concept, principles, and research methods of African environmental ethics. *The Journal of Pan African Studies, 11*(7), 123–141.

Idriss-Wheeler, D., Hajjar, J., & Yaya, S. (2021). Interventions directed at men for preventing intimate partner violence: A systematic review protocol. *Systematic Reviews, 10*(1), 161. https://doi.org/10.1186/s13643-021-01712-7

Inman, A. G., & Rao, K. (2018). Asian Indian women: Domestic violence, mental health, and resilience sites. *Women &*

Therapy, 41(1–2), 83–96.
https://doi.org/10.1080/02703149.2017.1324189

Irawati, S., Prayudeni, S., Rachmawati, R., Wita, I. W., Willfert, B., Hak, E., & Taxis, K. (2020). What are the key factors influencing the prescribing of statins behaviors through a qualitative study among physicians working in primary healthcare facilities in Indonesia? *B.M.J. Open, 10*(6), e035098. https://doi.org/10.1136/bmjopen-2019-035098

Islam, M. J., Broidy, L., Baird, K., & Mazerolle, P. (2017). Intimate partner violence around pregnancy and postpartum depression: The experience of women of Bangladesh. *PloS One, 12*(5), e0176211. https://doi.org/10.1371/journal.pone.0176211

Ivey, G., & Sonn, C. (2020). A psychosocial study of guilt and shame in white South African migrants to Australia. *Qualitative Psychology (Washington, D.C.), 7*(1), 114–130. https://doi.org/10.1037/qup0000133

Jacobs, R., & Niekerk, A. v. (2017). The role of spirituality as a coping mechanism for South African traffic officers. *Hervormde Teologiese Studies, 73*(3), 1–6. https://www.doi.org/10.4102/hts.v73i3.4344

Jacobs, Y., Myers, B., van der Westhuizen, C., Brooke-Sumner, C., & Sorsdahl, K. (2021). Task sharing or task dumping: Counsellor's experiences delivering a psychosocial intervention for mental health problems in South Africa. *Community Mental Health Journal, 57*(6), 1082–1093. https://doi.org/10.1007/s10597-020-00734-0

Jackson-Blott, K., Hare, D., Davies, B., & Morgan, S. (2019). Recovery-oriented training programs for mental health professionals: A narrative literature review. *Mental Health & Prevention, 13*, 113–127. https://doi.org/10.1016/j.mhp.2019.01.005

Jackson, C. L., Ciciolla, L., Crnic, K. A., Luecken, L. J., Gonzales, N. A., & Coonrod, D. V. (2015). Intimate partner violence before and during pregnancy: Related demographic and psychosocial factors and postpartum depressive symptoms among Mexican American women. *Journal of interpersonal violence, 30*(4), 659–679.

Jafar, T. H., Tavajoh, S., de Silva, H. A., Naheed, A., Jehan, I., Kanatiwela de Silva, C., Chakma, N., Huda, M., Legido-Quigley, H., COBRA-BPS Study Group, & on behalf of COBRA-BPS Study Group. (2023). Post-intervention acceptability of multicomponent intervention for management of hypertension in rural Bangladesh, Pakistan, and Sri Lanka- a qualitative study. *PloS One, 18*(1), e0280455. https://doi.org/10.1371/journal.pone.0280455

Jahns, R., Geiger, J., Schlünder, I., Strech, D., Brumhard, M., & von Kielmansegg, S. G. (2019). Broad donor consent for human biobanks in Germany and Europe: A strategy to help cross-border sharing and exchange of human biological materials and related data. *Journal of Laboratory Medicine, 43*(6), 291–299. https://doi.org/10.1515/labmed-2017-0064

Janelle, C., O'Connor, K., & Dupuis, G. (2016). Evaluating illness representations in heart transplant patients. *Journal of Health Psychology, 21*(9), 1850–1859. https://doi.org/10.1177/1359105314567210

Jayamaha, S. D., Antonellis, C., & Overall, N. C. (2016). Attachment insecurity and inducing guilt produce the desired change in romantic partners. *Personal Relationships, 23*(2), 311–338. https://doi.org/10.1111/pere.12128

Javed, S., Malik, A., & Mutaz Minwer Hala Alharbi. (2020). The relevance of leadership styles and Islamic work ethics in managerial effectiveness. *PSU Research Review, 4*(3), 189–207. https://doi.org/10.1108/PRR-03-2019-0007

Jarvis, J. (2021). Empathetic-reflective-dialogical re-storying: A teaching–learning strategy for life orientation. *Journal for Transdisciplinary Research in Southern Africa, 17*(1), e1–e7. https://doi.org/10.4102/td.v17i1.1077

References

Jewkes, R., Milovanovic, M., Otwombe, K., Chirwa, E., Hlongwane, K., Hill, N., Mbowane, V., Matuludi, M., Hopkins, K., Gray, G., & Coetzee, J. (2021). Intersections of sex work, mental ill-health, IPV, and other violence experienced by female sex workers: Findings from a cross-sectional community-centric national study in South Africa. International *Journal of Environmental Research and Public Health, 18*(22), 11971. https://doi.org/10.3390/ijerph182211971

Jöbges, S., Mouton Dorey, C., Porz, R., Ricou, B., & Biller-Andorno, N. (2022). What does coercion mean for patients and their relatives in intensive care? A thematic qualitative study. *BMC Medical Ethics, 23*(1), 9. https://doi.org/10.1186/s12910-022-00748-1

Joe, J. R., Norman, A. R., Brown, S., & Diaz, J. (2020). The intersection of HIV and intimate partner violence: An application of relational-cultural theory with black and Latina women. *Journal of Mental Health Counseling, 42*(1), 32–46. https://doi.org/10.17744/mehc.42.1.03

Johannesen, D. T. S., & Wiig, S. (2020). Exploring hospital certification processes from the certification body's perspective — A qualitative study. *BMC Health Services Research, 20*(1), 242. https://doi.org/10.1186/s12913-020-05093-w

Johnson, W. L., Johnson, W. L., Giordano, P. C., Giordano, P. C., Manning, W. D., Manning, W. D., & Longmore, M. A. (2015). The Age–IPV curve: Changes in the perpetration of intimate partner violence during adolescence and young adulthood. *Journal of Youth and Adolescence, 44*(3), 708–726. https://doi.org/10.1007/s10964-014-0158-z

Johnson, L., Cusano, J. L., Nikolova, K., Steiner, J. J., & Postmus, J. L. (2022). Do you believe your partner can kill you? An examination of female IPV survivors' beliefs of fatality risk indicators. *Journal of Interpersonal Violence, 37*(1–2), NP594–NP619. https://doi.org/10.1177/0886260520916273

Johnston, C. M., Wallis, M., Oprescu, F. I., & Gray, M. (2017). Methodological considerations related to nursing researchers using their own experience of a phenomenon within phenomenology. *Journal of Advanced Nursing, 73*(3), 574–584. https://doi.org/10.1111/jan.13198

Johnson, S. M., & Whiffen, V. E. (1999). Made to measure: Adapting emotionally focused couple therapy to partners' attachment styles. *Clinical Psychology (New York, N.Y.), 6*(4), 366–381. https://doi.org/10.1093/clipsy.6.4.366

Jones, S. R., Torres, V., & Arminio, J. (2006). *Negotiating the complexities of qualitative research in higher education: Fundamental elements and issues.* Taylor & Francis Group.

Jong, K., Ariti, C., van der Kam, S., Mooren, T., Shanks, L., Pintaldi, G., & Kleber, R. (2016). Monitoring and evaluating psychosocial intervention outcomes in humanitarian aid. *PloS One, 11*(6), e0157474. https://doi.org/10.1371/journal.pone.0157474

Jorba, M., & Moran, D. (2016). Conscious thinking and cognitive phenomenology: Topics, views, and future developments. *Philosophical Explorations, 19*(2), 95–113. https://doi.org/10.1080/13869795.2016.1176230de

Jordan, D. J., & Bedi, R. P. (2021). Addiction recovery as transformative learning: Identity change in men who taken part in residential Treatment/La guerison de la dependance en tant qu'apprentissage transformateur: Le changement identitaire chez des hommes ayant participe a un traitement en etablissement. *Canadian Journal of Counselling and Psychotherapy, 55*(4), 462. https://doi.org/10.47634/cjcp.v55i3.70980

Jose, R., & Novaco, R. W. (2016). Intimate partner violence victims seeking a temporary restraining order: Social support and resilience attenuating psychological distress. *Journal of Interpersonal Violence, 31*(20), 3352–3376.

Josilowski, C. S. (2019). Teachers' beliefs of the home-school collaboration: Enhancing learning for autistic children. *The Qualitative Report, 24*(12), 3008–3021.

http://library.capella.edu/login?qurl=https%3A%2F%2Fwww.proquest.com%2Fscholarly-journals%2Fteachers-perceptions-home-school-collaboration%2Fdocview%2F2331238758%2Fse-2%3Faccountid%3D27965

Joubert, D., & Van der Merwe, L. (2020). Phenomenology in five music education journals: Recent use and future directions. *International Journal of Music Education, 38*(3), 337–351. https://doi.org/10.1177/0255761419881492

June, L. N. (1986). Enhancing mental health and counseling services delivery to black males: Critical agency and provider responsibilities. *Journal of Multicultural Counseling and Development, 14*(1), 39–45. https://doi.org/10.1002/j.2161-1912.1986.tb00164.x

Jung, H., Herrenkohl, T. I., Skinner, M. L., Lee, J. O., Klika, J. B., & Rousson, A. N. (2019). Gender differences in intimate partner violence: A predictive analysis of IPV by child abuse and domestic violence exposure during early childhood. Violence Against Women, 25(8), 903-924. https://doi.org/10.1177/1077801218796329

Kabir, Z. N., Nasreen, H., & Edhborg, M. (2014). Intimate partner violence and its association with maternal depressive symptoms 6–8 months after childbirth in rural Bangladesh. *Global Health Action, 7*(1), 24725. https://doi.org/10.3402/gha.v7.24725

Kafka, J. M., Moracco, K. E., Young, B., Taheri, C., Graham, L. M., Macy, R. J., & Proescholdbell, S. K. (2021). Fatalities related to intimate partner violence: Towards a comprehensive perspective. *Injury Prevention, 27*(2), 137–144. https://doi.org/10.1136/injuryprev-2020-043704

Kahlke, R. M. (2018). *Reflection/Commentary on a past article: "Generic qualitative approaches: Pitfalls and benefits of methodological mixology."* https://journals.sagepub.com/doi/full/10.1177/160940691401300119

Kahlke, R. M. (2014). Generic qualitative approaches: Pitfalls and benefits of methodological mixology. *International Journal of*

Qualitative Methods, 13(1), 37–52. https://doi.org/10.1177/160940691401300119

Kahrass, H., Strech, D., & Mertz, M. (2016). The full spectrum of clinical ethical issues in kidney failure. Findings of a systematic qualitative review. *PloS One, 11*(3), e0149357. https://doi.org/10.1371/journal.pone.0149357

Kagoyire, M. G., Kangabe, J., & Ingabire, M. C. (2023). "A calf cannot fail to pick a color from its mother": Intergenerational transmission of trauma and its effect on reconciliation among post-genocide Rwandan youth. *BMC Psychology, 11*(1), 104. https://doi.org/10.1186/s40359-023-01129-y

Kaligis, F., Hillary, R., Kusuma, N. M. P., Sianipar, H. R. P., Ramadhanti, C. S., Findyartini, A., Indraswari, M. T., Magdalena, C. C., & Nurraga, G. W. (2022). Medical students' attitudes toward psychiatry in Indonesia. *PloS One, 17*(3), e0265605. https://doi.org/10.1371/journal.pone.0265605

Kallio, H., Pietilä, A., Johnson, M., & Kangasniemi, M. (2016). Systematic methodological review: Developing a framework for a qualitative semi-structured interview guide. *Journal of Advanced Nursing, 72*(12), 2954–2965. https://doi.org/10.1111/jan.13031

Källström, Å., Hellfeldt, K., Howell, K. H., Miller-Graff, L. E., & Graham-Bermann, S. A. (2020). Young adults victimized as children or adolescents: Relationships between perpetrator patterns, poly-victimization, and mental health problems. *Journal of Interpersonal Violence, 35*(11–12), 2335–2357. https://doi.org/10.1177/0886260517701452

Kamimura, A., Ashby, J., Myers, K., Nourian, M. M., & Christensen, N. (2015). Satisfaction with healthcare services among free clinic patients. *Journal of Community Health, 40*, 62–72.

Kamran Ehsan, M., & Rowland, D. L. (2021). A possible role for imagery-based therapy in managing PTSD in Pakistani women experiencing domestic abuse: A pilot study using eidetic therapy. *International Journal of Environmental Research and Public Health, 18*(5), 2478. https://doi.org/10.3390/ijerph18052478

Kapoor, S., Domingue, H. K., Watson-Singleton, N. N., & Kaslow, N. J. (2018). *Childhood abuse, intrapersonal strength, and suicide resilience in African American females who attempted suicide.* https://doi.org/10.100710896-017-9943-2

Karanikola, M., Kaikoushi, K., Doulougeri, K., Koutrouba, A., & Papathanassoglou, E. (2018). Beliefs of a professional role in community mental health nurses: The interplay of power relations between nurses and mentally ill individuals. *Archives of Psychiatric Nursing, 32*(5), 677–687. https://doi.org/10.1016/j.apnu.2018.03.007

Karn, S. (2023). Historical empathy: A cognitive-affective theory for history education in Canada. *Canadian Journal of Education, 46*(1), 80–110. https://doi.org/10.53967/cje-rce.5483

Kaspersen, S. L., Kalseth, J., Stene-Larsen, K., & Reneflot, A. (2022). Use of health services and support resources by immediate family members bereaved of suicide: A scoping review. *International Journal of Environmental Research and Public Health, 19*(16), 10016. https://doi.org/10.3390/ijerph191610016

Keesler, J. M. (2016). Trauma-informed day services for individuals with Intellectual/Developmental disabilities: Exploring staff understanding and belief within an innovative program. *Journal of Applied Research in Intellectual Disabilities, 29*(5), 481–492. https://doi.org/10.1111/jar.12197

Kelly, A., & Garland, E. L. (2016). Trauma-informed mindfulness-based stress reduction for female survivors of interpersonal violence: Results from a stage I RCT. *Journal of Clinical Psychology, 72*(4), 311–328. https://doi.org/10.1002/jclp.22273

Keilholtz, B. M., Spencer, C. M., Vail, S., & Palmer, M. (2023). Relationship dynamics associated with emotional IPV perpetration and victimization: A meta-analysis. *Journal of Marital and Family Therapy, 49*(2), 411–430. https://doi.org/10.1111/jmft.12630

Kendall, C. E., Porter, J. E., Shoemaker, E. S., Seoyeon Kang, R., Fitzgerald, M., Keely, E., Afkham, A., Crowe, L., MacPherson, P., Rosenes, R., Lundrigan, P., Bibeau, C., & Liddy, C. (2019). Evolving toward shared H.I.V. care using the Champlain base consult service. *MDM Policy & Practice, 4*(2), 2381468319868216. https://doi.org/10.1177/2381468319868216

Kendall, C. E., Boucher, L. M., Donelle, J., Martin, A., Marshall, Z., Boyd, R., Oickle, P., Diliso, N., Pineau, D., Renaud, B., LeBlanc, S., Tyndall, M., & Bayoumi, A. M. (2020). Engagement in primary health care among marginalized people who use drugs in Ottawa, Canada. *BMC Health Services Research, 20*(1), 1–12. https://doi.org/10.1186/s12913-020-05670-z

Kennedy, A. M., Black, S., Watt, S., Vitkin, N., Young, J., Reeves, R., & Salway, T. (2022). *Health provider and sexual and gender minority service user perspectives on the provision of mental health services during the early phase of the COVID-19 pandemic in British Columbia, Canada.* Cold Spring Harbor: Cold Spring Harbor Laboratory Press. https://doi.org/10.1101/2022.02.18.22271151

Kennedy, D. (2016). Is it any clearer? Generic qualitative inquiry and the VSAIEEDC model of data analysis. *Qualitative Report, 21*(8), 1369–1379. https://doi.org/10.46743/2160-3715/2016.2444

Kern-Godal, A., Brenna, I. H., Kogstad, N., Arnevik, E. A., & Ravndal, E. (2016). Contribution of the patient-horse relationship to substance use disorder treatment: Patients' experiences. *International Journal of Qualitative Studies on Health and Well-being, 11*(1),1–12. https://doi.org/10.3402/qhw.v11.31636

Kidman, R., & Kohler, H. (2020). Emerging partner violence among young adolescents in a low-income country: Perpetration, victimization, and adversity. *PloS One, 15*(3), e0230085. https://doi.org/10.1371/journal.pone.0230085

Kilgallen, J. A., Schaffnit, S. B., Kumogola, Y., Galura, A., Urassa, M., & Lawson, D. W. (2022). A positive correlation between Women's status and intimate partner violence suggests violence backlash in

Mwanza, Tanzania. *Journal of Interpersonal Violence, 37*(21–22), NP20331–NP20360. https://doi.org/10.1177/08862605211050095

Khan, A. R., & Arendse, N. (2022). Females perpetrated domestic violence against men and the case for Bangladesh. *Journal of Human Behavior in the Social Environment, 32*(4), 519–533. https://doi.org/10.1080/10911359.2021.1927281

Kienzler, H., & Sapkota, R. P. (2020, 2019). The long-term mental health consequences of torture, loss, and insecurity: A qualitative study among survivors of armed conflict in the Dang district of Nepal. *Frontiers in Psychiatry, 10*, 941. https://doi.org/10.3389/fpsyt.2019.00941

Kim, E. E., Chen, E. C., & Brachfeld, C. (2019). Patients' experience of spirituality and change in individual psychotherapy at a Christian counseling clinic: A grounded theory analysis. *Spirituality in Clinical Practice, 6*(2), 110–123. https://doi.org/10.1037/scp0000176

Kim, H., Lee, I., & Lee, B. (2022). Nursing leaders' beliefs of the state of nursing leadership and the need for nursing leadership education reform: A qualitative content analysis from South Korea. *Journal of Nursing Management, 30*(7), 2216–2226. https://doi.org/10.1111/jonm.13596

Kim, E., & Hogge, I. (2015). Intimate partner violence among Asian Indian women in the United States: Recognition of abuse and help-seeking attitudes. *International Journal of Mental Health, 44*(3), 200–214. https://doi.org/10.1080/00207411.2015.1035073

Kim, M. J., Preis, M. W., & Lee, C. (2019). The effects of helping, self-expression, and enjoyment on social capital in social media: The moderating effect of avoidance attachment in tourism. *Behavior & Information Technology, 38*(8), 760–781. https://doi.org/10.1080/0144929X.2018.1552718

Kimber, M., Henriksen, C. A., Davidov, D. M., Goldstein, A. L., Pitre, N. Y., Tonmyr, L., & Afifi, T. O. (2015). *The association between immigrant generational status, child maltreatment history, and intimate* partner violence (IPV): Evidence from a nationally representative survey. https://doi.org/10.100700127-014-1002-1

Kimpinde, M. C., & Dreyer, Y. (2020). Pastoral care for young people suffering from depression in the context of Soweto. *Hervormde Teologiese Studies, 76*(3). https://doi.org/10.4102/hts.v76i3.6225

Kimuna, S., Tenkorang, E. Y., & Djamba, Y. (2018). Ethnicity and intimate partner violence in Kenya. *Journal of Family Issues, 39*(11), 2958–2981. https://doi.org/10.1177/0192513X18766192

Kinyenje, E. S., Yahya, T. A., Degeh, M. M., German, C. C., Hokororo, J. C., Mohamed, M. A., Nassoro, O. A., Bahegwa, R. P., Msigwa, Y. S., Ngowi, R. R., Marandu, L. E., Mwaisengela, S. M., & Eliakimu, E. S. (2022). Client satisfaction at primary healthcare facilities and its association with implementation of client service charter in Tanzania. *PloS One, 17*(8), e0272321. https://doi.org/10.1371/journal.pone.0272321

Kjellberg, S., & Haider, J. (2019). Researchers' online visibility: Tensions of visibility, trust, and reputation. *Online Information Review, 43*(3), 426–439. https://doi.org/10.1108/OIR-07-2017-0211

Klag, M., & Langley, A. (2013). Approaching the conceptual leap in qualitative research. *International Journal of Management Reviews, 15*(2), 149–166. https://doi.org/10.1111/j.1468-2370.2012.00349.x

Klein, E., Peters, B., & Higger, M. (2018). Ethical Considerations in Ending Exploratory brain-computer Interface Research Studies in Locked-in Syndrome. *Cambridge Quarterly of Healthcare Ethics, 27*(4), 660–674. https://doi.org/10.1017/S0963180118000154

Klein, M., & Milner, R. J. (2019). The use of body-mapping in interpretative phenomenological analyses: A methodological discussion. *International Journal of Social Research Methodology, 22*(5), 533–543. https://doi.org/10.1080/13645579.2019.1593378

References

Klimecki, O. M., Vuilleumier, P., & Sander, D. (2016). The impact of emotions and empathy-related traits on punishment behavior: Introduction and validation of the inequality game. *PloS One, 11*(3), e0151028. https://doi.org/10.1371/journal.pone.0151028

Knight, A. W., Tam, C. W. M., Dennis, S., Fraser, J., & Pond, D. (2022). The role of quality improvement collaboratives in general practice: A qualitative systematic review. *BMJ Open Quality, 11*(2), e001800. https://doi.org/10.1136/bmjoq-2021-001800

Koch, A. K., & Nafziger, J. (2019). Correlates of narrow bracketing. *The Scandinavian Journal of Economics, 121*(4), 1441–1472. https://doi.org/10.1111/sjoe.12311

Koning, N. R., Büchner, F. L., Leeuwenburgh, N. A., Paijmans, I. J., van Dijk-van Dijk, DJ Annemarie, Vermeiren, R. R., Numans, M. E., & Crone, M. (2022). Identification of child mental health problems by combining electronic health record information from different primary healthcare professionals: A population-based cohort study. *BMJ Open, 12*(1), e049151. https://doi.org/10.1136/bmjopen-2021-049151

Kopelovich, S. L., Strachan, E., Sivec, H., & Kreider, V. (2019). A stepped care program is an implementation protocol and service delivery model suitable for cognitive behavioral therapy and psychosis. *Community Mental Health Journal, 55*(5), 755–767. https://doi.org/10.1007/s10597-018-00365-6

Korsbek, L., Vilholt-Johannesen, S., Johansen, G. K., Thomsen, R., Johansen, M. B., & Rasmussen, K. S. (2021). The intentional differences: A qualitative study of the views and experiences of non-peer mental health providers on working together with peer support colleagues in mental health. *Community Mental Health Journal, 57*(8), 1435–1441. https://doi.org/10.1007/s10597-021-00807-8

Kosia, A., Kakoko, D., Ave Maria, E. S., Nyamhanga, T., & Frumence, G. (2016). Intimate partner violence and challenges facing women living with HIV/AIDS in accessing antiretroviral treatment at

Singita Regional Hospital, Central Tanzania. *Global Health Action, 9*(1). doi: http://dx.doi.org.library.capella.edu/10.3402/gha.v9.32307

Kostere, S., & Kostere, K. (2022, 2021). *The generic qualitative approach to a dissertation in the social sciences: A step-by-step guide* (1st ed.). Routledge. https://doi.org/10.4324/9781003195689

Kotera, Y., Maxwell-Jones, R., Edwards, A., & Knutton, N. (2021). Burnout in professional psychotherapists: Relationships with self-compassion, Work-life Balance, and tele-pressure. *International Journal of Environmental Research and Public Health, 18*(10), 5308. https://doi.org/10.3390/ijerph18105308

Krahé, B., Schuster, I., & Tomaszewska, P. (2021). Prevalence of sexual aggression victimization and perpetration in a German university student sample. *Archives of Sexual Behavior, 50*(5), 2109–2121. https://doi.org/10.1007/s10508-021-01963-4

Krimsky, S., & Schwab, T. (2017). Conflicts of interest among committee members in the national academies' genetically engineered crop study. *PloS One, 12*(2), e0172317. https://doi.org/10.1371/journal.pone.0172317

Krug, E. G., Mercy, J. A., Dahlberg, L. L., & Zwi, A. B. (2002). The world reports on violence and health. *The Lancet, 360*(9339), 1083–1088. https://doi.org/10.1016/S0140-6736(02)11133-0

Kulkarni, S., & Kulkarni, S. (2019). Intersectional trauma-informed intimate partner violence (IPV) services: Narrowing the gap between IPV service delivery and survivor needs. *Journal of Family Violence, 34*(1), 55–64. https://doi.org/10.1007/s10896-018-0001-5

Kyza, E. A., & Nicolaidou, I. (2017). Co-designing reform-based online inquiry learning environments as a situated approach to teachers' professional development. *Codesign, 13*(4), 261–286. https://doi.org/10.1080/15710882.2016.1209528

References

Labarre, M., Brodeur, N., Roy, V., & Bousquet, M. (2019). *What are Practitioners' views on IPV and its solutions: An integrative literature review?* Sage. https://doi.org/10.1177/1524838017728709

Lacity, M. C., & Janson, M. A. (1994). Understanding qualitative data: A framework of text analysis methods. *Journal of Management Information Systems, 11*(2), 137–155. https://doi.org/10.1080/07421222.1994.11518043

Lacey, K. K., West, C. M., Matusko, N., & Jackson, J. S. (2016). Prevalence and factors associated with severe physical intimate partner violence among U.S. black women: A comparison of African American and Caribbean blacks. *Violence Against Women, 22*(6), 651–670. https://doi.org/10.1177/1077801215610014

LaFrance, D. L., Weiss, M. J., Kazemi, E., Gerenser, J., & Dobres, J. (2019). Multidisciplinary teaming: Enhancing collaboration through increased understanding. *Behavior Analysis in Practice, 12*(3), 709–726. https://doi.org/10.1007/s40617-019-00331-y

Lagdon, S., Armour, C., & Stringer, M. (2014). Adult experience of mental health outcomes as a result of intimate partner violence victimization: A systematic review. *European Journal of Psychotraumatology, 5*(1), 1–12. https://doi.org/10.3402/ejpt.v5.24794

Lamb, J. (2011). Sympathy for animals and salvation of the soul. *The Eighteenth Century, 52*(1), 69–85. https://doi.org/10.1353/ecy.2011.0003

Lamothe, M., Rondeau, É., Malboeuf-Hurtubise, C., Duval, M., & Sultan, S. (2015, 2016). Outcomes of MBSR or MBSR-based interventions in health care providers: A systematic review focusing on empathy and emotional competencies. *Complementary Therapies in Medicine, 24*, 19–28. https://doi.org/10.1016/j.ctim.2015.11.001

LaMotte, A. D., Gower, T., Miles-McLean, H., Farzan-Kashani, J., & Murphy, C. M. (2018, 2019). Trauma's influence on relationships: Clients' perspectives at an intimate partner violence intervention program. *Journal of Family Violence, 34*(7), 655–662. https://doi.org/10.1007/s10896-018-0004-2

Langenderfer-Magruder, L., Alven, L., Wilke, D. J., & Spinelli, C. (2019, 2018). "Getting everyone on the same page": Child welfare workers' collaboration challenges on intimate partner violence cases. *Journal of Family Violence, 34*(1), 21–31. https://doi.org/10.1007/s10896-018-0002-4

Langenderfer-Magruder, L., Olson, C., Wilke, D. J., & Alven, L. (2021). Rise: Helping frontline responder collaboration on co-occurring child welfare and intimate partner violence cases. *Journal of Interpersonal Violence, 36*(15–16), 7067–7089. https://doi.org/10.1177/0886260519832921

Lane, S. D., Rubinstein, R. A., Bergen-Cico, D., Jennings-Bey, T., Fish, L. S., Larsen, D. A., Fullilove, M. T., Schimpff, T. R., Ducre, K. A., & Robinson, J. A. (2017). Neighborhood trauma due to violence: A multilevel analysis. *Journal of Health Care for the Poor and Underserved, 28*(1), 446–462. https://doi.org/10.1353/hpu.2017.0033

Lane, A. S., & Roberts, C. (2018). The learning pathways grid: Promoting reflexivity among learners and researchers in patient safety simulations. *International Journal of Qualitative Methods, 17*(1), 160940691879160. https://doi.org/10.1177/1609406918791605

Larance, L. Y., Goodmark, L., Miller, S. L., & Dasgupta, S. D. (2019). Understanding and addressing Women's use of force in intimate relationships: A retrospective. *Violence Against Women, 25*(1), 56–80. https://doi.org/10.1177/1077801218815776

Labarre, M., Brodeur, N., Roy, V., & Bousquet, M. (2019). Practitioners' views on IPV and its solutions: An integrative literature review. *Trauma, Violence, & Abuse, 20*(5), 679–692. https://doi.org/10.1177/1524838017728709

Laher, S. (2016). Ostinato rigor: Showing methodological rigor in quantitative research. *South African Journal of Psychology, 46*(3), 316–327. https://doi.org/10.1177/0081246316649121

References

Langenderfer-Magruder, L., Alven, L., Wilke, D. J., & Spinelli, C. (2019, 2018). "Getting everyone on the same page": Child welfare workers' collaboration challenges on intimate partner violence cases. *Journal of Family Violence, 34*(1), 21–31. https://doi.org/10.1007/s10896-018-0002-4

Laude, M. K., Shen, L., Zhu, Y., Schaefer, G. O., Ong, C., & Xafis, V. (2020). Perspectives of Singaporean biomedical researchers and research support staff on actual and ideal I.R.B. review functions and characteristics: A quantitative analysis. *PloS One, 15*(12), e0241783. https://doi.org/10.1371/journal.pone.0241783

Laur, C., Valaitis, R., Bell, J., & Keller, H. (2017). We are changing nutrition care practices in hospitals: A thematic analysis of hospital staff perspectives. *B.M.C. Health Services Research, 17*(1), 498. https://doi.org/10.1186/s12913-017-2409-7

Laur, C., Valaitis, R., Bell, J., & Keller, H. (2017). We are changing nutrition care practices in hospitals: A thematic analysis of hospital staff perspectives. *B.M.C. Health Services Research, 17*(1), 498. https://doi.org/10.1186/s12913-017-2409-7

Lau, I. W. W., Liu, D., Xu, L., Fan, Z., & Sun, Z. (2018). Clinical value of patient-specific three-dimensional printing of congenital heart disease: Quantitative and qualitative assessments. *PloS One, 13*(3), e0194333. https://doi.org/10.1371/journal.pone.0194333

Lawn, S., Delany, T., Pulvirenti, M., Smith, A., & McMillan, J. (2016). Examining the use of metaphors to understand the experience of community treatment orders for patients and mental health workers. *BMC Psychiatry, 16*(82), 82. https://doi.org/10.1186/s12888-016-0791-z

Lee, K. A., Bright, C. L., & Betz, G. (2022). Adverse childhood experiences (ACEs), alcohol use in adulthood, and intimate partner violence (IPV) perpetration by black men: A systematic review. *Sage.* https://doi.org/10.1177/1524838020953101

Lenzi, D., Trentini, C., Tambelli, R., & Pantano, P. (2015). Neural basis of attachment-caregiving systems interaction: Insights from neuroimaging studies. *Frontiers in Psychology, 6,* 1241. https://doi.org/10.3389/fpsyg.2015.01241

Lentz, L., Smith-MacDonald, L., Malloy, D. C., Anderson, G. S., Beshai, S., Ricciardelli, R., Bremault-Phillips, S., & Carleton, R. N. (2022). A qualitative analysis of the mental health training and educational needs of firefighters, paramedics, and public safety communicators in Canada. *International Journal of Environmental Research and Public Health, 19*(12), 6972. https://doi.org/10.3390/ijerph19126972

Lester, S., Lawrence, C., & Ward, C. L. (2017). What do we know about preventing school violence? A systematic review of systematic reviews. *Psychology, Health & Medicine, 22*(sup1), 187–223. https://doi.org/10.1080/13548506.2017.1282616

Lev, S., Zychlinski, E., & Kagan, M. (2022). Secondary traumatic stress among social workers: The contribution of resilience, social support, and exposure to violence and ethical conflicts. *Journal of the Society for Social Work and Research, 13*(1), 47–65. https://doi.org/10.1086/714015

Levenson, J. S., & Willis, G. M. (2019). Implementing trauma-informed care in correctional treatment and supervision. *Journal of Aggression, Maltreatment & Trauma, 28*(4), 481–501. https://doi.org/10.1080/10926771.2018.1531959

Lewis, J. (2021). The stability paradox: The two-parent paradigm and the perpetuation of violence against women in termination of parental rights and custody cases. *Michigan Journal of Gender & Law, 27*(2), 311–402. https://doi.org/10.36641/mjgl.27.2.stability

Lefèvre, L., Jourdain, M., & Fournier, J. (2019). Processes and determinants of integrating eGFR in physicians' drug prescriptions: A qualitative study of semi-structured interviews. *Primary Health Care Research & Development, 20,* e143. https://doi.org/10.1017/S1463423619000847

Lelaurain, S., Fonte, D., Aim, M., Khatmi, N., Decarsin, T., Lo Monaco, G., & Apostolidis, T. (2018). "One Does not Slap a Girl but . . ." social representations and conditional logic in the legitimization of intimate partner violence. *Sex Roles, 78*(9–10), 637–652. https://doi.org/10.1007/s11199-017-0821-4

Leitemo, K., Vestbø, H. S. B., Bakali, J. V., & Nissen-Lie, H. A. (2020). The role of attachment anxiety and avoidance for reduced interpersonal problems in training group analytic therapy. *Group Dynamics, 24*(1), 26–41. https://doi.org/10.1037/gdn0000112

Lenzi, D., Trentini, C., Tambelli, R., & Pantano, P. (2015). Neural basis of attachment-caregiving systems interaction: Insights from neuroimaging studies. *Frontiers in Psychology, 6*, 1241. https://doi.org/10.3389/fpsyg.2015.01241

Lesnik-Oberstein, K. (2015). Motherhood, evolutionary psychology, mirror neurons, or 'Grammar is politics by other means. *Feminist Theory, 16*(2), 171–187. https://doi.org/10.1177/1464700115586514

Le Provost, A., Loddé, B., Pietri, J., De Parscau, L., Pougnet, L., Dewitte, J., & Pougnet, R. (2018). Suffering at work among medical students: Qualitative study using semi-structured interviews. *Revue Médicale De Bruxelles, 39*(1), 6–14. https://doi.org/10.30637/2018.17-080

Lévesque, S., Rousseau, C., Raynault-Rioux, L., & Laforest, J. (2023). Canadian service providers' perspectives on reproductive coercion and abuse: Participatory action research to address their needs and support their actions. *Reproductive Health, 20*(1), 100. https://doi.org/10.1186/s12978-023-01640-w

Lévesque, E., Knoppers, B. M., & Simard, J. (2015). Ethical challenges and innovations in issuing genomic data: The experience of perspective projection. *Advances in Genomics and Genetics, 5*, 283. https://doi.org/10.2147/AGG.S66286

Levitt, H. M. (2020). Reporting qualitative research in psychology: How to meet APA style journal article reporting standards (Revis ed.).

American Psychological Association. https://doi.org/10.1037/0000179-000

Levett-Jones, T., & Can't, R. (2020). The empathy continuum: An evidenced-based teaching model derived from an integrative review of contemporary nursing literature. *Journal of Clinical Nursing, 29*(7–8), 1026–1040. https://doi.org/10.1111/jocn.15137

Li, G. Y., Zhu, X., & Cheong, C. M. (2020). Secondary teachers' conceptions of integrated writing skills: Are teachers' conceptions aligned with the curriculum goals? *Asia Pacific Education Review, 21*(3), 379–391. https://doi.org/10.1007/s12564-020-09629-x

Li, F., Long, J., & Zhao, W. (2023). Mining braces of innovation linking to digital transformation grounded in TOE framework. *Sustainability (Basel, Switzerland), 15*(1), 301. https://doi.org/10.3390/su15010301

Liao, K., Peng, C., Snell, L., Wang, X., Huang, C., & Saroyan, A. (2021). Understanding the lived experiences of medical learners in a narrative medicine course: A phenomenological study. *B.M.C. Medical Education, 21*(1), 321. https://doi.org/10.1186/s12909-021-02741-5

Liebling, H., Davidson, L., Akello, G. F., & Ochola, G. (2016). The experiences of survivors and trauma counseling service providers in northern Uganda: Implications for mental health policy and legislation. *International Journal of Law and Psychiatry, 49*(Pt A), 84–92. https://doi.org/10.1016/j.ijlp.2016.06.012

Lim, B. H., Valdez, C. E., & Lilly, M. M. (2015). Making meaning out of interpersonal victimization: The narratives of IPV survivors. *Violence Against Women, 21*(9), 1065–1086. https://doi.org/10.1177/1077801215590670

Lindsay, S. M. (2022). The "Problem" of multispecies families: Speciesism in emergency intimate partner violence (IPV) shelters. *Social Sciences (Basel), 11*(6), 242. https://doi.org/10.3390/socsci11060242

References

Lin, K., Sun, I. Y., Wu, Y., & Liu, J. (2016). College students' attitudes toward intimate partner violence: A comparative study of China and the U.S. *Journal of Family Violence, 31*(2), 179–189. https://doi.org/10.1007/s10896-015-9759-x

Lin, C., Lin, M., Wen, C., & Chu, S. (2016). A word-count approach to analyze linguistic patterns in the reflective writings of medical students. *Medical Education Online, 21*(1), 29522–7. https://doi.org/10.3402/meo.v21.29522

Lin, B. B., Chang, C., Astell-Burt, T., Feng, X., Gardner, J., & Andersson, E. (2023). Nature experience from yards provides an important space for mental health during COVID-19. *Npj Urban Sustainability, 3*(1), 14. https://doi.org/10.1038/s42949-023-00094-0

Lino, V. T. S., Portela, M. C., Camacho, L. A. B., Atie, S., Lima, M. J. B., Rodrigues, N. C. P. & Andrade, M. K. N. (2014). Screening for depression in low-income elderly patients at the primary care level: Use of the patient health questionnaire 2. *PloS One, 9*(12), e113778. https://doi.org/10.1371/journal.pone.0113778

Liu, L. (2016). Using the generic inductive approach in qualitative educational research: A case study analysis. *Journal of Education and Learning, 5*(2), 129. https://doi.org/10.5539/jel.v5n2p129

Liu, L., Chui, W. H., Deng, Y., & Li, H. (2020). Dealing with resistance: Working with involuntary clients in community-based drug treatment programs in China. *Australian Social Work, 73*(3), 309–320. https://doi.org/10.1080/0312407X.2019.1688367

Løkkegaard, S. S., Hansen, N. B., Wolf, N. M., & Elklit, A. (2019). When daddy stalks mommy: Experiences of intimate partner stalking and involvement of social and legal authorities when stalker and victim have children together. *Violence Against Women, 25*(14), 1759–1777. https://doi.org/10.1177/1077801219826738

Locke, L., & Boyle, M. (2016). Avoiding the A.B.D. Abyss: A grounded theory study of a dissertation-focused course for doctoral students in an educational leadership program. *Qualitative Report, 21*(9), 1574. https://doi.org/10.46743/2160-3715/2016.2167

Locke, K., Feldman, M., & Golden-Biddle, K. (2022). Coding practices and iteratively: Beyond templates for analyzing qualitative data. *Organizational Research Methods, 25*(2), 262–284. https://doi.org/10.1177/1094428120948600

Lohmann, J., John, D., & Dzay, A. (2022). A scoping review of the methodological quality of research on the mental health of healthcare professionals in low- and lower-middle-income countries. *Welcome, Open Research, 7*, 169. https://doi.org/10.12688/wellcomeopenres.17916.2

Logan, T., & Landhuis, J. (2022). Should we be paying more attention to firearm threats in ex-partner stalking cases? *Behavioral Sciences & the Law, 40*(5), 619–639. https://doi.org/10.1002/bsl.2589

Loo, S., Almazan, A. N., Vedilago, V., Stott, B., Reisner, S. L., & Keuroghlian, A. S. (2021). Understanding community members and health care professional perspectives on gender-affirming care—A qualitative study. *PloS One, 16*(8), e0255568. https://doi.org/10.1371/journal.pone.0255568

López, G., Bogen, K. W., Meza-Lopez, R. J., Nugent, N. R., & Orchowski, L. M. (2022). Domestic violence during the COVID-19 global pandemic: An analysis of public commentary via Twitter. *Digital Health, 8*, 205520762211150–20552076221115024. https://doi.org/10.1177/20552076221115024

Lopez, R. (2010). *Our Social Brains Empathy 101*. Psychology Today.

Long, L., & Ullman, S. E. (2016). Correlates of problem drinking and drug use in black sexual assault victims. Springer. https://doi.org/10.1891/0886-670814-0002.

Lømo, B., Haavind, H., & Tjersland, O. A. (2021). Finding common ground: Therapist responsiveness to male clients who have acted violently against their female partner. *Journal of Interpersonal*

Violence, 36(17–18), NP9930–NP9958.
https://doi.org/10.1177/0886260519862271

Lotz, S. (2015). Spontaneous giving under structural inequality: Intuition promotes cooperation in asymmetric social dilemmas. *PloS One, 10*(7), e0131562.
https://doi.org/10.1371/journal.pone.0131562

Lovegrove, C. J., & Bannigan, K. (2021). What is the lived experience of anxiety for people with Parkinson's? A phenomenological study. *PloS One, 16*(4), e0249390.
https://doi.org/10.1371/journal.pone.0249390

Luke, C., Beeson, E. T., Miller, R., Field, T. A., & Jones, L. K. (2020). Counselors' beliefs of ethical considerations for integrating neuroscience with counseling. *The Professional Counselor (Greensboro, N.C.), 10*(2), 204–219.
https://doi.org/10.15241/cl.10.2.204

Lukosch, H. K., Bekebrede, G., Kurapati, S., & Lukosch, S. G. (2018). A scientific foundation of simulation games for analyzing and designing complex systems. *Simulation & Gaming, 49*(3), 279–314.
https://doi.org/10.1177/1046878118768858

Lundt, A., Henseler, C., Wormuth, C., Soos, J., Seidel, R., Muller, R., Arshaad, M. I., Broich, K., Hescheler, J., Sachinidis, A., Ehninger, D., Papazoglou, A., & Weiergraber, M. (2019). Gender-specific click and tone burst evoked A.B.R. datasets from mice lacking the Cav3.2 T-type voltage-gated calcium channel. *B.M.C. Research Notes, 12*(1), 157. https://doi.org/10.1186/s13104-019-4169-4

Luodonpää-Manni, M., Penttilä, E., & Viimaranta, J. (2017). In Luodonpää-Manni M., Penttilä E. and Viimaranta J. (Eds.), *Empirical approaches to cognitive linguistics: Analyzing real-life data (1st ed.)*. Cambridge Scholars.

Luo, Y., Li, H. C. W., Xia, W., Cheung, A. T., Ho, L. L. K., & Chung, J. O. K. (2022). The lived experience of resilience in parents of children with cancer: A phenomenological study. *Frontiers in Pediatrics, 10,* 871435. https://doi.org/10.3389/fped.2022.871435

Lysova, A., Hanson, K., Dixon, L., Douglas, E. M., Hines, D. A., & Celi, E. M. (2022). Internal and external barriers to help-seeking: Voices of men who experienced abuse in intimate relationships. *International Journal of Offender Therapy and Comparative Criminology, 66*(5), 538–559. https://doi.org/10.1177/0306624X20919710

Machado, A., Sousa, C., & Cunha, O. (2024). *Bidirectional violence in intimate relationships: A systematic review.* Sage. https://doi.org/10.1177/15248380231193440

Machado, A., Hines, D., & Douglas, E. M. (2020). Male victims of female-perpetrated partner violence: A qualitative analysis of men's experiences, the impact of violence, and beliefs of their worth. *Psychology of Men & Masculinity, 21*(4), 612–621. https://doi.org/10.1037/men0000285

Machado, A., Santos, A., Graham-Kevan, N., & Matos, M. (2017). Exploring help-seeking experiences of male victims of female perpetrators of IPV. *Journal of Family Violence, 32*(5), 513–523. https://doi.org/10.1007/s10896-016-9853-8

Machado, A., Hines, D., & Matos, M. (2016). Help-seeking and needs of male victims of intimate partner violence in Portugal. *Psychology of Men & Masculinity, 17*(3), 255–264. https://doi.org/10.1037/men0000013

Machisa, M. T., Christofides, N., & Jewkes, R. (2016). Structural pathways between child abuse, poor mental health outcomes, and male-perpetrated intimate partner violence (IPV). *PloS One, 11*(3), e0150986. https://doi.org/10.1371/journal.pone.0150986

Machisa, M. T., Christofides, N., & Jewkes, R. (2018). Social support factors associated with psychological resilience among women survivors of intimate partner violence in Gauteng, South

Africa. *Global Health Action, 11*(sup3), 1491114. https://doi.org/10.1080/16549716.2018.1491114

Machisa, M. T., Christofides, N., & Jewkes, R. (2017). Mental ill health in structural pathways to women's experiences of intimate partner violence. *PloS One, 12*(4), e0175240. https://doi.org/10.1371/journal.pone.0175240

Mackenzie, C., & Sorial, S. (2022). The empathy dilemma: Democratic deliberation, epistemic injustice and the problem of empathetic imagination. *Res Publica (Liverpool, England), 28*(2), 365–389. https://doi.org/10.1007/s11158-021-09534-z

Mackley, M. P., Fletcher, B., Parker, M., Watkins, H., & Ormondroyd, E. (2017). Stakeholder views on secondary findings in whole-genome and whole-exome sequencing: A systematic review of quantitative and qualitative studies. *Genetics in Medicine, 19*(3), 283–293. https://doi.org/10.1038/gim.2016.109

Mackowiak, C., & Scoglio, A. A. J. (2018). The Saving Center: A specialty clinic for treating and preventing IPV among veterans. *Psychological Services, 15*(4), 371–378. https://doi.org/10.1037/ser0000181

MacLeod, A. (2019). Interpretative phenomenological analysis (IPA) as a tool for participatory research within critical autism studies: A systematic review. *Research in Autism Spectrum Disorders, 64*, 49–62. https://doi.org/10.1016/j.rasd.2019.04.005

MacGregor JCD, Wathen CN, Olszowy LP, Saxton MD, & MacQuarrie BJ (2016). Gender differences in workplace disclosure and supports for domestic violence: Results of a Pan-Canadian Survey. *Violence and Victims, 31*(6), 1135–1154. doi: 10.1891/0886-6708.VV-D-15-00078 [PubMed] [Cross Ref] [Google Scholar]

MacLeod, M. (2019). Using the narrative approach with adolescents at risk for suicide. *Canadian Journal of Counselling and Psychotherapy (Online), 53*(1), 59–77.

Madden, R. H., Lukersmith, S., Zhou, Q., Glasgow, M., & Johnston, S. (2020). Disability-related questions for administrative datasets. *International Journal of Environmental Research and Public Health, 17*(15), 5435. https://doi.org/10.3390/ijerph17155435

Magaletta, P. R., Hom, M. A., Stanley, I. H., & Joiner, T. E. (2020). Strategies and solutions to address the mental health needs of protective service workers: An introduction. *Psychological Services, 17*(2), 127–128. https://doi.org/10.1037/ser0000371

Magezi, V., & Manzanga, P. (2020). COVID-19 and intimate partner violence in Zimbabwe: Towards being church in gender-based violence from a public pastoral care perspective. *In Die Skriflig: Tydskrif Van Die Gereformeerde Teologiese Vereniging, 54*(1), e1–e9. https://doi.org/10.4102/ids.v54i1.2658

Maia, E., Vieira, P., & Praça, I. (2023). Empowering preventive care with GECA chatbot. *Healthcare (Basel), 11*(18), 2532. https://doi.org/10.3390/healthcare11182532

Mahamid, F., Veronese, G., & Bdier, D. (2022). Gender-based violence experiences among Palestinian women during the COVID-19 pandemic: Mental health professionals' beliefs and concerns. *Conflict and Health, 16*(1), 13. https://doi.org/10.1186/s13031-022-00444-2

Mak, W. W. S., Chan, R. C. H., & Yau, S. S. W. (2019). Brief psychoeducation program to enhance recovery knowledge and attitudes of mental health service providers and users: Randomized controlled trials. *Administration and Policy in Mental Health and Mental Health Services Research, 46*(2), 200–208. https://doi.org/10.1007/s10488-018-0905-7

Malatras, A., Duguez, S., & Duddy, W. (2019). Muscle gene sets: A versatile methodological aid to functional genomics in the neuromuscular field. *Skeletal Muscle, 9*(1), 10. https://doi.org/10.1186/s13395-019-0196-z

References

Maldonado, A. I., & Murphy, C. M. (2021). Does trauma help explain the need for power and control in perpetrators of intimate partner violence? *Journal of Family Violence, 36*(3), 347–359. https://doi.org/10.1007/s10896-020-00174-0

Malihi, Z. (2021). Factors influencing help-seeking by those who have experienced intimate partner violence: Results from a New Zealand population-based study. *PloS One, 16*(12), e0261059. https://doi.org/10.1371/journal.pone.0261059

Malik, T., Ambrose, A. J., & Sinha, C. (2022). Evaluating user feedback for an artificial intelligence-enabled, cognitive behavioral therapy-based mental health app (wysa): *Qualitative thematic analysis. JMIR Human Factors, 9*(2), e35668. https://doi.org/10.2196/35668

Malik, J., Heyman, R. E., & Smith Slep, A. M. (2020). Emotional flooding in response to negative effect in couple conflicts: Individual differences and correlates. *Journal of Family Psychology, 34*(2), 145–154. https://doi.org/10.1037/fam0000584

Malone, J. C., & Dayton, C. J. (2015). What is the container/contained when there are ghosts in the nursery? Joining Bion and Freiberg in dyadic interventions with mother and infant. *Infant Mental Health Journal, 36*(3), 262–274. https://doi.org/10.1002/imhj.21509

Manning, N. (2019). Assessing violence and sexual risk among offenders with cognitive intellectual difficulties. In J. L. Ireland, C. A. Ireland & P. Birch (Eds.), *Violent and sexual offenders (1st ed.)*, 151–165. Routledge. https://doi.org/10.4324/9781315310411-9

Manjunatha, N. (2023). Trishul division of mental health: Conveying all sadness or stress of life is NOT a mental illness to people, the public, professionals, and policymakers. *Indian Journal of Psychiatry, 65*(9), 983–984. https://doi.org/10.4103/indianjpsychiatry.indianjpsychiatry_286_23

Mao, Z., Ahmed, S., Graham, C., & Kind, P. (2020). Exploring subjective constructions of health in China: A Q-methodological investigation. *Health and Quality of Life Outcomes, 18*(1), 1–165. https://doi.org/10.1186/s12955-020-01414-z

Martin, J., Paul, L., & Robertson, M. (2018). Continuing professional development for accredited mental health social workers: An evaluative study. *Advances in Social Work and Welfare Education, 20*(2), 129–143.

Martin, J., Raby, K. L., Labella, M. H., & Roisman, G. I. (2017). Childhood abuse and neglect, attachment states of mind, and nonsuicidal self-injury. *Attachment & Human Development, 19*(5), 425–446. https://doi.org/10.1080/14616734.2017.1330832

Martin, K., Ricciardelli, R., & Dror, I. (2020). What a forensic mental health nurses' perspective of their patients can bias healthcare: A qualitative review of nursing documentation. *Journal of Clinical Nursing, 29*(13–14), 2482–2494. https://doi.org/10.1111/jocn.15264

Martin, G., Litherland, G., & Duys, D. (2022). Trauma-informed supervision experiences: A preliminary phenomenological study. *Qualitative Report, 27*(10), 2059–2078. https://doi.org/10.46743/2160-3715/2022.5533

Mariscal, T. L., Hughes, C. M. L., & Modrek, S. (2020). Changes in incidents and payment methods for intimate partner violence-related injuries in women living in the United States, 2002 to 2015. *Women's Health Issues, 30*(5), 338–344. https://doi.org/10.1016/j.whi.2020.05.002

Mason, R., & O'Rinn, S. E. (2014). A scoping review of co-occurring intimate partner violence, mental health, and substance use problems. *Global Health Action, 7*(1), 24815. https://doi.org/10.3402/gha.v7.24815

Mathur, R., Thakur, K., & Hazam, R. (2019). Highlights of Indian Council of Medical Research National Ethical Guidelines for Biomedical and health research involving human participants. *Indian Journal of Pharmacology, 51*(3), 214–221. https://doi.org/10.4103/0253-7613.262456

References

Matlala, M. S., & Lumadi, T. G. (2019). Midwives' Perceptions on shortage and retention of staff at a public hospital in Tshwane district. *Curationis (Pretoria), 42*(1), e1–e10. https://doi.org/10.4102/curationis.v42i1.1952

Matope, N., & Khau, M. (2022). Women educators' narratives on intimate partner violence: The case of a state university in Zimbabwe. *Cogent Social Sciences, 8*(1). https://doi.org/10.1080/23311886.2022.2084889

Mawn, L., Welsh, P., Kirkpatrick, L., Webster, L. A. D., & Stain, H. J. (2016). Getting it right! Enhancing youth involvement in mental health research. *Health Expectations: An International Journal of Public Participation in Health Care and Health Policy, 19*(4), 908–919. https://doi.org/10.1111/hex.12386

Mayfield, J., Mayfield, M., & Sharbrough, W. C. (2015). Strategic vision and values in top leaders' communications: Motivating language at a higher level. *International Journal of Business Communication, 52*(1), 97–121. https://doi.org/10.1177/2329488414560282

Mayanja, Y., Kamacooko, O., Lunkuse, J. F., Kyegombe, N., & Ruzagira, E. (2023). Prevalence, perpetrators, and factors associated with intimate partner violence among adolescents living in urban slums of Kampala, Uganda. *Journal of Interpersonal Violence, 38*(13–14), 8377–8399. https://doi.org/10.1177/08862605231155128

Merchant, L. V., & Whiting, J. B. (2018). A grounded theory study of how couples desist from intimate partner violence. *Journal of Marital and Family Therapy, 44*(4), 590–605. https://doi.org/10.1111/jmft.12278

McCabe, R., & Day, E. (2022). Counselors' experiences of using mindfulness in treating depression and anxiety: An interpretative phenomenological analysis. *Counseling and Psychotherapy Research, 22*(1), 166–174. https://doi.org/10.1002/capr.12428

McCarrick, J., Davis-McCabe, C., Davis-McCabe, C., Hirst-Winthrop, S., & Hirst-Winthrop, S. (2016). Men's criminal justice system experiences following female perpetrated intimate partner violence. *Journal of Family Violence, 31*(2), 203–213. https://doi.org/10.1007/s10896-015-9749-z

McCauley, M., Brown, A., Ofosu, B., & van den Broek, N. (2019). "I just wish it becomes part of routine care": Healthcare providers' knowledge, attitudes, and beliefs of screening for maternal mental health during and after pregnancy: A qualitative study. *BMC Psychiatry, 19*(1), 279. https://doi.org/10.1186/s12888-019-2261-x

McCormack, L., Tillock, K., & Walmsley, B. D. (2017). Holding on while letting go: Trauma and growth on the pathway of dementia care in families. *Aging & Mental Health, 21*(6), 658–667. https://doi.org/10.1080/13607863.2016.1146872

McCrudden, M. T., & Marchand, G. (2020). Multilevel mixed methods research and educational psychology. *Educational Psychologist, 55*(4), 197–207. https://doi.org/10.1080/00461520.2020.1793156

McClure, M. M., & Parmenter, M. (2020). Childhood trauma, trait anxiety, and anxious attachment as predictors of intimate partner violence in college students. *Journal of Interpersonal Violence, 35*(23–24), 6067–6082. https://doi.org/10.1177/0886260517721894

McGinn, T., McColgan, M., & Taylor, B. (2020). Male IPV Perpetrator's perspectives on intervention and change: A systematic synthesis of qualitative studies. *Sage*. https://doi.org/10.1177/1524838017742167

McGinn, T., Taylor, B., & McColgan, M. (2021). A qualitative study of the perspectives of domestic violence survivors on behavior change programs with perpetrators. *Journal of Interpersonal Violence, 36*(17–18), NP9364–NP9390. https://doi.org/10.1177/0886260519855663

McGinn, T., Taylor, B., McColgan, M., & Lagdon, S. (2016). Survivor perspectives on IPV perpetrator interventions: A systematic narrative review. *Trauma, Violence & Abuse, 17*(3), 239–255. https://doi.org/10.1177/1524838015584358

McIntyre, J., Daley, A., Rutherford, K., & Ross, L. E. (2011). Systems-level barriers in accessing supportive mental health services for sexual and gender minorities: Insights from the provider's perspective. *Canadian Journal of Community Mental Health, 30*(2), 173–186. https://doi.org/10.7870/cjcmh-2011-0023

McKee, S. A., & Hilton, N. Z. (2019). Co-occurring substance use, PTSD, and IPV victimization: Implications for female offender services. *Trauma, Violence & Abuse, 20, Violence & Abuse, 20*(3), 303–314. https://doi.org/10.1177/1524838017708782

McKinley, C. E., Ka'apu, K., Scarnato, J. M., & Liddell, J. (2020). Cardiovascular health among U.S. indigenous peoples: A holistic and sex-specific systematic review. *Journal of Evidence-Based Social Work (2019), 17*(1), 24–48. https://doi.org/10.1080/26408066.2019.1617817

McLaughlan, T. (2023). International undergraduates' feelings of social engagement in online and face-to-face learning environments: A photo-elicitation approach to thematic analysis. *Smart Learning Environments, 10*(1), 1–18. https://doi.org/10.1186/s40561-023-00230-4

McMahon, T. R., Griese, E. R., & Kenyon, D. B. (2019). Cultivating native American scientists: An application of an indigenous model to an undergraduate research experience. *Cultural Studies of Science Education, 14*(1), 77–110. https://doi.org/10.1007/s11422-017-9850-0

McMillan, I. F., Schroeder, G. E., & Langhinrichsen-Rohling, J. (2023). Heterogeneity in college Students' technology-facilitated intimate partner violence perpetration occurring post-breakup: A latent profile analysis. *Journal of Interpersonal Violence, 38*(17–18), 10388–10408. https://doi.org/10.1177/08862605231171416

McTavish, J. R., Chandra, P. S., Stewart, D. E., Herrman, H., & MacMillan, H. L. (2022). Child maltreatment and intimate partner violence in mental health settings. *International Journal of Environmental Research and Public Health, 19*(23), 15672. https://doi.org/10.3390/ijerph192315672

McTavish, J. R., Chandra, P. S., Stewart, D. E., Herrman, H., & MacMillan, H. L. (2022). Child maltreatment and intimate partner violence in mental health settings. *International Journal of Environmental Research and Public Health, 19*(23), 15672. https://doi.org/10.3390/ijerph192315672

Meighan, P. J. (2022). Dùthchas is a Scottish Gaelic method that guides self-decolonization and conceptualizes a centric and relational approach to community-led research. *International Journal of Qualitative Methods, 21*, 160940692211424. https://doi.org/10.1177/16094069221142451

Melchiorre, M. G., Di Rosa, M., Macassa, G., Eslami, B., Torres-Gonzales, F., Stankunas, M., Lindert, J., Ioannidi-Kapolou, E., Barros, H., Lamura, G., & J. F. Soares, J. (2021). The prevalence, severity, and chronicity of abuse towards older men: Insights from a multinational European survey. *PloS One, 16*(4), e0250039. https://doi.org/10.1371/journal.pone.0250039

Mermillod, M., Grynberg, D., Pio-Lopez, L., Rychlowska, M., Beffara, B., Harquel, S., Vermeulen, N., Niedenthal, P. M., Dutheil, F., & Droit-Volet, S. (2018). Evidence of rapid modulation by social information of subjective, physiological, and neural responses to emotional expressions. *Frontiers in Behavioral Neuroscience, 11*, 231. https://doi.org/10.3389/fnbeh.2017.00231

Meuwly, N., & Davila, J. (2019). Feeling bad when your partner is away: The role of dysfunctional cognition and affect regulation strategies in insecurely attached individuals. *Journal of Social and Personal Relationships, 36*(1), 22–42. https://doi.org/10.1177/0265407517718389

Meyer, S., & Frost, A. (2019). *Responding to domestic and family violence: Good practices (1st ed.)*. 140–163. Routledge. https://doi.org/10.4324/9781315148281-10

Meyer, S., & Frost, A. (2019). *Theoretical strands (1st ed.)*. 19–35. Routledge. https://doi.org/10.4324/9781315148281-3

References

Michael, K. D., & Jameson, J. P. (2017). *Handbook of rural school mental health (1st ed.)*. Springer.

Micklitz, H. M., Nagel, Z., Jahn, S., Oertelt-Prigione, S., Andersson, G., & Sander, L. B. (2023). Digital self-help for people experiencing intimate partner violence: A qualitative study on user experiences and needs including people with lived experiences and services providers. *BMC Public Health, 23*(1), 1471. https://doi.org/10.1186/s12889-023-16357-5

Mihalache, G. (2019). Heuristic inquiry: Differentiated from descriptive phenomenology and aligned with transpersonal research methods. *The Humanistic Psychologist, 47*(2), 136–157. https://doi.org/10.1037/hum0000125

Mikulincer, M., & Shaver, P. R. (2017). Augmenting the sense of attachment security in group contexts: The effects of a responsive leader and a cohesive group. *International Journal of Group Psychotherapy, 67*(2), 161–175. https://doi.org/10.1080/00207284.2016.1260462

Miles, M. B., & Huberman, A. M. (1994). *Qualitative data analysis: An expanded source reference book* (2nd ed.). Sage.

Miller, E. (2016). Beyond bingo: A phenomenological exploration of leisure in aged care. *Journal of Leisure Research, 48*(1), 35–49. http://dx.doi.org.library.capella.edu/10.18666/jlr-2016-v48-i1-6254

Miller, S. L., Kafonek, K., & Iovanni, L. (2021). Agency and paternalism: Balancing acts between a domestic violence survivors' task force and a state coalition. *Violence Against Women, 27*(10), 1655–1677. https://doi.org/10.1177/1077801220947179

Miller, W. R. (2016). Sacred cows and greener pastures: Reflections from 40 years in addiction research. *Alcoholism Treatment Quarterly, 34*(1), 92–115. https://doi.org/10.1080/07347324.2015.1077637

Millar, A., Saxton, M., Øverlien, C., & Elliffe, R. (2022). Police officers do not need more training, but different training is needed. Policing domestic violence and abuse involving children: A rapid review. *Journal of Family Violence, 37*(7), 1071–1088. https://doi.org/10.1007/s10896-021-00325-x

Miranda, C., Veach, P. M., Martyr, M. A., & LeRoy, B. S. (2015, 2016). Portrait of the master genetic counselor clinician: A qualitative investigation of ability in genetic counseling. *Journal of Genetic Counseling, 25*(4), 767–785. https://doi.org/10.1007/s10897-015-9863-3

Mittal, M., Paden McCormick, A., Palit, M., Trabold, N., & Spencer, C. (2023). A meta-analysis and systematic review of community-based intimate partner violence interventions in India. *International Journal of Environmental Research and Public Health, 20*(7), 5277. https://doi.org/10.3390/ijerph20075277

Mitran, C. L. (2023). Experiences of licensed counselors and other licensed mental health providers working with neurodiverse adults: An instrumental case study. *The Family Journal (Alexandria, Va.), 31*(3), 357–366. https://doi.org/10.1177/10664807221104138

Mjøsund, N. H., Eriksson, M., Espnes, G. A., Haaland-Øverby, M., Jensen, S. L., Norheim, I., Kjus, S. H. H., Portaasen, I., & Vinje, H. F. (2017). Service user involvement enhanced the research quality in a study using interpretative phenomenology analysis—the power of multiple perspectives. *Journal of Advanced Nursing, 73*(1), 265–278. https://doi.org/10.1111/jan.13093

Moeini, S., Shahriari, M., & Shamali, M. (2020). Ethical challenges of obtaining informed consent from surgical patients. *Nursing Ethics, 27*(2), 527–536. https://doi.org/10.1177/0969733019857781

Mohamed, A., MacDonagh, E., & Giridhar, R. (2023). Mental health and contraception—are we doing enough? A study exploring the current practice of providing contraceptive advice by mental health professionals. *BJPsych Open, 9*(S1), S63. https://doi.org/10.1192/bjo.2023.218

Mokitimi, S., Jonas, K., Schneider, M., & de Vries, P. J. (2022). Child and adolescent mental health services in the Western Cape province of South Africa: Service providers' perspectives. *Child and Adolescent Psychiatry and Mental Health, 16*(1), 1–57. https://doi.org/10.1186/s13034-022-00491-w

Molas, A. (2022). The limits of simulation for understanding mental illness: Defending a Steinian theory of empathy. *Dialogue - Canadian Philosophical Association, 61*(3), 395–405. https://doi.org/10.1017/S0012217322000270

Molenaar, J., Hanlon, C., Alem, A., Wondimagegn, D., Medhin, G., Prince, M., & Stevenson, E. G. J. (2020). Perinatal mental distress in a rural Ethiopian community: A critical examination of psychiatric labels. *B.M.C. Psychiatry, 20*(1), 223. https://doi.org/10.1186/s12888-020-02646-5

Monteleone, R., & Forrester-Jones, R. (2017). 'Disability means, um, dysfunctioning people': A qualitative analysis of the meaning and experience of disability among adults with intellectual disabilities. *Journal of Applied Research in Intellectual Disabilities, 30*(2), 301–315. https://doi.org/10.1111/jar.12240

Montgomery, L., Wilson, G., Houston, S., Davidson, G., & Harper, C. (2019). An evaluation of mental health service provision in Northern Ireland. *Health & Social Care in the Community, 27*(1), 105–114. https://doi.org/10.1111/hsc.12627

Mookerjee, S., Cerulli, C., Fernandez, I. D., & Chin, N. P. (2015). Do Hispanic and non-Hispanic women survivors of intimate partner violence differ in their help-seeking? A qualitative study. *Journal of Family Violence, 30*(7), 839–851. https://doi.org/10.1007/s10896-015-9734-6

Morrison, P. K., Cluss, P. A., Miller, E. P., Fleming, R., Hawker, L., Bicehouse, T., & George, D. (2017). Elements needed for quality batterer intervention programs: Perspectives of professionals who deal with intimate partner violence. *Journal of Family Violence, 32*(5), 481–491. https://doi.org/10.1007/s10896-016-9835

Morgan, C., Badawi, N., & Novak, I. (2023). "A different ride": A qualitative interview study of parents' experience with early diagnosis and goals, activity, motor enrichment (GAME) intervention for infants with cerebral palsy. *Journal of Clinical Medicine, 12*(2), 583. https://doi.org/10.3390/jcm12020583

Mørk, M., Soberg, H. L., Hoksrud, A. F., Heide, M., & Groven, K. S. (2023). The struggle to stay physically active—A qualitative study exploring experiences of individuals with persistent plantar fasciopathy. *Journal of Foot and Ankle Research, 16*(1), 20. https://doi.org/10.1186/s13047-023-00620-4

Morris, M., Okoth, V., Prigmore, H. L., Ressler, D. J., Mbeya, J., Rogers, A., Moon, T. D., & Audet, C. M. (2022, 2020). The prevalence of interpersonal violence (IPV) against women and its associated variables: An exploratory study in the Rongo sub-county of Migori county, Kenya. *Journal of Interpersonal Violence, 37*(5–6), 2083–2101. https://doi.org/10.1177/0886260520935484

Moreira, P. A. S., Pinto, M., Cloninger, C. R., Rodrigues, D., & da Silva, C. F. (2019). Understanding the experience of psychopathology after intimate partner violence: The role of personality. *PeerJ 7*, e6647. https://doi.org/10.7717/peerj.6647

Moreira, A., Moreira, A. C., & Rocha, J. C. (2022). Randomized controlled trial: Cognitive-narrative therapy for IPV victims. *Journal of Interpersonal Violence, 37*(5–6), NP2998–NP3014. https://doi.org/10.1177/0886260520943719

Morgan, K., Buller, A. M., Evans, M., Trevillion, K., Williamson, E., & Malpass, A. (2016). The role of gender, sexuality, and context upon help-seeking for intimate partner violence: A synthesis of data across five studies. *Aggression and Violent Behavior, 31*, 136–146. https://doi.org/10.1016/j.avb.2016.09.001

Morgan, W., & Wells, M. (2016). 'it's deemed unmanly': Men's experiences of intimate partner violence (IPV). *The Journal of Forensic Psychiatry & Psychology, 27*(3), 404–418. https://doi.org/10.1080/14789949.2015.1127986

Morriss, L. (2015). Nut clusters and crisps: Atrocity stories and co-narration in interviews with approved mental health professionals. *Sociology of Health & Illness, 37*(7), 1072–1085. https://doi.org/10.1111/1467-9566.12285

Morse, D. S., Cerulli, C., Hordes, M., El-Bassel, N., Bleasdale, J., Wilson, K., Henry, O., & Przybyla, S. M. (2022). "I was 15 when I started doing drugs with my dad": Victimization, social determinants of health, and criminogenic risk among women opioid intervention court participants. *Journal of Interpersonal Violence, 37*(21–22), NP20513–NP20541. https://doi.org/10.1177/08862605211052053

Morton, S., & Hohman, M. (2016). "That is the weight of knowing": Practitioner skills and impact when delivering psychoeducational group work for women who have experienced IPV. *Social Work with Groups, 39*(4), 277–291. https://doi.org/10.1080/01609513.2015.1052915

Moser, A., & Korstjens, I. (2018, 2017). Series: Practical guidance to qualitative research. Part 3: Sampling, data collection, and analysis. *The European Journal of General Practice, 24*(1), 9–18. https://doi.org/10.1080/13814788.2017.1375091

Moskalewicz, M., Kordel, P., & Wiertlewska-Bielarz, J. (2023). Chemotherapy, clocks, and the awareness of death: A quantitative phenomenological study. *Frontiers in Psychology, 14*, 1097928. https://doi.org/10.3389/fpsyg.2023.1097928

Mossière, A., Maeder, E. M., & Pica, E. (2018). The racial composition of couples in battered spouse syndrome cases: A look at juror feelings and decisions. *Journal of Interpersonal Violence, 33*(18), 2867–2890. https://doi.org/10.1177/0886260516632355

Mott, J., & Martin, L. A. (2019). Adverse childhood experiences, self-care, and compassion outcomes in mental health providers working with trauma. *Journal of Clinical Psychology, 75*(6), 1066–1083. https://doi.org/10.1002/jclp.22752

Moudatsou, M., Stavropoulou, A., Philalithis, A., & Koukouli, S. (2020). The Role of Empathy in Health and Social Care Professionals. *Healthcare, 8*(1), 26. https://doi.org/10.3390/healthcare8010026

Moullin, J. C., Sabater-Hernández, D., Fernandez-Llimos, F., & Benrimoj, S. I. (2015). A systematic review of implementation frameworks of innovations in healthcare and resulting generic implementation framework. *Health Research Policy and Systems, 13*(1), 16. https://doi.org/10.1186/s12961-015-0005-z

Moulding, N., Franzway, S., Wendt, S., Zufferey, C., & Chung, D. (2021). Rethinking Women's mental health after intimate partner violence. *Violence Against Women, 27*(8), 1064–1090. https://doi.org/10.1177/1077801220921937

Moustakas, C. (1994). *Phenomenological research methods.* Sage.

Moxham, L., & Patterson, C. (2017). Why phenomenology is increasingly relevant to nurse researchers. *Nurse Researcher, 25*(3), 6–7. https://doi.org/10.7748/nr.25.3.6.s2

Murray, C. E., Davis, J., Rudolph, L., Graves, K. N., Colbert, R., Fryer, M., Mason, A., & Thigpen, B. (2016). Domestic violence training experiences and needs among mental health professionals: Implications from a statewide survey. *Violence and Victims, 31*(5), 901–920. https://doi.org/10.1891/0886-6708.VV-D-14-00092

Mushonga, D. R., Rasheem, S., & Anderson, D. (2021). Moreover, I raise Resilience factors contributing to posttraumatic growth in African American women. *Journal of Black Psychology, 47*(2–3), 151–176. https://doi.org/10.1177/0095798420979805

Muir, H. J., Coyne, A. E., Morrison, N. R., Boswell, J. F., & Constantino, M. J. (2019). Ethical implications of routine outcomes checking for patients, psychotherapists, and mental health care systems. *Psychotherapy (Chicago, Ill.), 56*(4), 459–469. https://doi.org/10.1037/pst0000246

Murphy, C. M., Eckhardt, C. I., Clifford, J. M., LaMotte, A. D., & Meis, L. A. (2020). Individual versus group cognitive-behavioral therapy for partner-violent men: A preliminary randomized trial. *Journal of Interpersonal Violence, 35*(15–16), 2846–2868. https://doi.org/10.1177/0886260517705666

Murali-Larson, J. (2023). CORR insights®: What is the prevalence of intimate partner violence and traumatic brain injury in fracture clinic patients? *Clinical Orthopaedics and Related Research, 481*(1), 143–144. https://doi.org/10.1097/CORR.0000000000002444

Murshid, N. S., & Bowen, E. A. (2018). A trauma-informed analysis of the Violence Against Women Act's provisions for undocumented immigrant women. *Violence Against Women, 24*(13), 1540–1556. https://doi.org/10.1177/1077801217741991

Musa, A., Chojenta, C., Loxton, D., & Lopez-Goni, J. J. (2020). High rate of partner violence during pregnancy in eastern Ethiopia: Findings from a facility-based study. *PloS One, 15*(6), e0233907. https://doi.org/10.1371/journal.pone.0233907

Muzik, M., Rosenblum, K. L., Alfafara, E. A., Schuster, M. M., Miller, N. M., Waddell, R. M., & Kohler, E. S. (2015). Mom power: Preliminary outcomes of a group intervention to improve mental health and parenting among high-risk mothers. *Archives of Women's Mental Health, 18*(3), 507–521. doi: http://dx.doi.org.library.capella.edu/10.1007/s00737-014-0490-z

Mwendera, C. A., de Jager, C., Longwe, H., Phiri, K., Hongoro, C., & Mutero, C. M. (2016). Facilitating factors and barriers to malaria research use for policy development in Malawi. *Malaria Journal, 15*(1), 512. https://doi.org/10.1186/s12936-016-1547-4

Mwayuli, S. M., Ongolly, F. K., Casmir, E. N., & Ondicho, T. G. (2019). Intimate partner violence against men: A socio-legal perspective of their experiences in Mathira East sub-county, central Kenya. *International Journal of Criminal Justice Sciences, 14*(2), 148–162. https://doi.org/10.5281/zenodo.3712681

Myers, M. W., & Hodges, S. D. (2013). Empathy: Perspective taking and prosocial behavior: Caring for others as we care for the self. In J. J. Froh & A. C. Parks (Eds.), Activities for teaching positive psychology: A guide for instructors (77–83). *American Psychological Association.* https://doi.org/10.1037/14042-013

Mystakidis, S., & Lympouridis, V. (2023). Immersive learning. *Encyclopedia (Basel, Switzerland), 3*(2), 396–405. https://doi.org/10.3390/encyclopedia3020026

Myszkowski, N., Brunet-Gouet, E., Roux, P., Robieux, L., Malézieux, A., Boujut, E., & Zenasni, F. (2017). Is the questionnaire on cognitive and affective empathy measuring two or five dimensions? Evidence in a French sample. *Psychiatry Research, 255,* 292–296. https://doi.org/10.1016/j.psychres.2017.05.047

Nafziger, J., & Koch, A. K. (2019). Correlates of Narrow Bracketing. *The Scandinavian Journal of Economics, 121*(4), 1441–1472. https://doi.org/10.1111/sjoe.12311

Nakalyowa-Luggya, D., Lutwama-Rukundo, E., Kabonesa, C., & Kwiringira, J. (2022). "It is such a shameful experience." barriers to help-seeking among male survivors of intimate partner violence (IPV) in Uganda. *Gender & Behaviour, 20*(4), 20502–20517.

Nally, T., Taket, A., & Graham, M. (2019). Exploring the use of resources to support gender equality in Australian workplaces. *Health Promotion Journal of Australia, 30*(3), 359–370. https://doi.org/10.1002/hpja.227

Nasrallah, F., Bellapart, J., Walsham, J., Jacobson, E., To, X. V., Manzanero, S., Brown, N., Meyer, J., Stuart, J., Evans, T., Chandra, S. S., Ross, J., Campbell, L., Senthuran, S., Newcombe, V., McCullough, J., Fleming, J., Pollard, C., & Reade, M. (2023). Prediction and diagnosis using imaging and clinical biomarkers trial in traumatic brain injury (Predict-TBI) study protocol: An observational, prospective, multicenter cohort study for predicting outcome in moderate-to-severe TBI. *BMJ Open, 13*(4), e067740. https://doi.org/10.1136/bmjopen-2022-067740

References

National Organization of Human Services (NOHS). (2018). Retrieved from NOHS.org, 2018.

National Commission for the Protection of Human Subjects of Biomedical and Behavioral Research. (1979). *Belmont report* (45 CFR 46). https://www.hhs.gov/ohrp/regulations-and-policy/belmont-report/read-the-belmont-report/index.html

National Institute of Clinical Excellence. (2014). PH50: Domestic violence and abuse: How health services, social care, and the organizations they work with can respond effectively. *London, England: National Institute of Clinical Excellence.*

Naweed, A., Stahlut, J., & O'Keeffe, V. (2022). The essence of care: Versatility as an adaptive response to challenges in delivering quality aged care by personal care attendants. *Human Factors, 64*(1), 109–125. https://doi.org/10.1177/00187208211010962

Nayak, S., Bhatnagar, J., & Budhwar, P. (2018). Leveraging social networking for talent management: An exploratory study of Indian firms. *Thunderbird International Business Review, 60*(1), 21–37. https://doi.org/10.1002/tie.21911

Neale, J. (2021). Iterative categorization (IC) (part 2): Interpreting qualitative data. *Addiction (Abingdon, England), 116*(3), 668–676. https://doi.org/10.1111/add.15259

Neal, A. M., & Edwards, K. M. (2017). Perpetrators and victims' attributions for IPV: A critical review of the literature. *Trauma, Violence, & Abuse, 18*(3), 239–267. https://doi.org/10.1177/1524838015603551

Neelakantan, L., Hetrick, S., & Michelson, D. (2019). Users' experiences of trauma-focused cognitive behavioral therapy for children and adolescents: A systematic review and meta-synthesis of qualitative research. *European Child & Adolescent Psychiatry, 28*(7), 877–897. https://doi.org/10.1007/s00787-018-1150-z

Negus, N. H., & Grobler, G. (2021). How can 6-week training course shape mental healthcare professionals to understand mindfulness? Experiences at Weskoppies Psychiatric Hospital. *The South African Journal of Psychiatry, 27*(1), 1489. https://doi.org/10.4102/sajpsychiatry.v27i0.1489

Ndlovu, S. M., Mutshidzi, Tsoka-Gwegweni, J., & Ndirangu, J. (2022). COVID-19 effect on gender-based violence among women in South Africa during lockdown: A narrative review. *African Journal of Reproductive Health, 26*(7), 59–71. https://doi.org/10.29063/ajrh2022/v26i7.7

Nesset, M. B., Lara-Cabrera, M. L., Dalsbø, T. K., Pedersen, S. A., Bjørngaard, J. H., & Palmstierna, T. (2019). Cognitive behavioral group therapy for male perpetrators of intimate partner violence: A systematic review. *BMC Psychiatry, 19*(1), 11. https://doi.org/10.1186/s12888-019-2010-1

Neuwirth, L. S. (2019). Basic psychopharmacology. In K. M. Carpenter, & S. M. Evans (Eds.), (41–59*). American Psychological Association.* https://doi.org/10.1037/0000133-003

Ngoubene-Atioky, A. J., Williamson-Taylor, C., Inman, A. G., & Case, J. (2017). Psychotherapists' empathy for childfree women of intersecting age and socioeconomic status. *Journal of Mental Health Counseling, 39*(3), 211–224. https://doi.org/10.17744/mehc.39.3.03

Nguyen, Q. P., Flynn, N., Kitua, M., Muthumbi, E. M., Mutonga, D. M., Rajab, J., & Miller, E. (2016). The health care sector response to intimate partner violence in Kenya: Exploring health care providers' feelings of care for victims. *Violence and Victims, 31*(5), 888–900. https://doi.org/10.1891/0886-6708.VV-D-13-00146

Nhedzi, A., Haffejee, S., O'Reilly, M., & Vostanis, P. (2022). Scoping child mental health serviceability in South Africa disadvantaged communities: Community provider perspectives. *Journal of Children's Services, 17*(4), 281–297. https://doi.org/10.1108/JCS-05-2022-0017

Nicolaidis, C., Raymaker, D., Kapp, S. K., Baggs, A., Ashkenazy, E., McDonald, K., Weiner, M., Maslak, J., Hunter, M., & Joyce, A. (2019). They aspire to practice-based guidelines for including autistic adults in research as co-researchers and study participants. *Autism: The International Journal of Research and Practice, 23*(8), 2007–2019. https://doi.org/10.1177/1362361319830523

Nikolova, K., Cardenas, I., Steiner, J. J., & Khetarpal, R. (2023). *Women's help-seeking in China and Papua New Guinea: Factors that change survivors of intimate partner violence.* Sage. https://doi.org/10.1177/21582440231221329

Nijjar, R., Ellenbogen, M. A., & Hodgins, S. (2016). Sexual risk behaviors in the adolescent offspring of parents with bipolar disorder: Prospective associations with parents' personality and externalizing behavior in childhood. *Journal of Abnormal Child Psychology, 44*(7), 1347–1359. https://doi.org/10.1007/s10802-015-0112-x

Nijdam-Jones, A., Livingston, J. D., Verdun-Jones, S., & Brink, J. (2015). Using social bonding theory to examine 'recovery' in a forensic mental health hospital: A qualitative study. *Criminal Behaviour and Mental Health, 25*(3), 157–168. https://doi.org/10.1002/cbm.1918

Nnawulezi, N., Sullivan, C. M., & Hacskaylo, M. (2019). Examining the setting characteristics that promote survivor empowerment: A mixed-method study. *Journal of Family Violence, 34*(4), 261–274. https://doi.org/10.1007/s10896-018-0016-y

Noel, L., Chen, Q., Petruzzi, L. J., Phillips, F., Garay, R., Valdez, C., Aranda, M. P., & Jones, B. (2022). Interprofessional collaboration between social workers and community health workers to address health and mental health in the United States: A systematized review. *Health & Social Care in the Community, 30*(6), e6240–e6254. https://doi.org/10.1111/hsc.14061

Nottingham, S. L., Mazerolle, S. M., Bowman, T. G., & Coleman, K. A. (2018). Alignment of athletic training doctoral education and faculty workload. *Athletic Training Education Journal, 13*(3), 268–280. https://doi.org/10.4085/1303268

Nowell, L. S., Norris, J. M., White, D. E., & Moules, N. J. (2017). Thematic analysis: Striving to meet the trustworthiness criteria. *International Journal of Qualitative Methods, 16*(1), 160940691773384. https://doi.org/10.1177/1609406917733847

Novak, M., Drummond, K., & Kumar, A. (2022). Healthcare professionals' experiences with education in short term medical missions: An inductive thematic analysis. *BMC Public Health, 22*(1), 997. https://doi.org/10.1186/s12889-022-13349-9

Noyes, J., Booth, A., Flemming, K., Garside, R., Harden, A., Lewin, S., Pantoja, T., Hannes, K., Cargo, M., & Thomas, J. (2018). Cochrane qualitative and implementation methods group guidance series—paper 3: Methods for assessing methodological limitations, data extraction and synthesis, and confidence in synthesized qualitative findings. *Journal of Clinical Epidemiology, 97*, 49–58. https://doi.org/10.1016/j.jclinepi.2017.06.020

Nusbaum, L., Douglas, B., Damus, K., Paasche-Orlow, M., & Estrella-Luna, N. (2017). Communicating risks and benefits in informed consent for research: A qualitative study. *Global Qualitative Nursing Research, 4*, 2333393617732017. https://doi.org/10.1177/2333393617732017

Nusir, M., Louati, A., Louati, H., Tariq, U., Zitar, R. A., Abualigah, L., & Gandomi, A. H. (2022). Design research insights on text mining analysis: Proving the most used and trends in keywords of design research journals. *Electronics (Basel), 11*(23), 3930. https://doi.org/10.3390/electronics11233930

Nyberg, L., Nyberg, L., Enander, V., Enander, V., Krantz, G., Krantz, G., & Department of Social Work. (2016). Theoretical considerations on Men's experiences of intimate partner violence: An interview-based study. *Journal of Family Violence, 31*(2), 191–202. https://doi.org/10.1007/s10896-015-9785-8

References

Nyström, M. E., Hansson, J., Garvare, R., Andersson-Bäck, M., Institutionen för socialt arbete, Göteborgs universitet, Gothenburg University, Samhällsvetenskapliga fakulteten, Faculty of Social Sciences, & Department of Social Work. (2015). Locally based research and development units as knowledge brokers and change facilitators in health and social care of older people in Sweden. *Evidence & Policy, 11*(1), 57–80. https://doi.org/10.1332/174426514X14098428292539

O'Connor, T. S. J., & Meakes, E. (2021). Three emerging spiritual practices in the Canadian Association for Spiritual Care (CASC): From pastoral care and counseling to multi-faith, evidence-based spiritual care and psycho-spiritual therapy. *The Journal of Pastoral Care & Counseling, 75*(4), 278–283. https://doi.org/10.1177/15423050211036662

O'Dwyer, C., Tarzia, L., Fernbacher, S., & Hegarty, K. (2021). *Health professionals' experiences of providing trauma-informed care in acute psychiatric inpatient settings: A scoping review*. Sage. https://doi.org/10.1177/1524838020903064

O'Brien, R. B. (2016). Intersectionality and adolescent domestic violence and abuse: Addressing "classed sexism" and improving service provision. *International Journal of Human Rights in Healthcare, 9*(3), 161–173. https://doi.org/10.1108/IJHRH-08-2015-0026

O'Dea, B., King, C., Achilles, M. R., Calear, A. L., & Subotic-Kerry, M. (2021). Delivering A digital mental health service in Australian secondary schools: Understanding school counselors' and parents' experiences. *Health Services Insights, 14*, 11786329211017689. https://doi.org/10.1177/11786329211017689

O'Donohue, W., Carlson, G. C., Benuto, L. T., & Bennett, N. M. (2014). Examining the scientific validity of rape trauma syndrome. *Psychiatry, Psychology, and Law, 21*(6), 858–876. https://doi.org/10.1080/13218719.2014.918067

Ogbe, E., Harmon, S., Van den Bergh, R., & Degomme, O. (2020). A systematic review of intimate partner violence interventions focused on improving survivors' social support and/or mental health outcomes. *PloS One, 15*(6), e0235177. https://doi.org/10.1371/journal.pone.0235177

Okenwa-Emegwa, L., & Eriksson, H. (2020). Lessons learned from teaching nursing students about equality, equity, human rights, and forced migration through roleplay in an inclusive classroom. *Sustainability (Basel, Switzerland), 12*(17), 7008. https://doi.org/10.3390/su12177008

Okeke-Ihejirika, P., Tetreault, B., Punjani, N., & Olukotun, M. (2022). Intimate partner violence interventions within immigrant populations: A scoping review of the G7 nations, including Canada. *Canadian Ethnic Studies, 54*(2), 67–97. https://doi.org/10.1353/ces.2022.0014

Olani, A. B., Degefa, N., Aschalew, Z., Kassa, M., Feleke, T., Gura, G., & Wambete, S. N. (2022). Exploring experiences of quarantined people during the early phase of COVID-19 outbreak in southern nations nationalities and peoples' region of Ethiopia: A qualitative study. *PloS One, 17*(9), e0275248. https://doi.org/10.1371/journal.pone.0275248

Oliffe, J. L., Kelly, M. T., Gonzalez Montaner, G., Seidler, Z. E., Kealy, D., Ogrodniczuk, J. S., & Rice, S. M. (2022). Mapping Men's mental health help-seeking after an intimate partner relationship break-up. *Qualitative Health Research, 32*(10), 1464–1476. https://doi.org/10.1177/10497323221110974

Oliffe, J. L., Han, C., Maria, E. S., Lohan, M., Howard, T., Stewart, D. E., & MacMillan, H. (2014). Gay men and intimate partner violence: A gender analysis. *Sociology of Health & Illness, 36*(4), 564–579. https://doi.org/10.1111/1467-9566.12099

Ohlsson-Nevo, E., Andersson, G., & Nilsing Strid, E. (2020, 2019). In the hands of nurses: A focus group study of how nurses perceive and promote inpatients' needs for physical activity. *Nursing Open, 7*(1), 334–344. https://doi.org/10.1002/nop2.401

References

Onnis, L. (2016). Restoring the mind-body unity: A new alliance between neurosciences and psychotherapy. *Journal of Family Psychotherapy, 27*(1), 1-9. https://doi.org/10.1080/08975353.2016.1136544

Onwuegbuzie, A. J., & Collins, K. M. T. (2017). The role of sampling in mixed methods-research: Enhancing inference quality. *Kölner Zeitschrift Für Soziologie Und Sozialpsychologie, 69*(Suppl 2), 133–156. https://doi.org/10.1007/s11577-017-0455-0

O'Reilly-de Brún, M., de Brún, T., Okonkwo, E., Bonsenge-Bokanga, J., De Almeida Silva, Maria Manuela, Ogbebor, F., Mierzejewska, A., Nnadi, L., van Weel-Baumgarten, E., van Weel, C., van den Muijsenbergh, M., & MacFarlane, A. (2016). Using participatory learning action research to access and engage with 'hard to reach' migrants in primary healthcare research. *BMC Health Services Research, 16*(23), 25. https://doi.org/10.1186/s12913-015-1247-8

Ornell, F., Schuch, J. B., Sordi, A. O., & Kessler, F. H. P. (2020). "Pandemic fear" and COVID-19: Mental health burden and strategies. *Revista Brasileira De Psiquiatria, 42*(3), 232–235. https://doi.org/10.1590/1516-4446-2020-0008

Oshri, A., Carlson, M. W., Kwon, J. A., Zeichner, A., & Wickrama, Kandauda K. A. S. (2017). Developmental growth trajectories of self-esteem in adolescence: Associations with child neglect and drug use and abuse in young adulthood. *Journal of Youth and Adolescence, 46*(1), 151–164. https://doi.org/10.1007/s10964-016-0483-5

Otto, N., & Brunson, M. (2021). Cross-boundary weed management in protected area–centered ecosystems: How can it work and what makes it harder to achieve? *Invasive Plant Science and Management, 14*(3), 183–189. https://doi.org/10.1017/inp.2021.24

Overstreet, N. M., Willie, T. C., Hellmuth, J. C., & Sullivan, T. P. (2015). Psychological, intimate partner violence and sexual risk behavior: Examining the role of distinct posttraumatic stress disorder symptoms in the partner Violence–Sexual risk link. *Women's Health Issues, 25*(1), 73–78. https://doi.org/10.1016/j.whi.2014.10.005

Ozodiegwu, I. D., Ogunwale, A. O., Surakat, O., Akinyemi, J. O., Bamgboye, E. A., Fagbamigbe, A. F., Bello, M. M., Adamu, A. Y., Uhomobhi, P., Ademu, C., Okoronkwo, C., Adeleke, M., & Ajayi, I. O. (2023). Description of the design of a mixed-methods study to assess the burden and determinants of malaria transmission for tailoring of interventions (microstratification) in Ibadan and Kano metropolis. *Malaria Journal, 22*(1), 1–255. https://doi.org/10.1186/s12936-023-04684-2

Ozturk, M. B., & Berber, A. (2022). Racialized professionals' experiences of selective incivility in organizations: A multi-level analysis of subtle racism. *Human Relations (New York), 75*(2), 213–239. https://doi.org/10.1177/0018726720957727

Paat, Y., & Markham, C. (2019). The roles of family factors and relationship dynamics on dating violence victimization and perpetration among college men and women in emerging adulthood. *Journal of Interpersonal Violence, 34*(1), 81–114. https://doi.org/10.1177/0886260516640544

Päivinen, H., & Holma, J. (2017). Towards gender awareness in couple therapy and treatment of intimate partner violence. *Journal of Gender-Based Violence, 1*(2), 221–234. https://doi.org/10.1332/239868017X15090095287019

Palasinski, M. (2019). Mirror on the wall, which is the most convincing of them all? Exploring anti-domestic violence posters. *Journal of Interpersonal Violence, 34*(9), 1755–1771. https://doi.org/10.1177/0886260516654931

Papageorgiou, A., Loke, Y. K., & Fromage, M. (2018). Communication skills training for mental health professionals working with people with severe mental illness. *BJPsych Advances, 24*(4), 220. https://doi.org/10.1192/bja.2018.18

Papp, L. M., Kouros, C. D., & Cummings, E. M. (2010). Emotions in marital conflict interactions: Empathic accuracy, assumed similarity, and the moderating context of depressive symptoms. *Journal of Social and Personal Relationships, 27*(3), 367–387. https://doi.org/10.1177/0265407509348810

Parameswaran, U. D., Ozawa-Kirk, J. L., & Latendresse, G. (2020). To live (code) or to not: A new method for coding in qualitative research. *Qualitative Social Work: QSW: Research and Practice, 19*(4), 630–644. https://doi.org/10.1177/1473325019840394

Paris, P. (2017). Skepticism about virtue and the five-factor model of personality. *Utilitas, 29*(4), 423–452. https://doi.org/10.1017/S0953820816000327

Parker, J. (2010). Approved social worker to an approved mental health professional: Evaluating the impact of changes within education and training. *The Journal of Mental Health Training, Education, and Practice, 5*(2), 19–26. https://doi.org/10.5042/jmhtep.2010.0362

Park, S., Bang, S.-H., & Jeon, J. (2021). "This Society Ignores Our Victimization": Understanding the Experiences of Korean Male Victims of Intimate Partner Violence. *Journal of Interpersonal Violence, 36*(23–24), 11658–11680. https://doi.org/10.1177/0886260519900966

Park, T., Thompson, K., Wekerle, C., Al-Hamdani, M., Smith, S., Hudson, A., Goldstein, A., & Stewart, S. H. (2019). Posttraumatic stress symptoms and coping motives mediate the association between childhood maltreatment and alcohol problems. *Journal of Traumatic Stress, 32*(6), 918–926. https://doi.org/10.1002/jts.22467

Park, T., Mutoni, L., Sridhar, R., Hegadoren, K., & Workun, B. (2022). Mental healthcare providers understanding and experiences of palliative care: A qualitative analysis. *Journal of Palliative Care*, 82585972211348. https://doi.org/10.1177/08258597221134865

Park A. L, Boustani M. M, Saifan D, Gellatly R, Letamendi A, Stanick C, Regan J, Perez G, Manners D, Reding MEJ, Chorpita BF. (2020). Community Mental Health Professionals' Perceptions About Engaging Underserved Populations. *Adm Policy Ment Health, 47*(3), 366–379. doi: 10.1007/s10488-019-00994-3. PMID: 31721005.

Parth, K., Wolf, I., & Löffler-Stastka, H. (2019). Capturing the unconscious is the "Psychoanalytic core competency assessment." An innovative tool for investigating psychodynamic therapeutic skills. *International Journal of Environmental Research and Public Health, 16*(23), 4700. https://doi.org/10.3390/ijerph16234700

Parveen, A., Allmark, P., Booth, A., Seedat, F., Woods, H. B., & McGarry, J. (2021). How correct and useful are UK prevalence rates of intimate partner violence (IPV) published? Rapid review and methodological commentary. *Journal of Criminal Psychology, 11*(2), 129–140. https://doi.org/10.1108/JCP-11-2020-0048

Parsons, T., & Bales, R. F. (1956). *Family socialization and interaction process.* London, UK: Routledge.

Patton, M.Q. (1990). *Qualitative Evaluation and Research Methods.* Sage.

Patton, M. Q. (2002). *Qualitative research and evaluation methods* (3rd ed.). Sage.

Patton, M. Q. (2015). *Qualitative research & evaluation methods* (4th ed.). Sage.

Patten, K. K. (2022). Finding our strengths: Recognizing professional bias and interrogating systems. *The American Journal of Occupational Therapy, 76*(6). https://doi.org/10.5014/ajot.2022.076603

Paterson, J., Prah, P., Tautolo, E., & Iusitini, L. (2022). Pacific Islands families study Patterns of intimate partner violence among Pacific mothers. *Journal of Interpersonal Violence, 37*(5–6), 2598–2614. https://doi.org/10.1177/0886260520938510

Pearson, J. N., & Meadan, H. (2018). African American parents' beliefs of diagnosis and services for children with autism. *Education and Training in Autism and Developmental Disabilities, 53*(1), 17–32.

Peled, E., & Krigel, K. (2016). The path to economic independence among survivors of intimate partner violence: A critical review of the literature and courses for action. *Aggression and Violent Behavior, 31*, 127–135. https://doi.org/10.1016/j.avb.2016.08.005

Pelkowitz, L., Crossley, C., Greville, H., & Thompson, S. C. (2023). Dealing with intimate partner violence and family violence in a regional center of western Australia: A study of local social workers' knowledge, attitudes, and practices. *International Journal of Environmental Research and Public Health, 20*(9), 5628. https://doi.org/10.3390/ijerph20095628

Peluso, P. R., Freund, R., Gottman, J. M., Gottman, J. S., & Peluso, J. P. (2019). Validation of the Gottman unfavorable comparisons for alternatives scale. *The Family Journal, 27*(3), 261–267. https://doi.org/10.1177/1066480719843904

Peng, W., Kanthawala, S., Yuan, S., & Hussain, S. A. (2016). A qualitative study of user perceptions of mobile health apps. *BMC Public Health, 16*(1), 1158. https://doi.org/10.1186/s12889-016-3808-0

Penrose, J. (2020). Authenticity, authentication, and experiential authenticity: Telling stories in museums. *Social & Cultural Geography, 21*(9), 1245–1267. https://doi.org/10.1080/14649365.2018.1550581

Peraica, T., Kovačić Petrović, Z., Barić, Ž., Galić, R., & Kozarić-Kovačić, D. (2021). Gender differences among domestic violence help-seekers: Socio-demographic characteristics, types and duration of violence, perpetrators, and interventions. *Journal of Family Violence, 36*(4), 429–442. https://doi.org/10.1007/s10896-020-00207-8

Perales, J., Reininger, B. M., Lee, M., & Linder, S. H. (2018). Participants' beliefs of interactions with community health workers who promote behavior change: A qualitative characterization from participants with normal, depressive, and anxious mood states. *International Journal for Equity in Health, 17*(1), 19. https://doi.org/10.1186/s12939-018-0729-9

Percy, W., Kostere, K., & Kostere, S. (2015). Generic qualitative research in psychology. *Qualitative Report, 20*(2), 76. https://doi.org/10.46743/2160-3715/2015.2097

Peretz, T., Lehrer, J., & Dworkin, S. L. (2020). Impacts of Men's gender-transformative personal narratives: A qualitative evaluation of the Men's Story Project. *Men and Masculinities, 23*(1), 104–126. https://doi.org/10.1177/1097184X18780945

Pernebo, K., Pernebo, K., Almqvist, K., & Almqvist, K. (2017). Young children exposed to intimate partner violence describe their abused parent: A qualitative study. *Journal of Family Violence, 32*(2), 169–178. https://doi.org/10.1007/s10896-016-9856-5

Perryman, S. M., & Appleton, J. (2016). Male victims of domestic abuse: Implications for health visiting practice. *Journal of Research in Nursing, 21*(5–6), 386–414. https://doi.org/10.1177/1744987116653785

Peiró, J. M., Martínez-Tur, V., Nagorny-Koring, N., & Auch, C. (2021). A framework of professional transferable competencies for system innovation: Enabling leadership and agency for sustainable development. *Sustainability (Basel, Switzerland), 13*(4), 1737. https://doi.org/10.3390/su13041737

Phipps, D. L., Giles, S., Lewis, P. J., Marsden, K. S., Salema, N., Jeffries, M., Avery, A. J., & Ashcroft, D. M. (2018). Mindful organizing in patients' contributions to primary care medication safety. Health Expectations: *An International Journal of Public Participation in Health Care and Health Policy, 21*(6), 964–972. https://doi.org/10.1111/hex.12689

Pinto, R. J., Correia-Santos, P., Levendosky, A., & Jongenelen, I. (2019). Psychological distress and posttraumatic stress symptoms: The role of maternal satisfaction, parenting stress, and social support among mothers and children exposed to intimate partner violence. *Journal of Interpersonal Violence, 34*(19), 4114–4136. https://doi.org/10.1177/0886260516674199

References

Piotrowski, C. C., & Cameranesi, M. (2018, 2017). Aggression by children exposed to IPV: Exploring the role of child depressive symptoms, trauma-related symptoms, & warmth in family relationships. *Child Psychiatry and Human Development, 49*(3), 360–371. https://doi.org/10.1007/s10578-017-0755-7

Piwowarczyk, L. A., & Ona, F. (2019). BeWell: Quality assurance health promotion pilot. *International Journal of Health Care Quality Assurance, 32*(2), 321–331. https://doi.org/10.1108/IJHCQA-08-2017-0152

Plata-bello, J., Modroño, C., Acosta-lópez, S., Pérez-martín, Y., Marcano, F., García-marín, V., & González–mora, J. L. (2017). Subarachnoid hemorrhage and visuospatial and visuoperceptive impairment: disruption of the mirror neuron system. *Brain Imaging and Behavior, 11*(5), 1538–1547. http://dx.doi.org.library.capella.edu/10.1007/s11682-016-9609-3

Pletzer, J. L., Sanchez, X., & Scheibe, S. (2015). Practicing psychotherapists are more skilled at downregulating negative emotions than other professionals. *Psychotherapy, 52*(3), 346–350. https://doi.org/10.1037/a0039078

Pointet Perizzolo, V. C., Glaus, J., Stein, C. R., Willheim, E., Vital, M., Arnautovic, E., Kaleka, K., Rusconi Serpa, S., Pons, F., Moser, D. A., & Schechter, D. S. (2022). Impact of mothers' IPV-PTSD on their ability to predict their child's emotional comprehension and its relationship to their child's psychopathology. *European Journal of Psych traumatology, 13*(1), 2008152. https://doi.org/10.1080/20008198.2021.2008152

Poleshuck, E., Mazzotta, C., Resch, K., Rogachefsky, A., Bellenger, K., Raimondi, C., Thompson Stone, J., & Cerulli, C. (2018). Development of an innovative treatment paradigm for intimate partner violence victims with depression and pain using community-based participatory research. *Journal of Interpersonal Violence, 33*(17), 2704–2724. https://doi.org/10.1177/0886260516628810

Pollard, D. L., & Cantos, A. L. (2021). Attachment, emotion dysregulation, and physical IPV in predominantly Hispanic, young adult couples. *International Journal of Environmental Research and Public Health, 18*(14), 7241. https://doi.org/10.3390/ijerph18147241

Pomey, M., Ghadiri, D. P., Karazivan, P., Fernandez, N., & Clavel, N. (2015). Patients as partners: A qualitative study of patients' engagement in their health care. *PloS One, 10*(4), e0122499. https://doi.org/10.1371/journal.pone.0122499

Pope, J., Redsell, S., Houghton, C., & Matvienko-Sikar, K. (2023). Healthcare professionals' experiences and beliefs of supporting mental health from pregnancy to two years postpartum. *Midwifery, 118*, 103581. https://doi.org/10.1016/j.midw.2022.103581

Pope, M. A., Jordan, G., Venkataraman, S., Malla, A. K., & Iyer, S. N. (2019). "Everyone has a role": Perspectives of service users with first-episode psychosis, family caregivers, treatment providers, and policymakers on responsibility for supporting individuals with mental health problems. *Qualitative Health Research, 29*(9), 1299–1312. https://doi.org/10.1177/1049732318812422

Pound, P., Langford, R., & Campbell, R. (2016). What do young people think about their school-based sex and relationship education? A qualitative synthesis of young people's views and experiences. *BMJ Open, 6*(9), e011329. https://doi.org/10.1136/bmjopen-2016-011329

Powers, A., & Lajoie, D. (2021). Understanding civilian mental health providers' knowledge in providing care for active-duty service members: Opportunities for improvement. *Journal of the American Psychiatric Nurses Association*, 10783903211011673. https://doi.org/10.1177/10783903211011673

Prange, C., Bruyaka, O., & Marmenout, K. (2018). Investigating the transformation and transition processes between dynamic capabilities: Evidence from DHL. *Organization Studies, 39*(11), 1547–1573. https://doi.org/10.1177/0170840617727775

References

Preiser, B., & Assari, S. (2017, 2018). Psychological predictors of sexual intimate partner violence against black and Hispanic women. *Behavioral Sciences, 8*(1), 3. https://doi.org/10.3390/bs8010003

Preshaw, D. H., Brazil, K., McLaughlin, D., & Frolic, A. (2016). Ethical issues experienced by healthcare workers in nursing homes: A literature review. *Nursing Ethics, 23*(5), 490–506. https://doi.org/10.1177/0969733015576357

Price, R. K., Bell, K. M., & Lilly, M. (2014). The interactive effects of PTSD, emotion regulation, and anger management strategies on female perpetrated IPV. *Violence and Victims, 29*(6), 907–926. https://doi.org/10.1891/0886-6708.VV-D-12-00123

Procentese, F., Di Napoli, I., Tuccillo, F., Chiurazzi, A., & Arcidiacono, C. (2019). Healthcare professionals' feelings and concerns towards domestic violence during pregnancy in southern Italy. *International Journal of Environmental Research and Public Health, 16*(17), 3087. https://doi.org/10.3390/ijerph16173087

Pugh, B., Li, L., & Sun, I. Y. (2021). Beliefs of why women stay in physically abusive relationships: A comparative study of Chinese and U.S. college students. *Journal of Interpersonal Violence, 36*(7–8), 3778–3813. https://doi.org/10.1177/0886260518778264

Purcell, J. R., Lohani, M., Musket, C., Hay, A. C., Isaacowitz, D. M., & Gruber, J. (2018). Lack of emotional gaze preferences using eye-tracking in remitted bipolar I disorder. *International Journal of Bipolar Disorders, 6*(1), 1–10. https://doi.org/10.1186/s40345-018-0123-

Purvis, T., Busingye, D., Andrew, N. E., Kilkenny, M. F., Thrift, A. G., Li, J. C., Cameron, J., Thijs, V., Hackett, M. L., Kneebone, I., Lannin, N. A., & Cadilhac, D. A. (2022). Mixed methods evaluation to explore participant experiences of a pilot randomized trial to ease self-management of people living with stroke: Inspiring virtual enabled resources following vascular events (verve). *Health Expectations: An International Journal of Public Participation in Health*

Care and Health Policy, 25(5), 2570–2581. https://doi.org/10.1111/hex.13584

Pulliam, N., Paone, T. R., Malott, K. M., & Shannon, J. (2019). The experiences of students of color at a predominantly white institution: Implications for counselor training. *Journal of Multicultural Counseling and Development, 47*(4), 239–255. https://doi.org/10.1002/jmcd.12156

Pybis, J., Saxon, D., Hill, A., & Barkham, M. (2017). The comparative effectiveness and efficiency of cognitive behavior therapy and genetic counseling in treating depression: Evidence from the 2nd U.K. national audit of psychological therapies. *BMC Psychiatry, 17*(1), 215. https://doi.org/10.1186/s12888-017-1370-7

Pyke, J., Rabin, K., Phillips, J., Moffs, J., & Balbirnie, M. (2002). Sexuality and the mental health client: Paternalistic attitudes, resistance, lack of information—there are many reasons why sex is infrequently addressed in the lives of people with severe mental health problems. *Canadian Nurse (1924), 98*(5), 19.

Quintal, A., Messier, V., Rabasa-Lhoret, R., & Racine, E. (2020). A qualitative study of individuals with type 1 diabetes on the ethical considerations raised by the artificial pancreas. *Narrative Inquiry in Bioethics, 10*(3), 237–261. https://doi.org/10.1353/nib.2020.0072

Radcliffe, P., d'Oliveira, Ana Flávia Pires Lucas, Lea, S., Santos Figueiredo, W., & Gilchrist, G. (2017). They are accounting for intimate partner violence perpetration. A cross-cultural comparison of English and Brazilian male substance users' explanations. *Drug and Alcohol Review, 36*(1), 64–71. https://doi.org/10.1111/dar.12450

Radford, S. J., Moran, G. W., & Czuber-Dochan, W. (2022). The impact of inflammatory bowel disease-related fatigue on health-related quality of life: A qualitative semi-structured interview study. *Journal of Research in Nursing, 27*(8), 685–702. https://doi.org/10.1177/17449871211061048

References

Radzvilavicius, A. L., Stewart, A. J., & Plotkin, J. B. (2019). Evolution of empathetic moral evaluation. *Elife, 8*. https://doi.org/10.7554/eLife.44269

Raghavan, M., Bruce, J., Bair-Merritt, M., Lucha, S., Maya-Silva, J., Stebbins, E., & Chamberlain, L. (2018). Building a novel health curriculum for survivors of intimate partner violence in a transitional housing program. *Violence Against Women, 24*(3), 266–285. https://doi.org/10.1177/1077801217697206

Ragusa, A. T. (2017). Rurality influences women's intimate partner violence experiences and the support needed for escape and healing in Australia. *Journal of Social Service Research, 43*(2), 270–295. https://doi.org/10.1080/01488376.2016.1248267

Rajah, V., & Osborn, M. (2022*). Understanding the body and embodiment in the context of Women's resistance to intimate partner violence: A scoping review.* Sage. https://doi.org/10.1177/1524838021995941

Raj, V., Raykar, V., Robinson, A. M., & Islam, M. R. (2022). Child and adolescent mental health training programs for non-specialist professionals in low and middle-income countries: A scoping literature review. *Community Mental Health Journal, 58*(1), 154–165. https://doi.org/10.1007/s10597-021-00805-w

Ramalho, R., Sharma, V., Liang, R., Simon-Kumar, R., Ameratunga, S., Lee, A., Kang, K., & Peiris-John, R. (2023). An intersectional approach to exploring lived realities and harnessing the creativity of ethnic minority youth for health gains: Protocol for a multiphase mixed method study. *BMC Public Health, 23*(1), 1110. https://doi.org/10.1186/s12889-023-16011-0

Ramírez-Gutiérrez, A. G., Cardoso-Castro, P. P., & Tejeida-Padilla, R. (2021, 2020). A methodological proposal for the complementarity of the SSM and the VSM for analyzing organizational viability. *Systemic Practice and Action Research, 34*(3), 331–357. https://doi.org/10.1007/s11213-020-09536-7

Ramsay, N., Hossain, R., Moore, M., Milo, M., & Brown, A. (2019). Health care while homeless: Barriers, facilitators, and the lived experiences of homeless individuals accessing health care in a Canadian regional municipality. *Qualitative Health Research, 29*(13), 1839–1849. https://doi.org/10.1177/1049732319829434

Rapholo, S. F., Ramphabana, L. B., & Makhubele, J. C. (2019). The influence of socio-cultural practices amongst shaved towards showing child sexual abuse: Implications for practice. *Gender & Behaviour, 17*(4), 13948–13961.

Rathod, S., Pinninti, N., Irfan, M., Gorczynski, P., Rathod, P., Gega, L., & Naeem, F. (2017). Mental Health Service Provision in Low- and Middle-Income Countries. *Health services insights, 10*, 1178632917694350. https://doi.org/10.1177/1178632917694

Ravi, K. E., Robinson, S. R., & Schrag, R. V. (2022). *Facilitators of formal help-seeking for adult survivors of IPV in the United States: A systematic review*. Sage. https://doi.org/10.1177/1524838021995954

Rehan, W., Antfolk, J., Johansson, A., Jern, P., & Santtila, P. (2017). Experiences of severe childhood maltreatment, depression, anxiety, and alcohol abuse among adults in Finland. *PloS One, 12*(5), e0177252. https://doi.org/10.1371/journal.pone. 0177252

Regmi, P. R., Aryal, N., Kurmi, O., Pant, P. R., Teijlingen, E., & Wasti, S. P. (2017). Informed consent in health research: Poses challenges and barriers in low middle-income countries with specific reference to Nepal. *Developing World Bioethics, 17*(2), 84–89. https://doi.org/10.1111/dewb.12123

Reid, S., Katan, A., Ellithy, A., Della Stua, R., & Denisov, E. V. (2019). The perfect storm: Mapping the life course trajectories of serial killers. *International Journal of Offender Therapy and Comparative Criminology, 63*(9), 1621–1662. https://doi.org/10.1177/0306624X19838683

Rejeh, N., Heravi-Karimooi, M., Vaismoradi, M., Griffiths, P., Nikkhah, M., & Bahrami, T. (2017). Psychometric properties of the Farsi version of attitudes to aging questionnaire in Iranian older adults. *Clinical Interventions in Aging, 12,* 1531–1542. https://doi.org/10.2147/CIA.S139321

Remler, D. K., & Van Ryzin, G. G. (2015). *Research methods in practice: Strategies for description and causation* (2nd ed.). Sage.

Renate, K. (2018). Reflection/Commentary on a past article: "Generic qualitative approaches: Pitfalls and benefits of methodological mixology". *International Journal of Qualitative Methods, 17*(1). https://doi.org/10.1177/1609406918788193

Renedo, A., Komporozos-Athanasiou, A., & Marston, C. (2018). Experience as evidence: The dialogic construction of health professional knowledge through patient involvement. *Sociology (Oxford), 52*(4), 778–795. https://doi.org/10.1177/0038038516682457

Renzetti, C. M., Follingstad, D. R., & Coker, A. L. (2017). Renzetti C., Claire M. Renzetti, Follingstad D., Diane R. Follingstad, Coker A. and Ann L. Coker (Eds.), *Preventing intimate partner violence: Interdisciplinary perspectives* (1st ed.). Policy. https://doi.org/10.2307/j.ctt1t89gf6

Reuter, T. R., Newcomb, M. E., Whitton, S. W., & Mustanski, B. (2016). Intimate Partner Violence Victimization in LGBT Young Adults: Demographic Differences and Associations with Health Behaviors. *Psychology of Violence.* doi:10.1037/vio0000031

Rhodes, K. V., & Iwashyna, T. J. (2009). Male perpetrators of intimate partner violence: Support for health care interventions targeted at level of risk. *Behavior Change, 26*(3), 174–189. https://doi.org/10.1375/bech.26.3.174

Rhym, J. (2018). Historicizing feeling: Film theory, neuroscience, and the philosophy of mind. *Discourse, 40*(1), 83–109. https://doi.org/10.13110/discourse.40.1.0083

Richardson, J. A. (2018). The discovery of cumulative knowledge. Accounting, Auditing & *Accountability Journal, 31*(2), 563–585. https://doi.org/10.1108/AAAJ-08-2014-1808

Richards, P. S., Currier, J. M., Jones, R. S., Pearce, M., & Stephens, D. (2023). Training opportunities and resources for spiritually integrated psychotherapists and researchers. In D. K. Judd, G. E. K. Allen & P. S. Richards (Eds.), Handbook of spiritually integrated psychotherapies (423–447). *American Psychological Association.* https://doi.org/10.1037/0000338-022

Riches, S., Iannelli, H., Reynolds, L., Fisher, H. L., Cross, S., & Attoe, C. (2022). Virtual reality-based training for mental health staff: A novel approach to increase empathy, compassion, and subjective understanding of service user experience. *Advances in Simulation (London), 7*(1), 1–19. https://doi.org/10.1186/s41077-022-00217-0

Ridings, L. E., Beasley, L. O., & Silovsky, J. F. (2017). Considerable risk and protective factors for families at risk for child maltreatment: An intervention approach. *Journal of Family Violence, 32*(2), 179–188. https://doi.org/10.1007/s10896-016-982

Rioli, G., Ferrari, S., Henderson, C., & Galeazzi, G. M. (2020). Experiences, opinions and current policies on users' choice and change of the allocated primary mental health professional: A survey among directors of community mental health centers in the Emilia-Romagna region, Italy. *International Journal of Mental Health Systems, 14*(1), 41-41. https://doi.org/10.1186/s13033-020-00373-8

Rivas, C., Ramsay, J., Sadowski, L., Davidson, L. L., Dunne, D., Eldridge, S., & Feder, G. (2015). Advocacy interventions to reduce or drop violence and promote the physical and psychosocial well-being of women who experience intimate partner abuse. *The Cochrane Database of Systematic Reviews, 12,* Article CD005043.

Rivera, P. M., & Fincham, F. (2015). Forgiveness as a mediator of the intergenerational transmission of violence. *Journal of Interpersonal Violence, 30*(6), 895–910. https://doi.org/10.1177/0886260514539765

River, J., & Flood, M. (2021). Masculinity, emotions, and men's suicide. *Sociology of Health & Illness, 43*(4), 910–927. https://doi.org/10.1111/1467-9566.13257

Rizo, C. F., & Rizo, C. F. (2016). Intimate partner violence-related stress and the coping experiences of survivors: "There is only so much a person can handle." *Journal of Family Violence, 31*(5), 581–593. https://doi.org/10.1007/s10896-015-9787-6

Rizo, C. F., Givens, A., & Lombardi, B. (2017). A systematic review of coping among heterosexual female IPV survivors in the United States focuses on the conceptualization and measurement of coping. *Aggression and Violent Behavior, 34*, 35–50. https://doi.org/10.1016/j.avb.2017.03.006

Roberts, R.E. (2020). Qualitative interview questions: Guidance for novice researchers. *The Qualitative Report, 25*(9), 3185–3203. https://nsuworks.nova.edu/tqr/vol25/iss9/1

Roberts, K., Dowell, A., & Nie, J. (2019). Attempting rigor and replicability in the thematic analysis of qualitative research data: A case study of codebook development. *BMC Medical Research Methodology, 19*(1), 1–8. https://doi.org/10.1186/s12874-019-0707-y

Robertson, A., Cresswell, K., Takian, A., Petrakaki, D., Crowe, S., Cornford, T., Barber, N., Avery, A., Fernando, B., Jacklin, A., Prescott, R., Klecun, E., Paton, J., Lichtner, V., Quinn, C., Ali, M., Morrison, Z., Jani, Y., Waring, J., . . . Sheikh, A. (2010). Implementing and adopting nationwide electronic health records in secondary care in England: Qualitative analysis of interim results from a prospective national evaluation. *Bmj, 341*(7778), 872. https://doi.org/10.1136/bmj.c4564

Robinson, K. J., Rose, D., & Salkovskis, P. M. (2017). Seeking help for obsessive-compulsive disorder (OCD): A qualitative study of the enablers and barriers conducted by a researcher with personal experience of OCD. *Psychology and Psychotherapy, 90*(2), 193–211. https://doi.org/10.1111/papt.12090

Robinson, S. R., Ravi, K., & Voth Schrag, R. J. (2021). *A systematic review of barriers to formal help-seeking for adult survivors of IPV in the United States,* 2005–2019. Sage. https://doi.org/10.1177/1524838020916254

Robinson, S., Frawley, P., & Dyson, S. (2021). Access and accessibility in domestic and family violence services for women with disabilities: Widening the lens. *Violence Against Women, 27*(6–7), 918–936. https://doi.org/10.1177/1077801220909890

Rode, D., Rode, M., Marganski, A. J., & Januszek, M. (2019). The impact of physical abuse & exposure to parental IPV on young adolescents in Poland: A clinical assessment and comparison of psychological outcomes. *Journal of Family Violence, 34*(5), 435–447. https://doi.org/10.1007/s10896-019-00036-4

Rolfe, S. M., & Schroeder, R. D. (2020). "Sticks and stones may break my bones, but words will never hurt me": Verbal sexual harassment among middle school students. *Journal of Interpersonal Violence, 35*(17–18), 3462–3486. https://doi.org/10.1177/0886260517709802

Rogers, H. J., Hogan, L., Coates, D., Homer, C. S. E., & Henry, A. (2021). Cross-cultural workers for women and families from migrant and refugee backgrounds: A mixed-methods study of service providers beliefs. *BMC Women's Health, 21*(1), 1–222. https://doi.org/10.1186/s12905-021-01368-4

Rogers, L., De Brún, A., & McAuliffe, E. (2023). Exploring healthcare staff narratives to gain an in-depth understanding of changing multidisciplinary team power dynamics during the COVID-19 pandemic. *BMC Health Services Research, 23*(1), 419. https://doi.org/10.1186/s12913-023-09406-7

Rodríguez-Almagro, J., Hernández-Martínez, A., Rodríguez-Almagro, D., Quirós-García, J. M., Martínez-Galiano, J. M., & Gómez-Salgado, J. (2019). Women's beliefs of a traumatic childbirth experience and factors related to a birth experience. *International Journal of Environmental Research and Public Health, 16*(9), 1654. https://doi.org/10.3390/ijerph16091654

Rolls, L., & Relf, M. (2006). Bracketing interviews: Addressing methodological challenges in qualitative bereavement and palliative care interviewing. *Mortality, 11*(3), 286–305. https://doi.org/10.1080/13576270600774893

Rollins, W. (2020). Social worker-client relationships: Social worker perspectives. *Australian Social Work, 73*(4), 395–407. https://doi.org/10.1080/0312407X.2019.1669687

Román-Martínez, I., Gómez-Miranda, M. E., & Sánchez-Fernández, J. (2017). University research and the creation of spin-offs: The Spanish case: Román-Martínez et al. *European Journal of Education, 52*, 387–398. https://doi.org/10.1111/ejed.12231

Romero-Martínez, Á., Lila, M., & Moya-Albiol, L. (2016). Empathy impairments in intimate partner violence perpetrators with antisocial and borderline traits: A critical factor in the risk of recidivism. *Violence and Victims, 31*(2), 347–360. https://doi.org/10.1891/0886-6708.VV-D-14-00149

Romero-Martínez, Á., Lila, M., Gracia, E., & Moya-Albiol, L. (2019). Improving empathy with motivational strategies in batterer intervention programs: Results of a randomized controlled trial. *British Journal of Clinical Psychology, 58*(2), 125–139. https://doi.org/10.1111/bjc.12204

Romero-Martínez, Á., Lila, M., Martínez, M., Pedrón-Rico, V., & Moya-Albiol, L. (2016). Improvements in empathy and cognitive flexibility after court-mandated intervention program in intimate partner violence perpetrators: The role of alcohol abuse. *International Journal of Environmental Research and Public Health, 13*(4), 394. https://doi.org/10.3390/ijerph13040394

Romme, S., Bosveld, M. H., Van Bokhoven, M. A., De Nooijer, J., Van den Besselaar, H., & Van Dongen, Jerome J. J. (2020). Patient involvement in interprofessional education: A qualitative study yielding recommendations on incorporating the patient's perspective. Health Expectations: *An International Journal of Public Participation in Health Care and Health Policy, 23*(4), 943–957. https://doi.org/10.1111/hex.13073

Roncero, C., Remon-Gallo, D., Casado-Espada, N., Aguilar, L., Gamonal-Limcaoco, S., Gallego, M. T., Bote, B., Montejo, A. L., & Buch-Vicent, B. (2022). Healthcare professionals' feelings and satisfaction with mental health telemedicine during the COVID-19 outbreak: A real-world experience in telepsychiatry. *Frontiers in Psychiatry, 13*, 981346. https://doi.org/10.3389/fpsyt.2022.981346

Ronen, G. M., & Rosenbaum, P. L. (2017). Reflections on ethics and humanity in pediatric neurology: The value of recognizing ethical issues in standard clinical practice. *Current Neurology and Neuroscience Reports, 17*(5), 1–8. https://doi.org/10.1007/s11910-017-0749-7

Rosenbaum, M., Dineen, R., Schmitz, K., Stoll, J., Hsu, M., & Hodges, P. D. (2020). Interpreters' feelings of culture bumps in genetic counseling. *Journal of Genetic Counseling, 29*(3), 352–364. https://doi.org/10.1002/jgc4.1246

Roshi, E., Burazeri, G., Bjegovic, V., Georgieva, L., Donev, D., Scintee, G., Hysa, B., & Laaser, U. (2006). Building public health associations in the transition countries of south-eastern Europe: The example of Albania. *European Journal of Public Health, 16*(3), 243–245. https://doi.org/10.1093/eurpub/ckl017

Rossettini, G., Carlino, E., & Testa, M. (2018). Clinical relevance of contextual factors as triggers of placebo and nocebo effects in musculoskeletal pain. *BMC Musculoskeletal Disorders, 19*(1), 27. https://doi.org/10.1186/s12891-018-1943-8

Rossi, P., Crippa, M., & Scaccabarozzi, G. (2021). The relationship between practitioners and caregivers during palliative care treatment: A grounded theory of a challenging collaborative process. *International Journal of Environmental Research and Public Health, 18*(15), 8081. https://doi.org/10.3390/ijerph18158081

Rossman, G. B., Rallis, S. F., & SAGE Publications. (2017, 2016). *An introduction to qualitative research: Learning in the field* (4th ed.). Sage.

Rotor, E. R., & Capio, C. M. (2018). Clinical reasoning of Filipino physical therapists: Experiences in a developing nation. *Physiotherapy Theory and Practice, 34*(3), 181–193. https://doi.org/10.1080/09593985.2017.1390802

References

Rouleau, E., Barabe, T., & Blow, A. (2019). Creating structure in a time of intense stress: Treating intimate partner violence. *Journal of Couple & Relationship Therapy, 18*(2), 148–169. https://doi.org/10.1080/15332691.2018.1505573

Rovira, A., & Slater, M. (2022). Encouraging bystander helping behavior in a violent incident: A virtual reality study using reinforcement learning. *Scientific Reports, 12*(1), 3843. https://doi.org/10.1038/s41598-022-07872-3

Rowley, L., Morant, N., & Katona, C. (2020). Refugees who have experienced extreme cruelty: A qualitative study of mental health and wellbeing after being granted leave to remain in the UK. *Journal of Immigrant & Refugee Studies, 18*(4), 357–374. https://doi.org/10.1080/15562948.2019.1677974

Roy, D. (2020). Develop and confirm an empirical model to study the mediating role of empathic school leadership in India's high school students' motivation. *Metamorphosis, 19*(1), 7–20. https://doi.org/10.1177/0972622520926294

Roy, V., Brodeur, N., Labarre, M., Bousquet, M., & Sanhueza, T. (2020). How do practitioners and program managers work with male perpetrators view IPV? A Quebec studies. *Journal of Family Violence, 35*(8), 877–888. https://doi.org/10.1007/s10896-019-00104-9

Roy, K., Zvonkovic, A., Goldberg, A., Sharp, E., & LaRossa, R. (2015). Sampling richness and qualitative integrity: Challenges for research with families. *Journal of Marriage and Family, 77*(1), 243–260. https://doi.org/10.1111/jomf.12147

Rubin, H. J. & Rubin, I.S. (2012) *Qualitative Interviewing: The Art of Hearing Data.* (3rd ed.). Sage.

Rubini, E., Valente, M., Trentin, M., Facci, G., Ragazzoni, L., & Gino, S. (2023). Negative consequences of conflict-related sexual violence on survivors: A systematic review of qualitative evidence. *International Journal for Equity in Health, 22*(1), 1–227. https://doi.org/10.1186/s12939-023-02038-7

Rudolph, A. E., Young, A. M., & Havens, J. R. (2020, 2018). Privacy, confidentiality, and safety considerations for conducting geographic momentary assessment studies among persons who use drugs and men who have sex with men. *Journal of Urban Health, 97*(2), 306–316. https://doi.org/10.1007/s11524-018-0315-x

Rugkåsa, J., Tveit, O. G., Berteig, J., Hussain, A., & Ruud, T. (2020). Collaborative care for mental health: A qualitative study of the experiences of patients and health professionals. *BMC Health Services Research, 20*(1), 844. https://doi.org/10.1186/s12913-020-05691-8

Rus, M., & Groselj, U. (2021). Ethics of vaccination in a childhood framework based on the four principles of biomedical ethics. *Vaccines (Basel), 9*(2), 113. https://doi.org/10.3390/vaccines9020113

Russell, B. S., Hutchison, M., Tambling, R., Tomkins, A. J., & Horton, A. L. (2020). Initial challenges of caregiving during COVID-19: Caregiver burden, mental health, and the Parent-Child relationship. *Child Psychiatry and Human Development, 51*(5), 671–682. https://doi.org/10.1007/s10578-020-01037-x

Ruiz-Hernández, J. A., García-Jiménez, J. J., Llor-Esteban, B., & Godoy-Fernández, C. (2015). Risk factors for intimate partner violence in prison inmates/Factores de riesgo de violencia de pareja en población penitenciaria. *The European Journal of Psychology Applied to Legal Context, 7*(1), 41.

Saan, M., Van Wesel, F., Leferink, S., Hox, J., Boeije, H., & Van Der Velden, P. (2022). Social network responses to victims of potentially traumatic events: A systematic review using qualitative evidence synthesis. *PloS One, 17*(11), e0276476. https://doi.org/10.1371/journal.pone.0276476

Sadri, G. (2012). Emotional intelligence and leadership development. *Public Personnel Management, 41*(3), 535–548. https://doi.org/10.1177/009102601204100308

References

Saeedi, Z., Ghorbani, N., Sarafraz, M. R., & Shoar, T. K. (2020). A bias of self-reports among repressors: Examining the evidence for the validity of self-relevant and health-relevant personal reports. *International Journal of Psychology, 55*(1), 76–82. https://doi.org/10.1002/ijop.12560

Sá, Fernando Henrique de L., & Baeza, F. L. C. (2020). Mental health care for refugees and the need for cultural competence training in mental health professionals. *Revista Brasileira De Psiquiatria.* https://doi.org/10.1590/1516-4446-2020-1388

Saldana, J. (2012). *The Coding Manual for Qualitative Researchers*. United Kingdom: Sage.

Saldana, I. J., Scherer, R. W., Rodriguez-Barraquer, I., Jampel, H. D., & Dickersin, K. (2016). The author's financial conflict of interest in randomized ophthalmology research was associated with the conference-published abstracts. *Trials, 17*(1), 213. https://doi.org/10.1186/s13063-016-1343-z

Saldivar, J., Daniel, F., Cernuzzi, L., & Casati, F. (2019). Online idea management for civic engagement: A study on the benefits of integration with social networking. *ACM Transactions on Social Computing, 2*(1), 1–29. https://doi.org/10.1145/3284982

Saletti-Cuesta, L., Aizenberg, L., & Ricci-Cabello, I. (2018). Opinions and experiences of primary healthcare providers of violence against women: A systematic review of qualitative studies. *Journal of Family Violence, 33*(6), 405–420. https://doi.org/10.1007/s10896-018-9971-6

Salom, C. L., Williams, G. M., Najman, J. M., & Alati, R. (2015). Substance use and mental health disorders collaborated with different forms of intimate partner violence victimization. *Drug and Alcohol Dependence, 151*, 121–127. https://doi.org/10.1016/j.drugalcdep.2015.03.011

Sandler, I., Saini, M., Pruett, M. K., Pedro-Carroll, J. L., Johnston, J. R., Holtzworth-Munroe, A., & Emery, R. E. (2016). Convenient and inconvenient truths in family law: Preventing scholar-advocacy bias in using social science research for public policy. *Family Court Review, 54*(2), 150–166. https://doi.org/10.1111/fcre.12211

Sandri, S., Hussein, H., & Alshyab, N. (2020). Sustainability of the energy sector in Jordan: Challenges and opportunities. *Sustainability (Basel, Switzerland), 12*(24), 10465. https://doi.org/10.3390/su122410465

Sankar, S., Parker, N., Nichols, E., Carolan, M., & Escobar-Chew, A. R. (2019). Addressing couple violence in therapy training clinics: A human-centered approach to systems intervention design. *Journal of Couple & Relationship Therapy, 18*(4), 330–352. https://doi.org/10.1080/15332691.2019.1609383

San Cristobal, P., Santelices, M. P., & Miranda Fuenzalida, D. A. (2017). Manifestation of trauma: The effect of early traumatic experiences and adult attachment on parental reflective functioning. *Frontiers in Psychology, 8*, 449. https://doi.org/10.3389/fpsyg.2017.00449

Sanders, W. (2015). An Aristotelian model of moral development. *Journal of Philosophy of Education, 49*(3), 382–398. https://doi.org/10.1111/1467-9752.12109

San-Martín, M., Delgado-Bolton, R., & Vivace, L. (2017). Role of a semiotics-based curriculum in empathy enhancement: A longitudinal study in three Dominican medical schools. *Frontiers in Psychology, 8*, 2018. https://doi.org/10.10.3389/fpsyg.2017.02018

Santamaría-García, H., Baez, S., García, A. M., Flichtentrei, D., Prats, M., Mastandueno, R., & Ibáñez, A. (2017). Empathy for others' suffering and its mediators in mental health professionals. *Scientific Reports, 7*(1), 6391–13. https://doi.org/10.1038/s41598-017-06775-y

Santhanam, S. P., & Hewitt, L. E. (2021, 2020). Perspectives of adults with autism on social communication intervention. *Communication Disorders Quarterly, 42*(3), 156–165. https://doi.org/10.1177/1525740120905501

References

Santo-Tomás Muro, R., Sáenz de Tejada Granados, Carlota, & Rodríguez Romero, E. J. (2020). Green infrastructures in the peri-urban landscape: Exploring local belief of well-being through 'Go-along' and 'Semi-structured interviews. *Sustainability 12*(17), 6836. https://doi.org/10.3390/su12176836

Santos, A., Matos, M., & Machado, A. (2017). Effectiveness of a group intervention program for female victims of intimate partner violence. *Small-Group Research, 48*(1), 34–61. https://doi.org/10.1177/1046496416675226

Santos, A. J., Nunes, B., Kislaya, I., Gil, A. P., & Ribeiro, O. (2019). Older adults' emotional reactions to elder abuse: Individual and victimization determinants. *Health & Social Care in the Community, 27*(3), 609–620. https://doi.org/10.1111/hsc.12673

Santos, A., Matos, M., & Machado, A. (2017). Effectiveness of a group intervention program for female victims of intimate partner violence. *Small-Group Research, 48*(1), 34–61. https://doi.org/10.1177/1046496416675226

Sargent, J., MD, Afzal, K. I., MD, Radwan, K., MD, & Jones, P. M., MD. (2016). Evidence-based family assessment and interventions: Providing mental health professionals techniques for integrating mental health treatment into the family setting. *Journal of the American Academy of Child and Adolescent Psychiatry, 55*(10), S357. https://doi.org/10.1016/j.jaac.2016.07.114

Sathyanarayana Rao, T., Banerjee, D., Sawant, N., Narayan, C., Tandon, A., Manohar, S., & Rao, S. (2022). Forensic and legal aspects of sexuality, sexual offenses, sexual dysfunctions, and disorders. *Indian Journal of Psychiatry, 64*(7), 108–129. https://doi.org/10.4103/indianjpsychiatry.indianjpsychiatry_59_21

Sato, C., Adumattah, A., Abulencia, M. K., Garcellano, P. D., Li, A. T., Fung, K., Poon, M. K., Vahabi, M., & Wong, J. P. (2022). COVID-19 mental health stressors of health care providers in the pandemic acceptance and commitment to empowerment response (PACER) intervention: Qualitative study. *JMIR Formative Research, 6*(3), e35280. https://doi.org/10.2196/35280

Sattar, T., Ahmad, S., & Asim, M. (2022). Intimate partner violence against women in southern Punjab, Pakistan: A phenomenological study. *BMC Women's Health, 22*(1), 505. https://doi.org/10.1186/s12905-022-02095-0

Satyanarayana, V. A., & Krishnamachari, S. (2022). The integrated cognitive-behavioral intervention reduced alcohol use and perpetration of intimate partner violence in a man with alcohol dependence syndrome: A case study. *Journal of Clinical Psychology, 78*(1), 15–25. https://doi.org/10.1002/jclp.23297

Satyen, L., Hansen, A., Green, J. L., & Zark, L. (2022). The effectiveness of culturally specific male domestic violence offender intervention programs on behavior changes and mental health: A systematic review. *International Journal of Environmental Research and Public Health, 19*(22), 15180. https://doi.org/10.3390/ijerph192215180

Saunders, B., Sim, J., Kingstone, T., Baker, S., Waterfield, J., Bartlam, B., Burroughs, H., & Jinks, C. (2018). Saturation in qualitative research: Exploring its conceptualization and operationalization. *Quality & Quantity, 52*(4), 1893–1907. https://doi.org/10.1007/s11135-017-0574-8

Saviet, M., & Ahmann, E. (2022). Using conference sessions as research settings: A field note. *Qualitative Report, 27*(4), 890–896. https://doi.org/10.46743/2160-3715/2022.5204

Sawrikar, P. (2019). Child protection, domestic violence, and ethnic minorities: Narrative results from a mixed methods study in Australia. *PloS One, 14*(12), e0226031. https://doi.org/10.1371/journal.pone.0226031

Sawrikar, P., & Katz, I. (2018). Proposing a service delivery model for Victims/Survivors of child sexual abuse (CSA) from ethnic minority communities in Australia. *Journal of Social Service Research, 44*(5), 730–748. https://doi.org/10.1080/01488376.2018.1479338

Schadler, C. (2016). How do we define situated and ever-transforming family configurations? A new materialistic approach. *Journal of Family Theory & Review, 8*(4), 503–514. https://doi.org/10.1111/jftr.12167

Schermer, V. L. (2021). Building empathic bridges: Cross-cultural 'maternal' attunement in group psychotherapy for immigrants and refugees 1. *Group Analysis, 54*(2), 226–243. https://doi.org/10.1177/0533316420978359

Schmälzle, R., Hartung, F., Barth, A., Imhof, M. A., Kenter, A., Renner, B., & Schupp, H. T. (2019). Visual cues that predict intuitive risk perception in the case of HIV. *PloS One, 14*(2), e0211770. https://doi.org/10.1371/journal.pone.0211770

Schiavone, F., Leone, D., Sorrentino, A., & Scaletti, A. (2020). Re-designing the service experience in the value co-creation process: An exploratory study of a healthcare network. *Business Process Management Journal, 26*(4), 889–908. https://doi.org/10.1108/BPMJ-11-2019-0475

Schweinhart, A., Aramburú, C., Bauer, R., Simons-Rudolph, A., Atwood, K., & Luseno, W. K. (2023). Changes in mental health, emotional distress, and substance use affect women experiencing violence and their service providers during COVID-19 in a U.S. southern state. *International Journal of Environmental Research and Public Health, 20*(4), 2896. https://doi.org/10.3390/ijerph20042896

Segata, J., Beck, L., & Muccillo, L. (2021). Beyond exotic wet markets: COVID-19 ecologies in the global meat-processing industry in Brazil. *Entropic, 20*(1), 94–114. https://doi.org/10.25120/etropic.20.1.2021.3794

Sell, R., Goldberg, S., & Conron, K. (2015). The utility of an online convenience panel for reaching rare and dispersed populations. *PloS One, 10*(12), e0144011. https://doi.org/10.1371/journal.pone.0144011

Senneseth, M., Pollak, C., Urheim, R., Logan, C., & Palmstierna, T. (2022). Personal recovery and its challenges in forensic mental health: Systematic review and thematic synthesis of qualitative literature. *BJPsych Open, 8*(1), e17. https://doi.org/10.1192/bjo.2021.1068

Sengoelge, M., Ponce, A., Perry, E., Pauncz, A., & Geldschlager, H. (2021). Reaching out and seeking help from frontline professionals: Experiences of men perpetrating partner violence. *Journal of Gender-Based Violence, 5*(1), 149–161. https://doi.org/10.1332/239868020X16040660254792

Sesar, K., Dodaj, A., & Šimić, N. (2018). The mental health of perpetrators of intimate partner violence. *Mental Health Review Journal, 23*(4), 221–239. https://doi.org/10.1108/MHRJ-08-2017-0028

Sewamala, F. M., Bermudez, L. G., Neilands, T. B., Mellins, C. A., McKay, M. M., Garfinkel, I., Sensoy Bahar, O., Nakigozi, G., Mukasa, M., Stark, L., Damulira, C., Nattabi, J., & Kivumbi, A. (2018). Suubi4Her: A study protocol to examine the impact and cost associated with a combination intervention to prevent HIV risk behavior and improve mental health functioning among adolescent girls in Uganda. *BMC Public Health, 18*(1), 693. https://doi.org/10.1186/s12889-018-5604-5

Scantlebury, A., Parker, A., Booth, A., McDaid, C., & Mitchell, N. (2018). Implementing mental health training programs for non-mental health trained professionals: A qualitative synthesis. *PloS One, 13*(6), e0199746. https://doi.org/10.1371/journal.pone.0199746

Sciberras, A., & Pilkington, L. (2018). The lived experience of psychologists working in mental health services: An exhausting and exasperating journey. *Professional Psychology, Research, and Practice, 49*(2), 151–158. https://doi.org/10.1037/pro0000184

Schachner, E. R., Hedrick, B. P., Richbourg, H. A., Hutchinson, J. R., & Farmer, C. (2021). Anatomy, ontogeny, and evolution of the archosaurian respiratory system: A case study on alligator Mississippians and Struthio camelus. *Journal of Anatomy, 238*(4), 845–873. https://doi.org/10.1111/joa.13358

References

Schadler, C. (2016). How do we define situated and ever-transforming family configurations? A new materialistic approach. *Journal of Family Theory & Review, 8*(4), 503–514. https://doi.org/10.1111/jftr.12167

Shadish, W. R., Cook, T. D., & Campbell, D. T. (2002). *Experimental and quasi-experimental designs for generalized causal inference.* Belmont, CA: Wadsworth Cengage.

Shadish, W. R., Zelinsky, N. A. M., Vevea, J. L., & Kratochwill, T. R. (2016). A survey of publication practices of single-case design researchers when treatments have small or large effects. *Journal of Applied Behavior Analysis, 49*, 656–673. doi:10.1002/jaba.308

Schäfer, M., & Löwer, M. (2021). Ecodesign—A review of reviews. *Sustainability (Basel, Switzerland), 13*(1), 315. https://doi.org/10.3390/su13010315

Schäfer, S. J., Simsek, M., Jaspers, E., Kros, M., Hewstone, M., Schmid, K., Fell, B. F., Dorrough, A. R., Glöckner, A., & Christ, O. (2022). Dynamic contact effects: Individuals' positive and negative contact history influences intergroup contact effects in a behavioral game. *Journal of Personality and Social Psychology, 123*(1), 107–122. https://doi.org/10.1037/pspi000037

Schenkl, S., Muggenthaler, H., Hubig, M., Erdmann, B., Weiser, M., Zachow, S., Heinrich, A., Güttler, F. V., Teichgräber, U., & Mall, G. (2017). Automatic CT-based finite element model generation for temperature-based death time estimation: Feasibility study and sensitivity analysis. *International Journal of Legal Medicine, 131*(3), 699–712. https://doi.org/10.1007/s00414-016-1523-0

Schmidlin, K., Clough-Gorr, K. M., Spoerri, A., SNC study group, & for the SNC study group. (2015). Privacy-preserving probabilistic record linkage (P3RL): A novel method for linking existing health-related data and supporting participant confidentiality. *BMC Medical Research Methodology, 15*(1), 46. https://doi.org/10.1186/s12874-015-0038-6

Schrooten, I., & de Jong, Menno D. T. (2017). If you could read my mind: The role of healthcare providers' empathic and communicative competencies in clients' satisfaction with consultations. *Health Communication, 32*(1), 111–188. https://doi.org/10.1080/10410236.2015.1110002

Schwab-Reese, L., & Renner, L. M. (2017). Attitudinal acceptance of and experiences with intimate partner violence among rural adults. *Journal of Family Violence, 32*(1), 115–123. http://dx.doi.org.library.capella.edu/10.1007/s10896-016-9895-y

Schwartz, M. F., & Southern, S. (2018). An integrative model for treatment of sexual desire disorders: An update of the masters and Johnson Institute approach. *The Family Journal (Alexandria, Va.), 26*(2), 223–237. https://doi.org/10.1177/1066480718775734

Scoglio, A. A. J., Lincoln, A., Kraus, S. W., & Molnar, B. E. (2022). Chipped or whole? Listening to survivors' experiences with disclosure following sexual violence. *Journal of Interpersonal Violence, 37*(9–10), NP6903–NP6928. https://doi.org/10.1177/0886260520967745

Scott-Storey, K., O'Donnell, S., Ford-Gilboe, M., Varcoe, C., Wathen, N., Malcolm, J., & Vincent, C. (2023). *What about the Men? A Critical Review of Men's Experiences of Intimate Partner Violence*. Sage. https://doi.org/10.1177/15248380211043827

Shah, R., Von Mach, T., Fedina, L., Link, B., & DeVylder, J. (2018). Intimate partner violence and psychotic experiences in four U.S. cities. *Schizophrenia Research, 195*, 506–512. https://doi.org/10.1016/j.schres.2017.09.017

Sherratt, F., Ivory, C., Sherratt, S., & Crawley, S. (2022). Organizing construction work: A digital and cooperative way forwards for micro-projects. Building Research and Information: *The International Journal of Research, Development and Demonstration, 50*(5), 559–573. https://doi.org/10.1080/09613218.2021.2012118

References

Shesar, K., Dodaj, A., & Šimić, N. (2018). The mental health of perpetrators of intimate partner violence. [Mental health of perpetrators of IPV] *The Mental Health Review, 23*(4), 221–239. https://doi.org/10.1108/MHRJ-08-2017-0028

Shortland, N. D., & Palasinski, M. (2019). Mirror on the wall, which is the most convincing of them all? Exploring anti-domestic violence posters. *Journal of Interpersonal Violence, 34*(9), 1755–1771. https://doi.org/10.1177/0886260516654931

Showalter, K., & McCloskey, R. J. (2021). A qualitative study of intimate partner violence and employment instability. *Journal of Interpersonal Violence, 36*(23–24), NP12730–NP12755. https://doi.org/10.1177/0886260520903140

Shreffler, J., Shreffler, M., Murfree, J. R., & Huecker, M. (2021). A global pandemic and substance use disorder: Healthcare professionals' viewpoints on merging two crises. *Substance use & Misuse, 56*(10), 1476–1482. https://doi.org/10.1080/10826084.2021.1936052

Shruthi, G., Mundada, M. R., Sowmya, B. J., & Supreeth, S. (2022). Mayfly Taylor optimization-based scheduling algorithm with deep reinforcement learning for dynamic scheduling in fog-cloud computing. *Applied Computational Intelligence and Soft Computing, 2022*, 1–17. https://doi.org/10.1155/2022/2131699

Shultz, J. W. (2020). Supporting transmasculine survivors of sexual assault and intimate partner violence: Reflections from peer support facilitation. *Sociological Inquiry, 90*(2), 293–315. https://doi.org/10.1111/soin.12340

Schultz, K., Walls, M., & Grana, S. J. (2021). Intimate partner violence and health: The roles of social support and communal mastery in five American Indian communities. *Journal of Interpersonal Violence, 36*(13–14), NP6725–NP6746. https://doi.org/10.1177/0886260518821463

Sibeoni, J., Verneuil, L., Manolios, E., & Révah-Levy, A. (2020). A specific method for qualitative medical research: The IPSE (inductive process to analyze the structure of lived experience) approach. *BMC Medical Research Methodology, 20*(1), 216. https://doi.org/10.1186/s12874-020-01099-4

Siegal, F. P., Kadowaki, N., Shodell, M., Fitzgerald-Bocarsly, P. A., Shah, K., Ho, S., Antonenko, S., & Liu, Y. (1999). The nature of the principal type 1 interferon-producing cells in human blood. *Science (American Association for the Advancement of Science), 284*(5421), 1835–1837. https://doi.org/10.1126/science.284.5421.1835

Silander, N. C., Geczy, B., Marks, O., & Mather, R. D. (2020). Implications of ideological bias in social psychology on clinical practice. *Clinical Psychology, 27*(2), n/a. https://doi.org/10.1111/cpsp.12312

Sileoet, K. M., Luttinen, R., Muñoz, S., & Hill, T. D. (2022). Mechanisms linking masculine discrepancy stress and the perpetration of intimate partner violence among men in the United States. *American Journal of Men's Health, 16*(4), 15579883221119355. https://doi.org/10.1177/15579883221119355

Silvestri, V., Arioli, M., Baccolo, E., & Macchi Cassia, V. (2022). Sensitivity to trustworthiness cues in own- and other-race faces: The role of spatial frequency information. *PloS One, 17*(9), e0272256. https://doi.org/10.1371/journal.pone.0272256

Silva-Martínez, E. (2016). El Silencio: Conceptualizations of Latina immigrant survivors of intimate partner violence in the Midwest of the United States. *Violence Against Women, 22*(5), 523–544. https://doi.org/10.1177/1077801215607357

Silva-Martínez, G. A., Rodríguez-Ríos, D., Alvarado-Caudillo, Y., Vaquero, A., Esteller, M., Carmona, F. J., Moran, S., Nielsen, F. C., Wickström-Lindholm, M., Wrobel, K., Wrobel, K., Barbosa-Sabanero, G., Zaina, S., & Lund, G. (2016). Arachidonic and oleic acids exert distinct effects on the DNA methylome. *Epigenetics, 11*(5), 321–334. https://doi.org/10.1080/15592294.2016.1161873

References

Simmons, C. A., Delaney, M. J., Lindsey, L., Whalley, A., Murry-Drobot, O., & Gayle Beck, J. (2017). Should programs designed to help IPV survivors screen for mental health-related problems: Voices from the field. *Violence Against Women, 23*(5), 603–622. https://doi.org/10.1177/1077801216646225

Simmons, J., & Swahnberg, K. (2021). Lifetime prevalence of poly victimization among older adults in Sweden, associations with ill-heath, and the mediating effect of sense of coherence. *BMC Geriatrics, 21*(1), 129. https://doi.org/10.1186/s12877-021-02074-4

Simmons, J. M., Cintron, A., & Grappendorf, H. (2021). What do their partners say? Examining family conflict through the lens of sports fans' significant others. *Journal of Sport Behavior, 44*(4), 447–467.

Simons, L. G., Simons, L. G., Sutton, T. E., Sutton, T. E., Simons, R. L., Simons, R. L., Gibbons, F. X., Gibbons, F. X., Murry, V. M., & Murry, V. M. (2016). Mechanisms that link parenting practices to adolescents' risky sexual behavior: A test of six competing theories. *Journal of Youth and Adolescence, 45*(2), 255–270. https://doi.org/10.1007/s10964-015-0409-7

Sim, J., Saunders, B., Waterfield, J., & Kingstone, T. (2018). Can sample size in qualitative research be found a priori? *International Journal of Social Research Methodology, 21*(5), 619–634. https://doi.org/10.1080/13645579.2018.1454643

Smith, Bridget J., Mielke, Jeff, Magloughlin, Lyra, & Wilbanks, Eric. (2019). Sound change and coarticulatory variability involving English =ɹ=. *Glossa: A Journal of General Linguistics 4(1)*, 63. doi: 10.5334=gjgl.650

Smith-Clapham, A. M., Childs, J. E., Cooley-Strickland, M., Hampton-Anderson, J., Novacek, D. M., Pemberton, J. V., & Wyatt, G. E. (2023). Implications of the COVID-19 pandemic on interpersonal violence within marginalized communities: Toward a new prevention paradigm. *American Journal of Public Health (1971), 113*(S2), S149–S156. https://doi.org/10.2105/AJPH.2023.307289

Snowdon, C., Silver, E., Charlton, P., Devlin, B., Greenwood, E., Hutchings, A., Moug, S., Vohra, R., & Grieve, R. (2023). Adapting patient and public involvement processes in response to the Covid-19 pandemic. *Health Expectations: An International Journal of Public Participation in Health Care and Health Policy, 26*(4), 1658–1667. https://doi.org/10.1111/hex.13771

Sinclair, S., Hack, T. F., Raffin-Bouchal, S., McClement, S., Stajduhar, K., Singh, P., Hagen, N. A., Sinnarajah, A., & Chochinov, H. M. (2018). What are healthcare providers' understandings and experiences of compassion? The healthcare compassion model: A grounded theory study of healthcare providers in Canada. *BMJ Open, 8*(3), e019701. https://doi.org/10.1136/bmjopen-2017-019701

Singh, J. A., Siddiqi, M., Parameshwar, P., & Chandra-Mouli, V. (2019). World Health Organization guidance on ethical considerations in planning and reviewing research studies on sexual and reproductive health in adolescents. *Journal of Adolescent Health, 64*(4), 427–429. https://doi.org/10.1016/j.jadohealth.2019.01.008

Singh, V. (2016). Male victims of physical partner violence have poorer physical and mental health than men of the general population. *Evidence-Based Nursing, 19*(1), 26. https://doi.org/10.1136/eb-2015-102091

Sivagurunathan, M., Walton, D. M., Packham, T., Booth, R. G., & MacDermid, J. C. (2022). Discourses around male IPV-related systemic biases on Reddit. *Journal of Interpersonal Violence, 37*(19–20), NP17834–NP17859. https://doi.org/10.1177/08862605211030015

Sivagurunathan, M., Orchard, T., & Evans, M. (2019). Barriers to use of mental health services amongst male child sexual abuse survivors: Service providers' perspective. *Journal of Child Sexual Abuse, 28*(7), 819–839. https://doi.org/10.1080/10538712.2019.1610823

Skoczek, A. C., & Akram, H. (2023). Neurological complications secondary to intimate partner violence: A brief review and case of posterior cerebral artery cerebrovascular accident following domestic abuse. *Curēus (Palo Alto, CA), 15*(8). https://doi.org/10.7759/cureus.42823

Skynner, A. C. R. (1979). Family therapy in clinical practice Bowen, m.d; Jason Aronson, New York City, 1978, 565 pages. *Psychiatric Services (Washington, D.C.), 30*(4), 276–277. https://doi.org/10.1176/ps.30.4.276-a

Sorsa, M. A., Kiikkala, I., & Åstedt-Kurki, P. (2015). Bracketing is a skill in conducting unstructured qualitative interviews. *Nurse Researcher, 22*(4), 8–12. https://doi.org/10.7748/nr.22.4.8.e1317

Soule, K. E., & Freeman, M. (2019). So, you want to do post-intentional phenomenological research? *Qualitative Report, 24*(4), 857–872.

Sousa, C. A., Siddiqi, M., & Bogue, B. (2022). What Do We Know After Decades of Research About Parenting and IPV? A Systematic Scoping Review Integrating Findings. *Trauma, Violence, & Abuse, 23*(5), 1629–1642. https://doi.org/10.1177/15248380211016019

Spencer, C. M., Keilholtz, B. M., Palmer, M., & Vail, S. L. (2024). *Mental and physical health correlates for emotional, intimate partner violence perpetration and victimization: A meta-analysis.* Sage.

Spencer, C. M., Mallory, A. B., Cafferky, B. M., Kimmes, J. G., Beck, A. R., & Stith, S. M. (2019). Mental health factors and intimate partner violence perpetration and victimization: A meta-analysis. *Psychology of Violence, 9*(1), 1–17.

Sprague, C., Hatcher, A. M., Woollett, N., Black, V. (2015). How Nurses in Johannesburg Address Intimate Partner Violence in Female Patients: Understanding IPV Responses in Low- and Middle-Income Country Health Systems. *J Interpers Violence. 2017 Jun, 32*(11), 1591–1619. doi 10.1177/0886260515589929. Epub 2015 Jun 19. PMID: 26092654.

Sprague, S., Scott, T., Garibaldi, A., Bzovsky, S., Slobogean, G. P., McKay, P., . . . Swaminathan, A. (2017). A scoping review of intimate partner violence aid programs within health care settings. *European Journal of Psych traumatology, 8*(1). https://doi.org/10.1080/20008198.2017.1314159

Sparrow, K., Kwan, J., Howard, L., Fear, N., & MacManus, D. (2017). A systematic review of mental health disorders and intimate partner violence victimization among military populations. *Social Psychiatry and Psychiatric Epidemiology, 52*(9), 1059–1080. https://doi.org/10.1007/s00127-017-1423-8

Stapleton, S., & Pattison, N. (2015). The lived experience of men with advanced cancer concerning their perceptions of masculinity: A qualitative phenomenological study. *Journal of Clinical Nursing, 24*(7–8), 1069–1078. https://doi.org/10.1111/jocn.12713

Steffensen, K. D., Hansen, D. G., Espersen, K., Lauth, S., Fosgrau, P., Pedersen, A. M., Groen, P. S., Sauvr, C., & Olling, K. (2023). "SDM: HOSP"—A generic model for hospital-based implementation of shared decision-making. *PloS One, 18*(1), e0280547. https://doi.org/10.1371/journal.pone.0280547

Stern, E., & Carlson, K. (2019). Indashyikirwa Women's safe spaces: Informal response for survivors of IPV within a Rwandan prevention program. *Social Sciences (Basel), 8*(3), 76. https://doi.org/10.3390/socsci8030076

Stern, E., & Niyibizi, L. L. (2018). Shifting feelings of consequences of IPV among beneficiaries of indashyikirwa: An IPV prevention program in Rwanda. *Journal of Interpersonal Violence, 33*(11), 1778–1804. https://doi.org/10.1177/0886260517752156

Stiawa, M., Müller-Stierlin, A., Staiger, T., Kilian, R., Becker, T., Gündel, H., . . . & Krumm, S. (2020). Mental health professionals' view about the impact of male gender for the treatment of men with depression—A qualitative study. *BMC Psychiatry, 20*, 1–13.

Stöckl, H., Sardinha, L., Maheu-Giroux, M., Meyer, S. R., & García-Moreno, C. (2021). Physical, sexual, and psychological intimate partner violence and non-partner sexual violence against women and girls: A systematic review protocol for producing global, regional and country estimates. *BMJ Open, 11*(8), e045574. https://doi.org/10.1136/bmjopen-2020-045574

Storhaug, H. C., Mead, S. B., & Steinsbekk, A. (2017). A qualitative study of employees' opinions on establishing a generic call center. *BMC Family Practice, 18*(1), 90. https://doi.org/10.1186/s12875-017-0661-x

St-Pierre Bouchard, J., Brassard, A., Lefebvre, A., Dugal, C., Lafontaine, M., Savard, C., Daspe, M., Péloquin, K., & Godbout, N. (2023). Cumulative childhood trauma, communication patterns, and intimate partner violence perpetrated by men seeking help. *Journal of Interpersonal Violence, 38*(9–10), 6843–6864. https://doi.org/10.1177/08862605221138651

Strauss, A., & Corbin, J. (1990). *Basics of qualitative research.* Sage.

Stubbs, A., & Szoeke, C. (2022). *The effect of intimate partner violence on the physical health and health-related behaviors of women: A systematic review of the literature.* Sage. https://doi.org/10.1177/1524838020985541

Stuijfzand, S., Deforges, C., Sandoz, V., Sajin, C., Jaques, C., Elmers, J., & Horsch, A. (2020). Psychological impact of an epidemic/pandemic on the mental health of healthcare professionals: A rapid review. *BMC Public Health, 20*(1), 1230. https://doi.org/10.1186/s12889-020-09322-z

Stylianou, A. M. (2019, 2018). Family court survivor-centered practice: A qualitative study of advocate-IPV survivor safety planning interactions. *Journal of Family Violence, 34*(3), 245–259. https://doi.org/10.1007/s10896-018-0020-2

Stylianou, A. M., & Ebright, E. (2021). Providing Coordinated, Immediate, Trauma-Focused, and Interdisciplinary Responses to Children Exposed to Severe Intimate Partner Violence: Assessing Feasibility of a Collaborative Model. *Journal of Interpersonal*

Violence, 36(5–6), NP2773–NP2799. https://doi.org/10.1177/0886260518769359

Sualp, K., Ergüney Okumus, F. E., & Molina, O. (2022). Group work training for mental health professionals working with Syrian refugee children in Turkey: A needs assessment study. *Social Work with Groups (New York. 1978), 45*(3–4), 319–335. https://doi.org/10.1080/01609513.2021.1953283

Sugiyama, N. B., & Hunter, W. (2020). Do conditional cash transfers empower women? insights from Brazil's bolsa família. *Latin American Politics and Society, 62*(2), 53–74. https://doi.org/10.1017/lap.2019.60

Suleimenova, A., & Ivanova, O. (2018). Emotional competence and individual style of action of future higher education teachers in the education system for sustainable development. *Journal of Teacher Education for Sustainability, 20*(2), 44–63. https://doi.org/10.2478/jtes-2018-0014

Sutton, A., Beech, H., Ozturk, B., & Nelson-Gardell, D. (2021). Preparing mental health professionals to work with survivors of intimate partner violence: A comprehensive systematic review of the literature. *Affiliate, 36*(3), 426–440. https://doi.org/10.1177/0886109920960827

Sylaska, K. M., & Edwards, K. M. (2014). Disclosure of intimate partner violence to informal social support network members: A review of the literature. *Trauma, Violence & Abuse, 15*(1), 3–21. https://doi.org/10.1177/1524838013496335

Szcześniak, M., Kroplewski, Z., & Szałachowski, R. (2020). The mediating effect of coping strategies on Religious/Spiritual struggles and life satisfaction. *Religions (Basel, Switzerland), 11*(4), 195. https://doi.org/10.3390/rel11040195

Tagbo, B. N., Ughasoro, M. D., & Esangbedo, D. O. (2014). Parental acceptance of inactivated polio vaccine in southeast Nigeria: A qualitative cross-sectional interventional study. *Vaccine, 32*(46), 6157–6162. https://doi.org/10.1016/j.vaccine.2014.08.053

Taheri, E., Hosseini, T., Kafami, Z., Faridhosseini, F., Saghebi, A., Fayyazi Bordbar, M. R., Farhoudi, F., Asgharipour, N., Salimi, Z., Aghebati, A., Amiri, M., Akbari, A., & Mohaddes Ardabili, H. (2022). Mass management of mental health issues during COVID-19 pandemic: The role of professional volunteer groups; an Iranian experience. *International Journal of Mental Health, 51*(3), 286–290. https://doi.org/10.1080/00207411.2022.2072146

Tan, L., Strudwick, J., Deady, M., Bryant, R., & Harvey, S. B. (2023). Mind-body exercise interventions for the prevention of post-traumatic stress disorder in trauma-exposed populations: A systematic review and meta-analysis. *BMJ Open, 13*(7), e064758. https://doi.org/10.1136/bmjopen-2022-064758

Tandall, L., Mikocka-Walus, A., McMillan, D., Wright, B., Hewitt, C., & Gascoyne, S. (2017). Is behavioral activation effective in the treatment of depression in young people? A systematic review and meta-analysis. *Psychology and Psychotherapy, 90*(4), 770–796. https://doi.org/10.1111/papt.1212

Tashakkori, Abbas, and Charles Teddlie. (1998). *Mixed Methodology: Combining Qualitative and Quantitative Approaches*. Sage.

Tarshis, S., & Baird, S. L. (2019). Addressing the indirect trauma of social work students in intimate partner violence (IPV) field placements: A framework for supervision. *Clinical Social Work Journal, 47*(1), 90–102. https://doi.org/10.1007/s10615-018-0678-1

Tarshis, S., Alaggia, R., & Logie, C. H. (2022). Intersectional and trauma-informed approaches to employment services: Insights from intimate partner violence (IPV) service providers. *Violence Against Women, 28*(2), 617–640. https://doi.org/10.1177/1077801220988344

Tarzia, L., PhD, Murray, E., PhD, Humphreys, C., PhD, Glass, N., PhD, Taft, A., PhD, Valpied, Jodie, BA, MEd, PGDip (Psych), & Hegarty,

K., PhD. (2016). I-decide an online intervention drawing on the psychosocial readiness model for women experiencing domestic violence. *Women's Health Issues, 26*(2), 208–216. https://doi.org/10.1016/j.whi.2015.07.011

Tarzia, L., Forsdike, K., Feder, G., & Hegarty, K. (2020). Interventions in Health Settings for Male Perpetrators or Victims of Intimate Partner Violence. *Trauma, Violence, & Abuse, 21*(1), 123–137. https://doi.org/10.1177/1524838017744772

Tarzia, L., & Hegarty, K. (2023). "He'd tell me I was frigid and ugly and force me to have sex with him anyway": Women's experiences of co-occurring sexual violence and psychological abuse in heterosexual relationships. *Journal of Interpersonal Violence, 38*(1–2), 1299–1319. https://doi.org/10.1177/08862605221090563

Tavares, W., Bowles, R., & Donelon, B. (2016). Informing a Canadian paramedic profile: Framing concepts, roles, and crosscutting themes. *BMC Health Services Research, 16*(1), 477. https://doi.org/10.1186/s12913-016-1739-1

Taylor, J. C., & Bates, E. A. (2019). *Intimate partner violence: New perspectives in research and practice Taylor and Francis.* https://doi.org/10.4324/9781315169842

Taylor, J. C., Bates, E. A., Colosi, A., & Cree A. J. (2021). Barriers to Men's Help-Seeking for Intimate Partner Violence. *Journal of Interpersonal Violence.* https://doi.org/10.1177/08862605211035870

Taylor, A. K., Kingstone, T., Briggs, T. A., O'Donnell, C. A., Atherton, H., Blane, D. N., & Chew-Graham, C. A. (2021). 'Reluctant pioneer': A qualitative study of doctors' experiences as patients with long COVID. Health Expectations: *An International Journal of Public Participation in Health Care and Health Policy, 24*(3), 833–842. https://doi.org/10.1111/hex.13223

Taylor, P. L., O'Donnell, S., Wuest, J., Scott-Storey, K., Vincent, C., & Malcolm, J. (2021). The mental health effects of cumulative lifetime violence in men: Disruptions in the ability to connect with others and finding ways to reengage. *Global Qualitative Nursing Research, 8,* 233339362110215–23333936211021576. https://doi.org/10.1177/23333936211021576

Taylor, B., Henshall, C., Kenyon, S., Litchfield, I., & Greenfield, S. (2018). Can rapid approaches to qualitative analysis deliver prompt, valid findings to clinical leaders? A mixed-methods study compared rapid and thematic analysis. *BMJ Open, 8*(10), e019993. https://doi.org/10.1136/bmjopen-2017-019993

Taylor, J. C., Bates, E. A., Colosi, A., & Creer, A. J. (2022). Barriers to Men's help-seeking for intimate partner violence. *Journal of Interpersonal Violence, 37*(19–20), NP18417–NP18444. https://doi.org/10.1177/08862605211035870

Tedgård, E., Råstam, M., Wirtberg, I., Institute of Neuroscience and Physiology, Gillberg Neuropsychiatry Centre, Göteborgs universitet, Gothenburg University, Gillbergcentrum, Sahlgrenska Academy, Sahlgrenska akademin, & Institution för neuroretina och fysiologi. (2018). Struggling with one's parenting after an upbringing with substance-abusing parents. *International Journal of Qualitative Studies on Health and Well-being, 13*(1), 1435100–15. https://doi.org/10.1080/17482631.2018.1435100

The New English Bible. (1970). New English Bible, Cambridge University Press. https://www.cambridge.org/gb/bibles/bible-versions/new-english-bible

The Kaiser Family Foundation (KFF). (2021). *Federal Information & News Dispatch, LLC.* Retrieved from ProQuest Central. Retrieved from http://library.capella.edu/login?qurl=https%3A%2F%2Fwww.proquest.com%2Freports%2Fkaiser-family-foundation-kff-webinar%2Fdocview%2F2504584684%2Fse-2%3Faccountid%3D27965.

Theobald, D., Farrington, D. P., Coid, J. W., & Piquero, A. R. (2016). Are male perpetrators of intimate partner violence different from convicted violent offenders? Examination of psychopathic traits and life success in males from a community survey. *Journal of*

Interpersonal Violence, 31(9), 1687–1718. https://doi.org/10.1177/0886260515569061

Thomas, J. C., & Kopel, J. (2023). Male victims of sexual assault: A review of the literature. *Behavioral Sciences, 13*(4), 304. https://doi.org/10.3390/bs13040304

Thompson, R. (2018). A qualitative phenomenological study of emotional and cultural intelligence of international students in the United States of America. *Journal of International Students, 8*(2), 1220–1255. https://doi.org/10.52811250423

Thompson, J. (2018). 'Shared intelligibility' and two reflexive strategies as methods of supporting 'responsible decisions' in a hermeneutic phenomenological study. *International Journal of Social Research Methodology, 21*(5), 575–589. https://doi.org/10.1080/13645579.2018.1454641

Thorvaldsdottir, K. B., Halldorsdottir, S., & Saint Arnault, D. M. (2021). Understanding and measuring help-seeking barriers among intimate partner violence survivors: Mixed-methods validation study of the Icelandic barriers to help-seeking for trauma (BHS-TR) scale. *International Journal of Environmental Research and Public Health, 19*(1), 104. https://doi.org/10.3390/ijerph19010104

Tjaden, P., & Thoennes. N. (2016, 2000). Prevalence and consequences of male-to-female and female-to-male intimate partner violence as measured by the National Violence Against Women Survey. *Violence Against Women, 6*(2), 142–161. https://doi.org/10.1177/10778010022181769

Tobin, G. A., & Begley, C. M. (2004). Methodological rigor within a qualitative framework. *Journal of Advanced Nursing, 48*(4), 388–396. https://doi.org/10.1111/j.1365-2648.2004.03207.x

Tol, W. A., Murray, S. M., Lund, C., Bolton, P., Murray, L. K., Davies, T., . . . & Bass, J. K. (2019). Can mental health treatments help prevent or reduce intimate partner violence in low and middle-income countries? A systematic review. *BMC Women's Health, 19*, 1–15.

References

Tomaz, S. A., Ryde, G. C., Swales, B., Neely, K. C., Andreis, F., Coffee, P., Connelly, J., Kirkland, A., McCabe, L., Watchman, K., Martin, J. G., Pina, I., & Whittaker, A. C. (2022). ". . . exercise opportunities became very important": Scottish older adults' changes in physical activity during Covid19. *European Review of Aging and Physical Activity, 19*(1), 1–16. https://doi.org/10.1186/s11556-022-00295-z

Trabold, N., King, J., Paul R, Crasta, D., Iverson, K. M., Crane, C. A., Buckheit, K., Bosco, S. C., & Funderburk, J. S. (2023). Leveraging integrated primary care to enhance the health system response to IPV: Moving toward primary prevention primary care. *International Journal of Environmental Research and Public Health, 20*(9), 5701. https://doi.org/10.3390/ijerph20095701

Treloar, C., Jackson, L. C., Gray, R., Newland, J., Wilson, H., Saunders, V., Johnson, P., & Brener, L. (2016). Multiple stigmas, shame, and historical trauma compound the experience of Aboriginal Australians living with hepatitis C. *Health Sociology Review, 25*(1), 18–32. https://doi.org/10.1080/14461242.2015.1126187

Tripathi, S., Jain, M., Bagai, A., & Rao, K. V. (2022). Designing proper, acceptable and workable community-engagement approaches to improve routine immunization outcomes in low- and middle-income countries: A synthesis of 3ie-supported formative evaluations. *PloS One, 17*(10), e0275278. https://doi.org/10.1371/journal.pone.0275278

Tripathi, S., & Azhar, S. (2022). *A systematic review of intimate partner violence interventions changing South Asian women in the United States.* Sage. https://doi.org/10.1177/1524838020957987

Trevillion, K., Corker, E., Capron, L. E., & Oram, S. (2016). Improving mental health service responses to domestic violence and abuse. *International Review of Psychiatry, 28*(5), 423–432. https://doi.org/10.1080/09540261.2016.1201053

Trochim, W. M., & McLinden, D. (2017). Introduction to a special issue on concept mapping. *Evaluation and Program Planning, 60*, 166–175. https://doi.org/10.1016/j.evalprogplan.2016.10.006

Tsapalas, D., Parker, M., Ferrer, L., & Bernales, M. (2021). Gender-based violence, perspectives in Latin America and the Caribbean. *Hispanic Health Care International, 19*(1), 23–37. https://doi.org/10.1177/1540415320924768

Tufekcioglu, S., & Muran, J. C. (2015). Case formulation and the therapeutic relationship: The role of therapist self-reflection and self-revelation. *Journal of Clinical Psychology, 71*(5), 469–477. https://doi.org/10.1002/jclp.22183

Tufford, L., & Newman, P. (2012). Bracketing in qualitative research. *Qualitative Social Work: QSW: Research and Practice, 11*(1), 80–96. https://doi.org/10.1177/1473325010368316

Tucker, B. P., & Parker, L. D. (2020). The question of research relevance: A university management perspective. *Accounting, Auditing & Accountability Journal, 33*(6), 1247–1275. https://doi.org/10.1108/AAAJ-01-2018-3325

Turner, L. H., & West, R. (2015, 2014). *Communication and family violence: A review of recent scholarship.* In Lynn Turner, L. H. Turner, Richard West & R. West (Eds.), Sage.

The Sage Handbook of Family Communication (122). 66.n8. Sage. https://doi.org/10.4135/97814833753.

Turney, K., & Halpern-Meekin, S. (2017). Parenting in on/off relationships: The link between relationship churning and father involvement. *Demography, 54*(3), 861–886. https://doi.org/10.1007/s13524-017-0571-5

Turki, F. J., Jdaitawi, M., & Sheta, H. (2018). Fostering positive adjustment behavior: Social connectedness, achievement motivation, and emotional-social learning among male and female university students. *Active Learning in Higher Education, 19*(2), 145–158. https://doi.org/10.1177/1469787417731202

Tutty, L. M., Babins-Wagner, R., & Rothery, M. A. (2017). Women in IPV treatment for abusers and women in IPV survivor groups:

Different or two sides of the same coin? *Journal of Family Violence, 32*(8), 787–797. https://doi.org/10.1007/s10896-017-9927-2

Ufer, L. G., Moore, J. A., Hawkins, K., Gembel, G., Entwistle, D. N., & Hoffman, D. (2018). Care coordination: Empowering families is a promising practice that helps medical home use among children and youth with special health care needs. *Maternal and Child Health Journal, 22*(5), 648–659. https://doi.org/10.1007/s10995-018-2477-2

Uhl, S., Konnyu, K., Wilson, R., Adam, G., Robinson, K. A., & Viswanathan, M. (2023). Parent feelings and decision making about treatments for epilepsy: A qualitative evidence synthesis. *BMJ Open, 13*(1), e066872. https://doi.org/10.1136/bmjopen-2022-066872

Ulloa, E. C., & Hammett, J. F. (2016). The effect of gender and perpetrator–victim role on mental health outcomes and risk behaviors associated with intimate partner violence. *Journal of Interpersonal Violence, 31*(7), 1184–1207. https://doi.org/10.1177/0886260514564163

Ulloa, E. C., & Hammett, J. F. (2016). The role of empathy in violent intimate relationships. *Partner Abuse, 7*(2), 140–156. https://doi.org/10.1891/1946-6560.7.2.14

Ulloa, E. C., Hammett, J. F., Meda, N. A., & Rubalcaba, S. J. (2017). Empathy and romantic relationship quality among cohabitating couples: An actor–partner interdependence model. *The Family Journal, 25*(3), 208–214. https://doi.org/10.1177/1066480717710644

Ungar, T., Ungar, T., Knaak, S., Knaak, S., Szeto, A. C., & Szeto, A. C. (2016). Theoretical and practical considerations for combating mental illness stigma in health care. *Community Mental Health Journal, 52*(3), 262–271. https://doi.org/10.1007/s10597-015-9910-4

Valdez, C. E., Lim, B. H., & Lilly, M. M. (2013). "It will make the whole tower crooked": Victimization trajectories in IPV. *Journal of Family Violence, 28*(2), 131–140. https://doi.org/10.1007/s10896-012-9476-7

van der Aa, Jessica E., Aabakke, A. J. M., Ristorp Andersen, B., Settnes, A., Hornnes, P., Teunissen, P. W., Goverde, A. J., & Scheele, F.

(2020). From prescription to guidance: A European framework for generic competencies. *Advances in Health Sciences Education: Theory and Practice, 25*(1), 173–187. https://doi.org/10.1007/s10459-019-09910-8

van der Meij, L., Pulopulos, M. M., Hidalgo, V., Almela, M., Lila, M., Roney, J. R., & Salvador, A. (2022). Hormonal changes of intimate partner violence perpetrators in response to brief social contact with women. *Aggressive Behavior, 48*(1), 30–39. https://doi.org/10.1002/ab.21995

Vandewalle, J., Debyser, B., Beeckman, D., Vandecasteele, T., Van Hecke, A., & Verhaeghe, S. (2016). Peer workers' beliefs and experiences of barriers to implementing peer worker roles in mental health services: A literature review. *International Journal of Nursing Studies, 60*, 234–250. https://doi.org/10.1016/j.ijnurstu.2016.04.018

van Duin, L., Bevaart, F., Zijlmans, J., Luijks, M., Doreleijers, T. H., Wierdsma, A., Oldehinkel, A., Marhe, R., & Popma, A. (2019). The role of adverse childhood experiences and mental health care use in psychological dysfunction of male multi-problem young adults. *European Child & Adolescent Psychiatry, 28*(8), 1065–1078. https://doi.org/10.1007/s00787-018-1263-4

Van Duyne, I. M. (2020). Sticks and stones may break my bones, but words will hurt me: The "T" word. *Journal of Life Care Planning, 18*(1), 11–18.

van Leeuwen, K. M., van Loon, M. S., van Nes, F. A., Bosmans, J. E., de Vet, Henrica C. W, Ket, J. C. F., Widdershoven, G. A. M., & Ostelo, Raymond W. J. G. (2019). What does the quality of life mean to older adults: A thematic synthesis. *PloS One, 14*(3), e0213263. https://doi.org/10.1371/journal.pone.0213263

Valderrama, A., Martinez, A., Charlebois, K., Guerrero, L., & Forgeot d'Arc, B. (2023, 2022). For autistic persons by autistic persons: Acceptability of a structured peer support service according to key stakeholders. *Health Expectations: An International Journal of Public*

Participation in Health Care and Health Policy, 26(1), 463–475. https://doi.org/10.1111/hex.13680

Valandra, Higgins, B. M., Murphy-Erby, Y., & Brown, L. M. (2019). An exploratory study of African American men's perspectives of interracial, heterosexual intimate partner violence using a multisystem life course framework. *Journal of the Society for Social Work and Research, 10*(1), 69–95. https://doi.org/10.1086/701824

Vallerga, M., & Zurbriggen, E. L. (2022). Hegemonic masculinities in the 'Manosphere': A thematic analysis of beliefs about men and women on the red pill and incel. *Analyses of Social Issues and Public Policy, 22*(2), 602–625. https://doi.org/10.1111/asap.12308

Vanderende, K., Mercy, J., Shawa, M., Kalanda, M., Hamela, J., Maksud, N., . . . & Hillis, S. (2016). Violent childhood experiences are associated with young adult men intimate partner violence perpetration: a multistage cluster study survey in Malawi. *Annals of Epidemiology, 26*(10), 723–728. https://doi.org/10.1016/j.annepidem.2016.08.007

van Rosmalen, L., van der Horst, Frank C. P, & van der Veer, R. (2016). From secure dependency to attachment: Mary Ainsworth integrates Blatz's security theory into Bowlby's attachment theory. *History of Psychology, 19*(1), 22–39. https://doi.org/10.1037/hop0000015

Vatnar, S. K. B., Leer-Salvesen, K., & Bjørkly, S. (2021, 2019). *Mandatory reporting of intimate partner violence: A mixed methods systematic review.* Sage. https://doi.org/10.1177/15248380198691020

Vela, A. M., & Carroll, A. J. (2023). Cardiac psychology: Psychosocial and behavioral assessment and treatment for cardiovascular conditions. *Journal of Health Service Psychology (Online), 49*(1), 21–32. https://doi.org/10.1007/s42843-023-00079-8

Velotti, P., Rogier, G., Beomonte Zobel, S., Chirumbolo, A., & Zavattini, G. C. (2020). The relation of anxiety and avoidance dimensions of attachment to intimate partner violence: A meta-analysis about perpetrators. *Trauma, Violence & Abuse*, 152483802093386–1524838020933864. https://doi.org/10.1177/1524838020933864

Velotti, P., Beomonte Zobel, S., Rogier, G., & Tambelli, R. (2018). Exploring relationships: A systematic review on intimate partner violence and attachment. *Frontiers in Psychology, 9,* 1166. https://doi.org/10.3389/fpsyg.2018.01166

Venäläinen, S. (2020). Reversing positions: Constructions of male victimhood in online discussions about intimate partner violence committed by women. *Men and masculinities, 23*(3–4), 772–787. https://doi.org/10.1177/1097184X18824374

Verrocchio, M. C. (2018). Childhood maltreatment, pathological personality dimensions, and suicide risk in young adults. *Frontiers in Psychology, 9,* 806. doi:10.3389/2018.00806

Victor, K., & Barnard, A. (2016). Slaughtering for a living: A hermeneutic phenomenological perspective on the well-being of slaughterhouse employees. *International Journal of Qualitative Studies on Health and Well-being, 11*(1), 1–13. https://doi.org/10.3402/qhw.v11.30266

Vilamala, S., Puig, M., Ochoa, S., Martín-Martínez, J. R., Hernández, A., Balsera, J., Verdaguer-Rodríguez, M., Villellas, R., Arenas, O., & García-Franco, M. (2022). Assessment of the treatment needs of community recovery services in Spain: From the perspective of service users, families, and mental health professionals. *Health & Social Care in the Community, 30*(6), e5819–e5830. https://doi.org/10.1111/hsc.14013

Vil, N. M. S., Sperlich, M., Fitzpatrick, J., Bascug, E., & Elliott, J. (2022). "I thought it was normal:" Perspectives of black nursing students from high-risk IPV communities on causes and solutions to IPV in the black community. *Journal of Interpersonal Violence, 37*(13–14), NP12260–NP12283. https://doi.org/10.1177/0886260521997939

Vitoria-Estruch, S., Romero-Martínez, A., Lila, M., & Moya-Albiol, L. (2018). Differential cognitive profiles of intimate partner violence perpetrators based on alcohol consumption. *Alcohol, 70*, 61–71. https://doi.org/10.1016/j.alcohol.2018.01.006

Viverito, K. M., Mittal, D., Han, X., Messias, E., Chekuri, L., & Sullivan, G. (2018). Attitudes of seeking help for mental health problems and beliefs about treatment effectiveness: A comparison between providers and the public. *Stigma and Health (Washington, D.C.), 3(1)*, 35–41. https://doi.org/10.1037/sah0000053

Voges, J., Berg, A., & Niehaus, D. J. H. (2019). Revisiting the African origins of attachment research—50 years on from Ainsworth: A descriptive review. *Infant Mental Health Journal, 40*(6), 799–816. https://doi.org/10.1002/imhj.21821

Vollmann, M., Sprang, S., & van den Brink, F. (2019). Adult attachment and relationship satisfaction: The mediating role of gratitude toward the partner. *Journal of Social and Personal Relationships, 36*(11–12), 3875–3886. https://doi.org/10.1177/0265407519841712

Volpe, E. M., Quinn, C. R., Resch, K., Sommers, M. S., Wieling, E., & Cerulli, C. (2017). Narrative Exposure Therapy: A Proposed Model to Address Intimate Partner Violence-Related PTSD in Parenting and Pregnant Adolescents. *Family & Community Health, 40*(3), 258–277. https://doi.org/10.1097/FCH.0000000000000072

Volpe, M., Battistoni, A., Gallo, G., Rubattu, S., Tocci, G., On behalf of the Scientific Societies & the Writing Committee. (2018). Executive summary of the 2018 joint consensus document on cardiovascular disease prevention in Italy. *High Blood Pressure & Cardiovascular Prevention, 25*(3), 327–341. https://doi.org/10.1007/s40292-018-0278-8

Voth Schrag, R. J., Ravi, K., Robinson, S., Schroeder, E., & Padilla-Medina, D. (2021). Experiences with help-seeking among non-service-engaged survivors of IPV: Survivors' recommendations for service providers. *Violence Against Women, 27*(12–13), 2313–2334. https://doi.org/10.1177/1077801220963861

Voth Schrag, R., Ravi, K., & Robinson, S. (2020). The role of social support is the link between economic abuse and economic hardship. *Journal of Family Violence, 35*(1), 85–93.

Voth Schrag, R., Wood, L., & Busch-Armendariz, N. (2020). Pathways from intimate partner violence to academic disengagement among Women University students. *Violence and Victims, 35*(2), 227–245.

Waalkes, P. L., DeCino, D. A., LeBlanc, J., Phelps-Pineda, M. M., Somerville, T., & Flynn, S. V. (2023). Generic qualitative dissertations in counselor education: A content analysis. *Counselor Education and Supervision, 62*(1), 52–63. https://doi.org/10.1002/ceas.12261

Wagers, S. M., Piquero, A. R., Narvey, C., Reid, J. A., & Loughran, T. A. (2021). Variation in exposure to violence in early adolescence distinguishes between intimate partner violence victimization and perpetration among young men involved in the justice system. *Journal of Family Violence, 36*(1), 99–108. https://doi.org/10.1007/s10896-020-00170-4

Wakida, E. K., Obua, C., Rukundo, G. Z., Maling, S., Talib, Z. M., & Okello, E. S. (2018). Barriers and facilitators to integrating mental health services into primary healthcare: A qualitative study among Ugandan primary care providers using the COM-B framework. *BMC Health Services Research, 18*(1), 890. https://doi.org/10.1186/s12913-018-3684-7

Walburg, F., van Berkel-de Joode, J. W., Brandt, H., van Tulder, M., Aiaanse, M., & van Meijel, B. (2022). Experiences and beliefs of people with a severe mental illness and health care professionals of a one-year group-based lifestyle program (SMILE). *PloS One, 17*(8), e0271990. https://doi.org/10.1371/journal.pone.0271990

Walker, A., Lyall, K., Silva, D., Craigie, G., Mayshak, R., Costa, B., Hyder, S., & Bentley, A. (2020). Male victims of female-perpetrated intimate partner violence, help-seeking, and reporting behaviors: A qualitative study. *Psychology of Men & Masculinity, 21*(2), 213–223

References

Walker, A., Lyall, K., Silva, D., Craigie, G., Mayshak, R., Costa, B., Hyder, S., & Bentley, A. (2019). Male victims of female-perpetrated intimate partner violence, help-seeking, and reporting behaviors: A qualitative study. *Psychology of Men & Masculinities*. Advanced online publication. https://dx.doi.org/10.1037/men000022

Walker, J., Chaar, B. B., Vera, N., Pillai, A. S., Lim, J. S., Bero, L., & Moles, R. J. (2017). Medicine shortages in Fiji: A qualitative exploration of stakeholders' views. *PloS One, 12*(6), e0178429. https://doi.org/10.1371/journal.pone.0178429

Wall, J. T., Kaiser, B. N., Friis-Healy, E. A., Ayuku, D., & Puffer, E. S. (2020). What about lay counselors' experiences of task-shifting mental health interventions? Example from a family-based intervention in Kenya. *International Journal of Mental Health Systems, 14*(1), 9. https://doi.org/10.1186/s13033-020-00343-0

Waller, B. (2016). Broken fixes: A systematic analysis of the effectiveness of modern and postmodern interventions to decrease IPV perpetration among black males remanded to treatment. *Aggression and Violent Behavior, 27*, 42–49. https://doi.org/10.1016/j.avb.2016.02.003

Wallace, G. T., Conner, B. T., & Shillington, A. M. (2021). Classification trees name shared and distinct correlates of no suicidal self-injury and suicidal ideation across gender identities in emerging adults. *Clinical Psychology and Psychotherapy, 28*(3), 682–693. https://doi.org/10.1002/cpp.2530

Wansink, B., & van Ittersum, K. (2016). Boundary research: Tools and rules to change emerging fields. *Journal of Consumer Behavior, 15*(5), 396–410. https://doi.org/10.1002/cb.1570

Wands, Z. E., & Mirzoev, T. (2022). Intimate partner violence against Indigenous women in Sololá, Guatemala: Qualitative insights into service providers' perspectives. *Violence Against Women, 28*(1), 150–168. https://doi.org/10.1177/1077801220981145

Ward, B., Reupert, A., McCormick, F., Waller, S., & Kidd, S. (2017). Family-focused practice within a recovery framework: Practitioners' qualitative perspectives. *BMC Health Services Research, 17*(1), 234. https://doi.org/10.1186/s12913-017-2146-y

Watson, D. M. (2019). The counselor knows best: A grounded theory approach to understanding how working-class, rural women experience the mental health counseling process. *Journal of Rural Mental Health, 43*(4). https://doi.org/10.10370000120

Watson, E., Fletcher-Watson, S., & Kirkham, E. J. (2023). Views on sharing mental health data for research purposes: Qualitative analysis of interviews with people with mental illness. *BMC Medical Ethics, 24*(1), 1–99. https://doi.org/10.1186/s12910-023-00961-6

Weaver, T. L., Elrod, N. M., & Kelton, K. (2020). Intimate partner violence and body shame: Examining the associations between abuse components and body-focused processes. *Violence Against Women, 26*(12–13), 1538–1554. https://doi.org/10.1177/1077801219873434

Webber, J., Trothen, T. J., Finlayson, M., & Norman, K. E. (2022). Moral distress experienced by community service providers of home health and social care in Ontario, Canada. *Health & Social Care in the Community, 30*(5), e1662–e1670. https://doi.org/10.1111/hsc.13592

Weibl, J., & Hess, T. (2020). Turning data into value—exploring the role of constructive collaboration in using value among data. *Information Systems Management, 37*(3), 227–239. https://doi.org/10.1080/10580530.2020.1696585

Weingarten, K., Galván-Durán, A. R., D'Urso, S., & Garcia, D. (2020). The witness-to-witness program: Helping the helpers in the context of the COVID-19 pandemic. *Family Process, 59*(3), 883–897. https://doi.org/10.1111/famp.12580

Weiss, N. H., Duke, A. A., Overstreet, N. M., Swan, S. C., & Sullivan, T. P. (2016). Intimate partner aggression-related shame and posttraumatic stress disorder symptoms: The moderating role of substance use problems. *Aggressive Behavior, 42*(5), 427–440. https://doi.org/10.1002/ab.21639

Welland, C. & Ribner, N. (2008, 2007). *Healing from violence: Latino men's journey to new masculinity*. Springer.

Wen, W., Khatibi, S., Siamak Khatibi, & Wei Wen. (2018). The impact of curviness on four different image sensor forms and structures. *Sensors 18*(2), 429. https://doi.org/10.3390/s18020429

Weobong, B., Weiss, H. A., McDaid, D., Singla, D. R., Hollon, S. D., Nadkarni, A., . . . Patel, V. (2017). Sustained effectiveness and cost-effectiveness of the healthy activity program, brief psychological treatment for depression delivered by lay counselors in primary care: 12-month follow-up of a randomized controlled trial. *PLoS Medicine, 14*(9), e1002385. https://doi.org/10.1371/journal.pmed.1002385

Wessels, J. S., & Visagie, R. G. (2017). The eligibility of public administration research for ethics review: A case study of two international peer-reviewed journals. *International Review of Administrative Sciences, 83*(1_suppl), 156–176. https://doi.org/10.1177/0020852315585949

Westas, M., Mourad, G., Andersson, G., Neher, M., Lundgren, J., & Johansson, P. (2022). The experience of taking part in an internet-based cognitive behavioral therapy program among patients with cardiovascular disease and depression: A qualitative interview study. *BMC Psychiatry, 22*(1), 294. https://doi.org/10.1186/s12888-022-03939-

White, C., Goldberg, V., Hibdon, J., & Weisburd, D. (2019). Understanding the role of service providers, land use, and resident characteristics on the occurrence of mental health crisis calls to the police. *Journal of Community Psychology, 47*(8), 1961–1982. https://doi.org/10.1002/jcop.22243

Whitten, T., Vecchio, N., Radford, K., & Fitzgerald, J. A. (2017). Intergenerational care as a practical intervention strategy for children at risk of delinquency. *The Australian Journal of Social Issues, 52*(1), 48–62. https://doi.org/10.1002/ajs4.6

Wiglesworth, A. (2022). Commentary: Understanding how patient-specific factors might violate assumptions of suicide risk and change the well-being of mental health care providers following patient suicidal behavior. *Clinical Psychology (New York, N.Y.), 29*(2), 117–120. https://doi.org/10.1037/cps0000086

Williams, H. (2021). The meaning of "phenomenology": Qualitative and philosophical phenomenological research methods. *Qualitative Report, 26*(2), 366–385. https://doi.org/10.46743/2160-3715/2021.4587

Williams, V., Boylan, A., & Nunan, D. (2020). Critical appraisal of qualitative research: Necessity, partialities, and the issue of bias. *BMJ Evidence-Based Medicine, 25*(1), 9–11. https://doi.org/10.1136/bmjebm-2018-111132

Williams, M. E., Joyner, K., Matic, T., & Lakatos, P. P. (2019). Reflective supervision: A qualitative evaluation of a training program for infant and early childhood mental health supervisors. *The Clinical Supervisor, 38*(1), 158–181. https://doi.org/10.1080/07325223.2019.1568942

Wilson, L., Rouillard, M. C. M., & Weideman, S. (2016). Registered counselors' beliefs of their role in the South African context of providing mental health-care services. *South African Journal of Psychology, 46*(1), 63–73. https://doi.org/10.1177/0081246315591340

Wilson, E., Kenny, A., & Dickson-Swift, V. (2018). Ethical challenges of community-based participatory research: Exploring researchers' experience. *International Journal of Social Research Methodology, 21*(1), 7–24. https://doi.org/10.1080/13645579.2017.1296714

Wilson, J. L., Uthman, C., Nichols-Hadeed, C., Kruchten, R., Thompson Stone, J., & Cerulli, C. (2021). Mental health therapists' perceived barriers to addressing intimate partner violence and suicide. *Families Systems & Health, 39*(2), 188–197. https://doi.org/10.1037/fsh0000581

Winstok, Z. (2013). From a static to a dynamic approach to the study of partner violence. *Sex Roles, 69*(3–4), 193–204. https://doi.org/10.1007/s11199-013-0278-z

Wittmayer, J. M., & Schäpke, N. (2014). Action, research, and participation: Roles of researchers in sustainability transitions. *Sustainability Science, 9*(4), 483–496. https://doi.org/10.1007/s11625-014-0258-4

Woerner, J., Wyatt, J., & Sullivan, T. P. (2019). If you cannot say something nice: A latent profile analysis of social reactions to intimate partner violence disclosure and associations with mental health symptoms. *Violence Against Women, 25*(10), 1243–1261. https://doi.org/10.1177/1077801218811681

Wörmann, X., Wilmes, S., Seifert, D., & Anders, S. (2021). Males as victims of intimate partner violence—results from a clinical-forensic medical examination center. *International Journal of Legal Medicine, 135*(5), 2107–2115. https://doi.org/10.1007/s00414-021-02615-x

Wójcik, K., Ćmiel, A., Satława, T., Lichołai, S., Wawrzycka-Adamczyk, K., Biedroń, G., Masiak, A., Zdrojewski, Z., Storoniak, H., Bułło-Piontecka, B., Dębska-Ślizień, A., Jeleniewicz, R., Majdan, M., Jakuszko, K., Augustyniak-Bartosik, H., Krajewska, M., Brzosko, I., Brzosko, M., Kur-Zalewska, J., . . . Musiał, J. (2022). pos0253 personalized risk evaluation for outcome prediction in anca-associated vasculitis (AAV) using latent class analysis and machine learning. *Annals of Rheumatic Diseases, 81*(Suppl 1), 367. https://doi.org/10.1136/annrheumdis-2022-eular.1089

Wolf, L. E., Hammack, C. M., Brown, E. F., Brelsford, K. M., & Beskow, L. M. (2020). Protecting participants in genomic research: Understanding the "Web of protections" afforded by federal and state law. *The Journal of Law, Medicine & Ethics, 48*(1), 126–141. https://doi.org/10.1177/1073110520917000

Wolford-Clevenger, C., Vann, N. C., M.S., & Smith, P. N. (2016). The association of partner abuse types and suicidal ideation among men and women college students. *Violence and Victims, 31*(3), 471–485. https://doi.org/10.1891/0886-6708.VV-D-14-00083

Wong, J. S., & Bouchard, J. (2021). Preventing intimate partner violence: A formative evaluation of an intervention program serving immigrants, refugees, and visible minority men. *Journal of Gender-Based Violence, 5*(2), 331–347. https://doi.org/10.1332/239868020X16082303077492

Wood, L., Cook Heffron, L., Voyles, M., & Kulkarni, S. (2020). Playing by the rules: Agency policy and procedure in-service experience of IPV survivors. *Journal of Interpersonal Violence, 35*(21–22), 4640–4665. https://doi.org/10.1177/0886260517716945

Wood, S. N., Kennedy, S. R., Hameed Uddin, Z., Asira, B., Tallam, C., Akumu, I., Wanjiru, I., Glass, N., & Decker, M. R. (2021). "Being married does not mean you have to reach the end of the world": Safety planning with intimate partner violence survivors and service providers in three urban informal settlements in Nairobi, Kenya. *Journal of Interpersonal Violence, 36*(19–20), NP10979–NP11005. https://doi.org/10.1177/0886260519879237

Wood, L., Voth Schrag, R., & Busch-Armendariz, N. (2020). Mental health and academic impacts of intimate partner violence among IHE-attending women. *Journal of American College Health, 68*(3), 286–293. https://doi.org/10.1080/07448481.2018.1546710

Wörmann, X., Wilmes, S., Seifert, D., & Anders, S. (2021). Males as intimate partner violence victims result from a clinical-forensic medical examination center. *International Journal of Legal Medicine, 135*(5), 2107–2115. https://doi.org/10.1007/s00414-021-02615-x

Woerner, J., Wyatt, J., & Sullivan, T. P. (2019). If you cannot say something nice: A latent profile analysis of social reactions to intimate partner violence disclosure and associations with mental health symptoms. *Violence Against Women, 25*(10), 1243–1261. https://doi.org/10.1177/1077801218811681

WHO global consultation on violence and health. (1996). *Violence: a public health priority (WHO/EHA/SPI.POA.2)*. Geneva: World Health Organization.

World Health Organization. (2018). *WHO Global Consultation on Violence and Health. Violence: public health*. Geneva. Retrieved from http://www.who.int/violenceprevention/approach/defnition/en, 2018.

World Health Organization, W. H., & World Health Organization. (2013). *World Health Statistics 2013* (1st ed.). World Health Organization.

Wozniak, D. F., & Allen, K. N. (2012). Ritual and performance in domestic violence healing: From survivor to thriver through rites of passage. *Culture, Medicine and Psychiatry, 36*(1), 80–101. https://doi.org/10.1007/s11013-011-9236-9

Wyckoff, K. G., Narasimhan, S., Stephenson, K., Zeidan, A. J., Smith, R. N., & Evans, D. P. (2023). "COVID allowed him to tighten the reins around my throat": Perceptions of COVID-19 movement restrictions among survivors of intimate partner violence. *BMC Public Health, 23*(1), 199. https://doi.org/10.1186/s12889-023-15137-5

Xiao, B., Imel, Z. E., Georgiou, P., Atkins, D. C., & Narayanan, S. S. (2016). Computational analysis and simulation of empathic behaviors: A survey of empathy modeling with behavioral signal processing framework. *Current Psychiatry Reports, 18*(5),1–11. https://doi.org/10.1007/s11920-016-0682-5

Xiang, X., Cheng, J., Zuverink, A., & Wang, X. (2020, 2019). Beliefs and practice behaviors on late-life depression among private duty home care workers: A mixed-methods study. *Aging & Mental Health, 24*(11), 1904–1911. https://doi.org/10.1080/13607863.2019.1636207

Xu, A., Baysari, M. T., Stocker, S. L., Leow, L. J., Day, R. O., & Carland, J. E. (2020). Researchers' views on, and experiences with, the requirement to obtain informed consent in research involving human participants: A qualitative study. *BMC Medical Ethics, 21*(1), 1–11. https://doi.org/10.1186/s12910-020-00538-7

Xu, E. (2020). A generalizable model for frame identification: Towards an integrative approach. *Communication Research and Practice, 6*(3), 245–258. https://doi.org/10.1080/22041451.2020.1759925

Yamada, A., Vaivao, D. E. S., & Subica, A. M. (2019). Addressing mental health challenges of Samoan Americans in southern California: Perspectives of Samoan community providers. *Asian American Journal of Psychology, 10*(3), 227–238. https://doi.org/10.1037/aap0000140

Yang, T., Poon, A. W. C., & Breckenridge, J. (2019). Estimating the prevalence of intimate partner violence in mainland China—insights and challenges. *Journal of Family Violence, 34*(2), 93–105. https://doi.org/10.1007/s10896-018-9989-9

Yakeley, J. (2022). The search for tailored treatments: Discussion of five interventions for perpetrators of intimate partner violence. *Journal of Clinical Psychology, 78*(1), 80–98. https://doi.org/10.1002/jclp.232

Yaro, P. B., Asampong, E., Tabong, P. T., Anaba, S. A., Azuure, S. S., Dokurugu, A. Y., & Nantogmah, F. A. (2020). Stakeholders' perspectives about the impact of training and sensitization of traditional and spiritual healers on mental health and illness: A qualitative evaluation in Ghana. *International Journal of Social Psychiatry, 66*(5), 476–484. https://doi.org/10.1177/0020764020918284

Yates, C. M., DeLeon, A., & Rapp, M. C. (2017). Exploring experiential learning through an abstinence assignment within an addictions counseling course. *The Professional Counselor, 7*(4), 318–329. https://doi.org/10.15241/cmy.7.4.318

Yeomans, L. (2016). Imagining the lives of others: Empathy in public relations. *Public Relations Inquiry, 5*(1), 71–92. https://doi.org/10.1177/2046147X16632033

Yohannes, K., Berhane, Y., Bradby, H., Herzig Van Wees, Sibylle L, & Målqvist, M. (2023). *Contradictions hindering the provision of mental* healthcare and psychosocial services to women experiencing homelessness in Addis Ababa, Ethiopia: Service providers' and program coordinators' experiences and perspectives. https://doi.org/10.1186/s12913-023-09810-z

Yonga, A. M., Kiss, L., & Onarheim, K. H. (2022). A systematic review of the effects of intimate partner violence on HIV-positive pregnant women in sub-Saharan Africa. *BMC Public Health, 22*(1), 220. https://doi.org/10.1186/s12889-022-12619-w

Yoshihama, M., Hammock, A. C., & Baidoun, F. (2022). Analysis of bystander behavior towards intimate partner violence via performance. *Journal of Interpersonal Violence, 37*(11–12), NP10196–NP10219. https://doi.org/10.1177/0886260520985482

Younas, A., Porr, C., Maddigan, J., Moore, J., Navarro, P., & Whitehead, D. (2023). Behavioral indicators of compassionate nursing care of individuals with complex needs: A naturalistic inquiry. *Journal of Clinical Nursing, 32*(13–14), 4024–4036. https://doi.org/10.1111/jocn.16542

Young, M. J., Bodien, Y. G., & Edlow, B. L. (2022). Ethical considerations in clinical trials for disorders of consciousness. *Brain Sciences, 12*(2), 211. https://doi.org/10.3390/brainsci12020211

Yount, K. M., Anderson, K. M., Trang, Q. T., & Bergenfeld, I. (2023). Preventing sexual violence in Vietnam: Qualitative findings from high school, university, and civil society key informants across regions. *BMC Public Health, 23*(1), 1114. https://doi.org/10.1186/s12889-023-15973-5

Yue, C. A., Men, L. R., & Ferguson, M. A. (2021). Examining the effects of internal communication and vibrant culture on employees' organizational identification. *International Journal of Business Communication, 58*(2), 169–195. https://doi.org/10.1177/2329488420914066

Yuk-ha Tsang, E. (2020). Being bad to feel good: China's migrant men, displaced masculinity, and the commercial sex industry. *The*

Journal of Contemporary China, 29(122), 221–237. https://doi.org/10.1080/10670564.2019.1637563

Yuspendi, Handojo, V., Athota, V. S., Sihotang, M. Y. M., & Aryani, Putu Ngurah Asita Dewi. (2018). Adult attachment Stability–Instability before and after marriage between intimate partner violence (IPV) and non-IPV women separated from partners during military duty in Indonesia. *Australian and New Zealand Journal of Family Therapy, 39*(1), 103–116. https://doi.org/10.1002/anzf.1281

Zinzow, H. M., Littleton, H., Muscari, E., & Sall, K. (2022). Barriers to formal help-seeking following sexual violence: Review from within an ecological systems framework. *Victims & Offenders, 17*(6), 893–918. https://doi.org/10.1080/15564886.2021.1978023

Zosky, D. L. (2016). "I feel your pain": Do better intervention programs change the perpetrator's empathy for victims? *Partner Abuse, 7*(1), 70–86. https://doi.org/10.1891/1946-6560.7.1.70

Zhou, H., Majka, E. A., & Epley, N. (2017). Inferring perspective versus getting perspective: Underestimating the value of being in another person's shoes. *Psychological Science, 28*(4), 482–493. https://doi.org/10.1177/0956797616687124

Zhu, C., Lu, W., He, Y., Ke, S., Wu, H., & Zhang, L. (2018). Iron isotopic analyses of geological reference materials on MC-ICP-MS with instrumental mass bias corrected by three independent methods. *Acta Geochimica, 37*(5), 691–700. https://doi.org/10.1007/s11631-018-0284-5

Zhu, J., Wekerle, C., Lanius, R., & Frewen, P. (2019). Trauma- and stressor-related history and symptoms predict distress experienced during a brief mindfulness meditation sitting: Moving toward trauma-informed care in mindfulness-based therapy. *Mindfulness, 10*(10), 1985–1996. https://doi.org/10.1007/s12671-019-01173-z

References

Zygmunt, A., Tanuseputro, P., James, P., Lima, I., Tuna, M., & Kendall, C. E. (2020). Neighborhood-level marginalization and avoidable mortality in Ontario, Canada: A population-based study. *Canadian Journal of Public Health, 111*(2), 169–181. https://doi.org/10.17269/s41997-019-00270-9

Appendix A

PUBLISHING AGREEMENT

This Agreement is between the author (Author) and Capella University. Under this Agreement, in consideration for the opportunity to have his/her capstone project published on a Capella website, Author grants Capella certain rights to preserve, archive, and publish the Author's doctoral capstone (the Work), abstract, and index terms.

License for Inclusion in Capella Websites and Publications

Grant of Rights. Author hereby grants to Capella the **non-exclusive**, royalty-free, irrevocable, worldwide right to reproduce, distribute, display, and transmit the Work (in whole or in part) in such tangible and electronic formats as may be in existence now or developed in the future. Such forms include, but are not limited to, Capella University websites, where the Work may be made available for free download. Author further grants to Capella the right to include the abstract, bibliography and other metadata in Capella University's doctoral capstone repository and any successor or related index and/or finding products or services. The rights granted by Author automatically include (1) the right to allow for distribution of the Work, in whole or in part, by agents and distributors, and (2) the right to make the Abstract, bibliographic data and any metadata associated with the Work available to search engines.

Removal of Work from the Program. Capella may elect not to distribute the Work if it believes that all necessary rights of third parties have not been secured. In addition, if Author's degree is rescinded or found to be in violation of Capella University's Research Misconduct Policy or other University policies, Capella may expunge the Work from publication. Capella may also elect not to distribute the work in a manner supported by other Capella University policies.

Rights Verification. Author represents and warrants that Author is the copyright holder of the Work and has obtained all necessary rights to permit Capella to reproduce and distribute third party materials contained in any part of the Work, including all necessary licenses for any non-public, third-party software necessary to access, display, and run or print the Work. The author is solely responsible and will indemnify and defend Capella for any third-party claims related to the Work as submitted for publication, including but not limited to claims alleging the Work violates a third party's intellectual property rights.

STATEMENT OF ORIGINAL WORK

Capella University's Academic Honesty Policy (3.01.01) holds learners accountable for the integrity of work they submit, which includes but is not limited to discussion postings, assignments, comprehensive exams, and the dissertation or capstone project.

Established in the Policy are the expectations for original work, rationale for the policy, definition of terms that pertain to academic honesty and original work, and disciplinary consequences of academic dishonesty. Also stated in the Policy is the expectation that learners will follow APA rules for citing another person's ideas or works.

The following standards for original work and definition of *plagiarism* are discussed in the Policy:

> Learners are expected to be the sole authors of their work and to acknowledge the authorship of others' work through proper citation and reference. Use of another person's ideas, including another learners, without proper reference or citation, constitutes plagiarism and academic dishonesty and is prohibited conduct. (p. 1)
>
> Plagiarism is one example of academic dishonesty. Plagiarism is presenting someone else's ideas or work as your own. Plagiarism also includes copying verbatim or rephrasing ideas without properly acknowledging the source by author, date, and publication medium. (p. 2)

Capella University's Research Misconduct Policy (3.03.06) holds learners accountable for research integrity. What constitutes research misconduct is discussed in the Policy:

> Research misconduct includes but is not limited to falsification, fabrication, plagiarism, misappropriation, or other practices that seriously deviate from those that are commonly accepted within the academic community for proposing, conducting, or reviewing research, or in reporting research results. (p. 1)

Learners failing to abide by these policies are subject to consequences, including but not limited to dismissal or revocation of the degree.

Appendix A

Acknowledgments:

I have read, understand, and agree to this Capella Publishing Agreement, including all rights and restrictions included within the publishing option chosen by me as indicated above.

I have read, understood, and abided by Capella University's Academic Honesty Policy (3.01.01) and Research Misconduct Policy (3.03.06), including Policy Statements, Rationale, and Definitions.

I attest that this dissertation or capstone project is my own work. Where I have used the ideas or words of others, I have paraphrased, summarized, or used direct quotes following the guidelines set forth in the APA Publication Manual.

(Print Name) <u>**Moses Omane-Boateng**</u>

REQUIRED (print name) signature *[signature]*

<u>Date October 08, 2024</u>

Acknowledgments

My recognition of this dissertation indicates the presiding chair of my committee and the members, faculty and staff, the mental health professionals (respondents) participating in the data-collection protocol, the Capella Doctoral Academic Progress Reward Team, friends, and the church family. Accept my gratitude for your priceless support for this research study. The dissertation journey protocol was daunting, yet the Lord's Grace was sufficient to sustain me.

To my mentor and chair, Dr. Elaine M. Barclay, you have been my cheerleader, motivator, and critique. Dr. Barclay, thank you for the guidance throughout this daunting dissertation journey. The weekly inspirational drives and feedback invigorated resilience, challenging me to be a better independent researcher. Dr. B, you are an invaluable asset to this milestone. I compliment my committee members, Dr. Morgan McAfee and Dr. Pamela Klem, for their knowledge and critiques during the process. Please note that your time and guidance were priceless. I want to thank Dr. Philip Atkins, my first mentor, who laid the foundation for my dissertation journey. Dr. Atkins, thank you for the seed planted on solid and fertile grounds.

I want to acknowledge Dr. Tracee Washington for her encouraging words and empathic support for my academic progress. My gratitude goes to the Capella Doctoral Progress Reward team for the ten-thousand-dollar tuition award for the dissertation tuition. I want to compliment Dr.

Mahmoud Sadri of Texas Woman's University, who taught me my first doctoral course in sociology (SOCI 5900). Thank you for the academic genesis in the fall of 2006.

I want to acknowledge Sr. Pastor Kenneth D. Davis and my church family at EOC, Denton. Thank you for your prayers and support, which strengthened me. Youth Pastor Bobby Givens of St. Andrew COGIC, thank you for the weekly prayers for my strength and encouragement. You are an inspiration. Bro. and Sis. Young, I appreciate your empathy.

About the Author

Moses Omane-Boateng began his academic journey in his home country of Ghana, where he earned a Teacher's Certification "A" through the Ghana National Teachers Training Council at SDA Training College. He attended the University of North Texas, Denton, Texas, where he obtained a Bachelor of Business Administration in Economics and a Bachelor of Business Administration in Finance. His studies continued at UNT, Denton, Texas, where he completed a Master's in Public Administration (MPA). During this time, he participated in postgraduate studies in Economics and Medical Sociology. He completed his studies at Capella University, Minneapolis, Minnesota, earning a PhD in Human Services with a Specialization in Social and Community Services. His dissertation research topic for the PhD was Counselors' Perceptions of and Experiences with Empathy When Treating Male IPV Victims. IPV denotes intimate partner violence.

During his years of study, he was a member of the Delta Alpha Pi International Honor Society, the National Scholars Honor Society, and the National Society for Leadership and Success, Capella Chapter.

He has taught Economics and Government at Grayson County College, Denison, Texas. Additionally, he taught Economics, Government, and Sociology at North Central Texas

College at five separate campuses: Bowie, Corinth, Flower Mound, Gainesville, and Graham, Texas.

Moses is an elder and preacher at Empowered Outreach Church in Denton, Texas.

www.ingramcontent.com/pod-product-compliance
Lightning Source LLC
Chambersburg PA
CBHW052132070526
44585CB00017B/1791